FIND
KATHERINE

JAMES SWEETMAN

Published by TheExcellenceForum

www.theexcellenceforum.com
www.jamessweetman.com

ISBN 978-1-944247-61-4

Typesetting by
Gough Typesetting Services,
Dublin

Cover Design by
Hayes Design
www.hayesdesign.co.uk

Printed by
Eprint
35 Coolmine Industrial Estate, Dublin 15

*For everyone seeking the
courage to pursue their dreams.*

ALSO BY JAMES SWEETMAN

Books Non-Fiction

Graduate to Success
Soar – Powerful Questions That Will Transform Your life
How to Excel at Interviews (ebook)

Books Fiction

The Odyssey of Abraham Little

Audio CDs

How to Excel at Interviews
15 Ways to Boost your Self-Confidence

www.jamessweetman.com

*"Sound when stretched is music. Movement when stretched is dance.
Mind when stretched is meditation. Life when stretched is celebration."*

Ravi Shankar

Chapter 1

At the age of fifty-one Katherine Hunter was running away from home. She had done it once before when she was thirteen. On that occasion no one really missed her and she had been home in time for tea. It was different now.

Her official story was that she was spending a week at The Bliss Retreat in Teguise, on the island of Lanzarote, immersing herself in a few days of self care and self discovery workshops, or so the brochure said. The truth was she was fleeing. It had been a last minute decision. The escape route presented itself when Rhona broke her leg and suggested Katherine took her place.

Mags and Rhona said the holiday would do her good and she hoped they were right. It had been a tough few months; her mother dying, Claire moving out, the financial worries with Vincent's business. And then there was everything that Mags and Rhona knew nothing about.

On the plane, she had replayed yet again the recent conversations with Vincent, not that there were many of them. Together nearly thirty years and married for the last twenty-six, Katherine knew every different category of silence in her marriage. In the early years, the silent treatment was her weapon in the subtle power struggles that established the unwritten rules of their relationship. Lately, there was the silence of meal times, less obvious when a TV droned in the background. It was the same when they ate out. Over the years as the restaurants got pricier, the conversation got poorer. But since the blow up a week ago, when she came home unexpectedly from the hospital, a new type of silence was born, one that masked mutual disgust.

Vincent hadn't even offered to drive her to the airport. He

had golf. Katherine knew him well enough to know he was upset that she was going, but she also felt he wasn't upset enough.

When she had taken her seat on the plane, she had scanned the faces of the passengers snaking down the aisle. A tiny and well-hidden part of her wanted Vincent to confound every expectation and dash on board at the last minute. He would ask the man beside her to change seats, look at her and place his hand on hers. He wouldn't have to say a word. That was her favourite type of silence. But that didn't happen. When the air stewardess sealed the door, a part of her wondered if she was making the biggest mistake of her life.

If the plane had crashed, she knew that her children would miss her, especially her son Thom, but they were young and they would get on with their lives. Vincent would grieve, of course he would, but he wouldn't be alone too long. Even before recent events, Katherine always felt that if anything happened to her, Vincent would remarry. They used to joke about it. He wasn't conventionally handsome, but he had that aura of being a man on a mission and that certainty of purpose was a quality women found attractive. It was what Katherine used to find attractive.

She had imagined herself on the plane, a sophisticated woman, happily browsing through *Vogue* and *Harper's Bazaar*, excited about treating herself to a week of sun, rest and rejuvenation, in a retreat away from the tourist hubs. But the reality had been, seated in 11A, she felt like a frightened little girl extradited to a strange environment, desperate for an elusive panacea to cure her woes and where, in all likelihood, she'd just receive the judgemental stares of New Age hippies.

The sun was setting but the breeze ventilating the taxi was delightfully warm. The taxi driver was young, a bit of a poseur Katherine thought with his mirrored sunglasses, leonine mane and elbow jutting out the window. The black jagged rocks and dormant volcanoes presented a truly alien landscape. It was Katherine's first time in Lanzarote. Vincent referred to it as

4

'Lanzagrotty' because of its popularity as a cheap sun spot.

Katherine extracted the compact mirror from her handbag. It felt like she was gazing at the remnants of the woman she thought she was. She rubbed her top lip, and the few hairs that shouldn't be there. And you had to be laughing for the lines around your eyes to be called laughter lines. It wasn't the face she wanted to see. Katherine had always prided herself on not looking her age, but the dam holding back the years had broken, and age had overtaken her like a slingshot. How had Katherine Boyle, the girl who at twenty was considered a local beauty, she had the sashes to prove it, end up with high blood pressure? Vincent had even dared to hurl the words 'nervous breakdown' at her. She reapplied lipstick then snapped the compact shut.

It took the rock music on the radio to drown out the voice in her head. Katherine had never regretted marrying Vincent. They had made a good life for themselves. They had ticked all the boxes. Thomas arrived in time for her father to hold him and to be named after him. The baby was also how she got through her grief. Two years later Claire completed the family portrait. For several years she thought she would have liked a third child, but Vincent was happy with two, and his vasectomy put an end to the debate.

She had much to be thankful for, she knew that. As Rhona said her woes were first world problems. Vincent's insurance brokerage and estate agency business provided a good income, and Katherine never had to work outside the home. They had enjoyed all the trappings of the boom years; they rode the back of the Celtic Tiger as the phrase went. But apart from her children, their success, and it had to be called that, had seemed hollow to Katherine. For Vincent, more was never enough. But all that was before the recession.

Polite, that was the word that now described their marriage. Katherine wondered where was the man who used to come home from work and carry her upstairs over his shoulder. She would kick and scream and love every minute of it. Sometimes they never made it upstairs. She missed that man. She missed that woman too.

And now her life seemed fragile. She felt alone, unmoored and that felt strange because for the last twenty-six years she was one half of the duet that was Vincent and Katherine, Vinnie and Kay, Mr and Mrs Hunter.

At a large roundabout she noticed the first road sign for Teguise. She rooted around for The Bliss Retreat leaflet in her bag. She had read the brochure and visited the website several times. The list of workshops did sound appealing and the testimonials promising. *'After a week, my worries just seemed to disappear and I now feel like the woman I was meant to be.'* It was written by B Angelo. Lucky woman, Katherine thought. The place looked beautiful too. The owner of the retreat, Neide Witt, her name rhyming with Heidi according to a YouTube clip, was a dark-haired middle-aged woman, presumably Dutch or German. Her photo on the back of the brochure wasn't the most flattering, but her face looked kind. In the blurb she spoke about how it was her dream to transform the group of houses, or *fincas* as they were referred to, into a holistic retreat centre.

According to Rhona the week ahead was a special one at The Retreat because two guest lecturers would be attending. Katherine had researched it online. Ran Kaplan, an Israeli artist was running a workshop. Katherine had loved art at school and took classes after Claire was born. The idea of picking up a paintbrush again was the main pull factor when she told Rhona she would go. There had been plenty of push factors too. A writer, Bruno Reye was scheduled to lead a creative writing workshop. She hadn't heard of him, but Rhona was a fan.

The road bisected a vast lava field. Katherine had researched Teguise before she had left. It used to be the capital of the island and hosted a market every Sunday. She hoped she would have an opportunity to browse it tomorrow. She kept an eye on the signposts they passed; after all she was a single woman in a taxi not really knowing where she was going.

Cresting a hill, it seemed like the entire vista of the island opened before her. Long shadows stretched across the barren landscape. In the setting sun, the rust coloured mountains appeared illuminated from within. Solitary white houses and the occasional palm tree and cactus were the only signs of habitation, indeed life. Several science fiction movies had been filmed in Lanzarote, she could see why.

Above the thumping music the driver pointed to the clusters of white buildings on the horizon – Teguise. Katherine could feel her heart beat against her ribs. The road was straight. A floodlit citadel dominated the skyline and apart from the church tower the town was a series of low-rise whitewashed houses, just like the photograph in the brochure.

The taxi had been prepaid online but Katherine had a few euros ready to hand over when the driver heaved her case from the boot. He said he had left her as close as he could to the entrance to The Bliss Retreat. He pointed to a side street too narrow for a car. Grabbing her case and her determination she marched down the alley.

A light over the doorway illuminated a sign that read 'entrance' in English and Spanish. Disturbed from its preening, a cat darted from the doorway. She hoped the plaque on the wall read 'The Bliss Retreat', but it was hard to make it out in the fading light. There was no sign of a bell or buzzer, just a metal handle. A gust of wind pushed the door away from her and banged against the wall. Her entrance was not a silent one. Across a courtyard a few people were seated at a table. Though now almost dark, Katherine could see enough that was familiar to let her know she was in the right place.

"Welcome. Let me help you with that." The voice came from a barefoot young woman with fiery red hair who waved enthusiastically. Katherine heaved her case over the step.

"I'm in the right place? This is The Bliss Retreat?"

"Yes, you've found us. Let me take that for you." The girl's accent was English. She could be no more than twenty. Katherine wondered if the girl had the strength to drag it, let alone lift it.

"I warn you, it's heavy."

"Oh I'll manage; I'm stronger than I look. I'm Serendipity by the way and you must be Katherine."

"Katherine Hunter, that's right." The girl's name was odd, but her friendliness sincere.

"You're the last to arrive, so we'll get you settled in. How was your flight?"

"Bumpy, but on time that was the main thing."

"I love your Irish accent. Of course you swapped with your friend at the last minute, wasn't that it?"

"Well remembered." Katherine was impressed.

"Neide told me. Maybe it's serendipity."

"Sorry"

"Like my name. Maybe you are the one who was meant to be here all along."

"Who knows? You've an interesting name."

"I love it. I think it's really me. My real name is Sharon which I hate, but don't tell anyone. My nickname at school was Dippy and everyone says luck follows me wherever I go, so I'm sticking with Serendipity. Now let's get you to your room." The young woman hauled Katherine's stuffed suitcase over the paved courtyard towards an archway framed by deep purple bougainvillea, spotlit by the setting sun. Three women, one with peroxide blonde hair sat at a long table. They nodded as Katherine passed.

"Have you thought about your outcomes for the week? Tell me, what workshops are you looking forward to? I can't wait for Bruno Reye's, have you read any of his books?"

"I'm a novice to all this," Katherine said, trying to keep up

8

with the barrage of questions. "How long have you worked here?" She couldn't get herself to say the girl's name just yet.

"Oh, this is my first summer. I came here last year for a week with my mother and loved it. Then I met Neide again at a workshop in London. I'm an artist and she asked if I would like to come here for a few weeks, paint some murals to brighten up the walls and help out. It's been great cos I get to sit in on a lot of the workshops."

"Not bad for a summer job."

"Well I don't get paid, but it's free bed and board."

"I see." Katherine hoped the young woman wasn't being taken advantage of; she had an innocence and naivety that could easily be abused. "I used to paint years ago," Katherine said finding something they had in common.

"We're all really excited about Ran Kaplan being here."

Katherine followed the young hostess through the archway into a smaller courtyard with a palm tree in the centre.

"You're over here on the left Katherine, the last door, number 12."

"Tell me Serendipity," Katherine was careful to pronounce each syllable, "is it possible to get something to eat?"

"There's salad and quiche in the kitchen. Carlos always leaves something out for new guests, so help yourself. It's all included, vegetarian of course, very healthy. A few of the early arrivals went out for dinner; there are a few nice restaurants in Teguise too. Now here you are."

The doors off the courtyard were all painted different colours. Katherine's was emerald green. A wooden wind chime hung from the awning.

"Hard to believe these were once stables. Neide's done a wonderful job, hasn't she?" Serendipity said leading the way.

"It's very quiet."

The room was simple, almost cell-like. A single bed, a desk and chair beneath a window and thankfully her own toilet and shower. On first inspection everything seemed clean. A striking painting hung over the single bed.

"One of yours?" Katherine asked.

"No, a woman who stayed in this room last summer painted it. The Angel Nisroc, the Angel of Freedom, I believe."

Katherine never heard of such an angel, but she liked the mix of blues, violets and deep purples. The figure had massive wings and the face of a bird. Though not necessarily well painted, it had a power that was captivating.

"Neide's thinking about giving each room a name instead of a number. This will be the freedom room and next door I think will be courage. So, I'll let you settle in. The timetable for the week is on the desk and I'll be hovering around the common room if you need anything."

"You're very good. I appreciate it."

"It's great to have you here Katherine and I'm sure you'll have loads of breakthroughs this week."

Breakthroughs, there was that word Rhona was so fond of using.

"Oh is there a key or do I need to sign in or anything?"

"We don't use keys here, there's no need, just hang this little sign on the door if you want some privacy." Serendipity displayed a hand-painted 'privacy please' sign, then literally skipped out of the room.

Katherine tested the bed springs. It seemed comfortable enough though she couldn't remember the last time she had slept in a single bed. The room was stuffy and her blouse stuck to her back. A three-quarter height wall separated the bathroom from the bedroom. It wasn't the most private of spaces. A large sign informed her not to flush toilet paper but to use the adjacent basket. In other circumstances Katherine would have been appalled, but this was a time to be flexible.

There was only one small hand towel. She had shoved many items into her case that she would probably never use, but never dreamt of bringing a bath towel. Maybe she could ask for one or buy one.

An incense burner and a book of quotations sat on the bedside locker, a nice touch Katherine thought. She picked up the schedule for the week and scanned the workshops that lay ahead. An 'Art Masterclass with Ran Kaplan', on Tuesday caught her eye. There was a picture of the Israeli artist who was also going to facilitate a creativity workshop. His dark hair and brown eyes reminded Katherine of Mark Goodwin, but she wasn't going to think about him now. She had left that situation behind her.

First up in the morning was the welcome meeting at ten followed by an opportunity to explore the weekly market in Teguise. The afternoon workshop had the lofty title of 'Starting your journey to your authentic self'. From Monday there was optional dawn yoga followed by meditation, all before breakfast. For Vincent, this would be a circle of hell, but she could see why Rhona would have loved to be here. She owed it to her friend to make the most of the week. She owed it to herself as well.

CHAPTER 2

Neide Witt stood in front of the group, her hands clasped across her ample bosom. She was a large woman and her patterned skirt only accentuated her girth. The owner of The Retreat scanned the semicircle of faces. The eight women and two men facing her sat in watchful silence. Katherine wasn't sure if the woman who ran The Bliss Retreat was performing some sort of ritual. Neide's sandals slapped the soles of her feet as she circled the assembled participants.

Katherine liked the Big Room, the main workshop space. The dark orange walls were warm and in keeping with the colour of the land. An eye-catching turquoise and green mural dominated the far wall. The scattered beanbags and cushions looked more comfortable than the plastic chairs they were perched on. The previous night when Katherine had explored her surroundings, the room had been closed, but now the bi-fold doors were wide open and a welcome breeze cooled the backs of the ten people embarking on the first of the scheduled workshops.

Half-hidden in a large wooden cabinet, Katherine spied easels, boxes of paints and scrolls of papers. The thought of dabbling with a paintbrush later in the week enlivened her spirits. She took a deep breath, inhaling the earthy scent of smouldering sage leaves. Her shoulders began to loosen for the first time in weeks.

Imelda, an ex-nun she had chatted with in the kitchen the night before, had kept her a seat. Katherine had exchanged pleasantries with several of the others and none of them appeared to be what Vincent referred to as 'whacko'. She had particularly enjoyed the chat with Imelda over supper and was delighted that the older woman had sought out her company.

A spritely seventy-five, Imelda had been born in Wexford, in the sunny south-east, just like Katherine, but had moved to England as a child. Katherine didn't believe her at first when she said she had been a nun for forty-five years. She couldn't envisage this woman in a starched habit slapping the knuckles of hesitant students. At the age of seventy Imelda left her vocation, as she called it. With an infectious laugh she was quick to add that it wasn't to run off with a man. She hoped she had another good twenty years in her and the thought of spending it in a convent with other retired nuns did not appeal. Over mugs of camomile tea she told Katherine how she had just come back from travelling in Asia for six months, just like a gap year student. Imelda's eyes lit up when she recounted her experiences at the temples of Angkor Wat in Cambodia and how she skipped along the Great Wall of China because it had been a life-long ambition to see it. All Katherine could think was how brave this woman was and how full of life. Her admiration for Imelda was further enhanced when just after dawn, feeling far from rested, Katherine looked out her bedroom window and saw Imelda standing on one leg, arms raised in a yoga position smiling broadly, uttering a prayer, welcoming the new day.

***

Katherine hadn't slept well in weeks, and she had tossed and turned the whole night. The meagre benefits of the small fan by the bed were far out-weighed by the rattle it made, to say nothing of the issues with Vincent that spun around her head. A prowling cat leapt on to her window sill several times, always when she was just about to nod off, causing her heart to race. When a light sleep did descend she had dreamt that she had been standing at the end of Tramore harbour, a high tide lapping at her feet. Green algae covered every surface and she was afraid to move in case she slipped and fell in. The sea was a sinister brown. Someone called her name and when she turned, her feet went from under her. On all fours she tried to crawl away from the edge. A bald fisherman in oilskins stood in a boat calling her name. His big hands reached for her, but she didn't dare move.

It had been a horrible dream and she woke feeling uneasy and far from refreshed. Rhona always said that it's the emotion in the dream that's worth pondering. Katherine felt overwhelmed and powerless. She didn't need to be a genius to figure out what her unconscious mind was communicating. And she hated harbours. Her aunt Kay had drowned off Tramore harbour when Katherine was ten.

***

"You are all very welcome to The Bliss Retreat." Neide said perching herself on the edge of the table. There were smiles and nods all round.

"Now I see many of you have your own notebooks and pens, if anyone needs writing material I've loose pages here and there's a box of pencils in the cabinet." Her English was excellent. Katherine always admired people who could speak more than one language. Katherine wondered what age Neide was. She suspected she must be in her fifties, but it was hard to tell. She wasn't wearing a wedding ring.

"Now if you want something more special, a friend makes these beautiful journals from old leather and recycled paper. They are only fifteen euros. She has a beautiful little shop in the old town. Normally these are twenty five."

"I'll take one." Katherine raised her hand. From what she could tell, she was the only one in the group without a notebook of some kind on her lap. No towel and no notebook, yet she had packed six pairs of shoes.

The soft leather cover reminded Katherine of an old schoolbag she once had, it even smelled like it. The cream pages were thick and their edges rough. It was the sort of notebook that demanded profound thoughts and elegant handwriting.

"My wish for you is that you will have an enjoyable and worthwhile experience this week. I'm sure you will all learn something new about yourselves. Or maybe even unlearn and relearn, who knows?" Neide had a gap between her two front teeth. Katherine was reminded how her father used to say that that was a sign of a good singer.

"And you know you will learn from each other as well. A few weeks ago there was a lovely Swedish woman here and at the end of the week, when we were speaking about our experiences, she shared something she had learnt from everyone else in the group." A murmur of approval rippled down the line of chairs.

Katherine planned to record everything she learnt in her journal and she looked forward to good conversations with open and hopefully like-minded people. The night before, much to Katherine's surprise, she'd had a very interesting and enlightening conversation with Imelda. She tended to avoid discussion about religion or politics, especially with someone she'd just met, but Imelda knew of no such boundaries. Her analogy of God made perfect sense to Katherine. She learnt more after an hour with her than she had in many years of attending Mass, or religious instruction at school. Imelda said that now when she thinks of God she imagines an infinite loving presence residing at the top of a mountain, with many paths leading to the summit. Imelda had said that she had spent all her life climbing one path, a path she felt was getting narrower and narrower, a path that was more concerned with itself than with the people who wanted to climb it. Now she fully believed that there were many paths to God and that she had the freedom to explore them, or maybe even to forge her own one. Katherine planned to sketch a mountain in her notebook to remind her of the conversation.

"I'll take one of those notebooks as well; it's always nice to support local artists." All eyes turned to Bruce, the bearded man at the far end of the arc of chairs. He appeared isolated from the group as the two seats beside him were unoccupied. That morning at breakfast he had sat beside Katherine. He was a retired law professor, not the type Katherine expected to see in such a place. He looked just the part, long-faced with a neat grey beard and glasses that he played with more than wore. Rather than pushing them onto his head, he had the habit of resting them on his beard. She could easily imagine him dismissing a question from a student with a single condescending glance. Twice at breakfast he had referenced the fact that he had been divorced three times. Katherine couldn't help thinking that perhaps he thought The Retreat would be fertile hunting ground for wife number four.

It was easy to remember the names of the two men, outnumbered as they were. The other man in the group was Declan who was in his early thirties. He was with his friend Suzy. The two of them and Katherine had arrived for breakfast at the same time and they invited Katherine to join them at the long table in the courtyard. Both of them had decided they needed a fresh start, as they had both been dumped by their respective boyfriends at the beginning of the summer. Declan was rake thin and wore a white t-shirt with a deep v and had a tattoo on the side of his forearm. He was a handsome guy, with cheekbones Katherine envied. Suzy, a buxom blonde, was probably closer to forty than his thirty. She now sat on Katherine's left, an expensive looking shoe dangling from her foot. Katherine suspected she was the sort of woman that had regular pedicures.

"So let's get to know each other a little, yes?" Neide pulled a chair into the semicircle facing the others. Everyone in the group shifted in their seats. Katherine's eyes hit the floor. "Maybe we can speak one at a time and introduce ourselves? Who would like to start?"

"I will." Bruce positioned himself squarely in the chair his hands behind his head. He spoke about his spiritual journey and how he was seeking answers to the big questions in life. He crossed and re-crossed his legs as he spoke and announced yet again that he had been divorced three times. When he digressed into his opinion on the latest Richard Dawkins' book, Neide gently suggested that they keep the introductions short because there was another exercise to do and she wanted everyone to have sufficient time to wander up the town and explore the Sunday market. She had silenced him with real skill, Katherine thought.

Imelda went next and shared her story about being an ex-nun. When she spoke about wanting to find her own path, there was a ripple of applause from the group. She motioned for Katherine to go next. Katherine could feel herself blush and despite her dry mouth, she thought she might as well get it over with.

"Do you know I'm not really sure why I'm here? It was a last minute decision. A friend was due to come, but she broke her leg and I took her place only last week. When I saw the list of classes and workshops I thought I might enjoy it." Katherine wondered if she had said enough. Neide's head was tilted as if she was listening for something else to be said, so she continued. "The last few weeks have been quite stressful too and I felt I needed a break, some time for myself, some time to think."

"Thanks Katherine." Neide nodded and a cursory round of applause, led by Imelda, followed.

"Oh and I'm married to Vincent and have two grown children Thomas and Claire," Katherine said. There was much more she could have added.

A pattern was formed as people spoke in the order they

were seated. Suzy and Declan introduced themselves, then the two women from Scotland, Morag and Louise, who had been persuaded to come by a friend who had been before. Katherine suspected they were about her own age or maybe a little older. Morag spoke with a voice darkened by a lifetime of smoking. Her name reminded Katherine of an old daytime soap opera she used to watch when the kids were at school. Disappointment or sadness seemed etched into the features of her friend Louise. She shared that she was recently divorced after twenty plus years of marriage and that she was hoping The Retreat would help her start the next chapter of her life. Katherine wondered about the circumstances of her separation.

The next in line was a young girl with short brown hair. She stayed rooted to the chair, her eyes locked on the floor. She was about to speak when the next woman along broke the silence. Marie was her name and she confidently declared she was a life coach from Belfast. She had short bleached blonde hair and a strong Northern Ireland accent. Katherine felt her skirt was just a little too short and her top too low for her age. She spoke first about renovating an old mill she and her partner had bought and how they recently featured on one of those property programmes on TV. She spoke at length about how she felt it was important to invest in her own development and to take time out to sharpen her own saw, a phrase Katherine vaguely remembered from a book she once read. Katherine felt it was a little inappropriate when she offered her coaching services to the group. The throat-clearing from several of the others indicated they felt the same.

"Now who's left?" Neidi motioned to the young shy girl with short brown hair. "Sophie?"

Katherine felt sorry for her. She sat on her hands and rocked back and forth, her legs wrapped around the chair. English was not her first language. She was very young, barely eighteen Katherine surmised. She said she was from Bruges and that her mother, who was a friend of Neide's, had arranged the week for her.

"And is there anything in particular you would like to get from this week Sophie?" Neide asked.

"Maybe just to be a bit more confident." The young woman's honest words struck a chord with Katherine. She didn't put up a front, she didn't try to look or sound sorted, she was just herself and now she had the respect of everyone in the room.

The last of the group to speak was a very overweight woman. She introduced herself as Tonya, a barrister from London. Katherine couldn't help thinking there was something toad-like about her. Dressed head to toe in black and with a heavy brow and loud voice, Katherine could easily picture her arguing her cases in court. The pink bands that secured her pigtails and her large flower-shaped ring looked odd, as if she was playing at dressing up. She had heat rash on her arms and had a habit of making fists with her hands. There was something prickly about her demeanour that made Katherine feel uncomfortable.

"Great, thank you all for sharing. I know some of you found it more challenging than others, but as we are going to be together for the next five days, it is so much easier when we break the ice and get to know one another. Now, there is just one more exercise for this morning, then we will break and you can wander into the town and explore the Sunday market."

"The lace is a great buy. Our friend Rosemary got some when she was here," Morag said.

"There's another person due to join us, she won't be staying here but she will be joining the workshops. She should be here shortly," Neide said, glancing at the door and her watch. "Right on cue, you two." Neide motioned for Serendipity and another man to take a seat. "I think most of you will have met Serendipity and this is my partner." Neide said his name, but Katherine couldn't quite make it out. It sounded like Iwan. A difficult Welsh name to pronounce even without Neide's accent. Serendipity gave a little wave and took the spare seat beside Sophie. The man, dressed head to toe in white, placed his arm around Neide's shoulder. He towered over her. Morag whispered away to Louise before masking whatever she was saying with a cough.

"Believe it or believe it not, but two years ago I was sitting in one of those chairs," Iwan said. "If you told me then how my life would be transformed I wouldn't have believed you, but that story is for later in the week." He didn't sound Welsh, Katherine thought, more north of England. "So let me just say to you, this week could change your life." His overt enthusiasm grated.

"Now being aware of the time, let's make a start with the main exercise for this session, the gratitude list," Neide said when her partner paused for breath. "Most people are called to a retreat like this because they are seeking something, but before we are ready to receive new gifts, we have to be thankful for all the gifts we currently have in our lives."

Serendipity bounced out of her chair to ensure everyone had a pen and paper.

"Think of your life at the moment and write down at least five things you are grateful for. Of course don't limit yourself to five, write as many as you want."

Katherine stared at the empty page in her new notebook. Everyone else had begun writing. Iwan, if that was his name, bent and kissed Neide on the cheek. Katherine was not a fan of public displays of affection and she felt there was something a little showy about his stance.

Katherine began to write.

I'm grateful for my health.
I'm grateful for my children.
I'm grateful for the friends I have.
I'm grateful that I was able to come here.

Katherine needed another one. *I'm grateful for my lovely home.* She contemplated writing that she was grateful for having

Vincent in her life, but it wouldn't have felt sincere.

"Now maybe before the week is over you will add more to your gratitude list. Gratitude is the antidote to many things. You cannot be sad and grateful at the same time, or worried and grateful, or frustrated and grateful. When I get stressed, I ask myself what am I grateful for right now, and that always seems to help. Gratitude changes our focus," Neide said circling the room again.

Katherine could see a quizzical look on Bruce's face as if he was preparing to ask a question.

"Would anyone like to share what's on their list?" Neide asked. There were no volunteers and thankfully Bruce just re-crossed his legs.

"Imelda you were writing away. Would you mind sharing what you wrote?"

"It mightn't make sense to anyone else; I just jotted down what came into my head."

"That's the best way to do it, go for it."

In a measured tone, Imelda began to speak.

"I'm grateful that I've never known hunger.
I'm grateful that my mother gave birth to me and
kept me when others told her not to.
I'm grateful that my lungs have worked perfectly for seventy-
five years and that my heart has not missed one beat; even
though I'm told I occasionally have an irregular one.
I'm grateful for the love of God that nourishes me in every moment.
I'm grateful that I have the luxury of being able to
contemplate issues of well-being and spiritual growth,
when millions struggle to put food on the table.
I'm grateful that I have a table and a lovely home to put it in.
I'm grateful for the people who join me at my
table and the conversations we share.

21

*I'm grateful for all the teachers that have
come and will come into my life.
I'm grateful that I can read and write, knowing
that my father could do neither.
I'm grateful for the birds that welcomed the day with me this morning.
I'm grateful for the music of Tina Turner
that moves my feet and my soul.
I'm grateful for the grace of spirit that is always available to
me, even when I do my best to divorce myself from it.
I'm grateful to be in this room, in this moment,
which will never come again.*

The room was silent.

"That's as much as I had time to write." Imelda closed her pad.

"Wow, what a way to close our first session." Neidi placed her hand on her heart and Katherine could see that she was genuinely moved.

Katherine looked at her own paltry list. She picked up her pen and added another item. *I'm grateful that I know Imelda.*

A knock on the glass door stirred the room from their contemplation. All heads turned.

"Ah there you are," Neide said.

A tall black woman with close cropped white hair stepped into the Big Room. Her pale dress glowed in the sunlight. Neide directed her to the vacant chair.

"Everyone, this is Corinne, the final member of our group."

CHAPTER 3

Katherine would have liked company, but she found herself walking towards the market alone. Imelda had excused herself as soon as the morning workshop ended, saying she wanted to visit the church. Katherine hoped there might be a few people hovering in the courtyard ready to venture out, but only Serendipity and the shy young Belgian girl, Sophie were in sight, engrossed in conversation by the cactus garden.

Neide had said that you couldn't miss the market. It transformed the sleepy hilltop town every Sunday. Turn right and right again and head up the hill towards the town square, or just follow the people, Neide had said. Katherine hoped there would be a stall where she could pick up a towel.

A convoy of buses lined the street where the taxi had left Katherine the night before. Cars, jeeps and motorcycles parked wherever they could find space. The warren-like side streets were too narrow for traffic. A bus driver kept honking his horn in a futile attempt to reverse.

Not wanting to run the gauntlet of the congested street, Katherine turned into an appealing cobbled side street, with a tree growing right in the middle of it. Several cats slumbered in its shade. The one with white paws looked suspiciously like the cat that had scared her during the night when it stalked by her window.

The noonday sun glared off the whitewashed walls. Even behind her sunglasses Katherine was squinting. She could feel the sun bite at her arms and shoulders. Thankfully she had remembered her sun lotion.

The alleyway slowly wound uphill past boldly painted doors. Window boxes alive with colour, all framed by the foil of the brilliant white walls. It would be too easy to get lost in the maze of streets and passageways.

Ahead, stalls lined both sides of the street and beyond them Katherine could see the square heaving with people, tourists from all the coastal resorts who sacrificed their sunbathing for a few hours of retail therapy and some distraction for the kids. It was quite a contrast to the peaceful oasis of The Retreat. Music blared from a stall selling CDs. Children ran ahead of parents, warnings shouted after them in several languages.

The market stalls were a curious mix of trinkets, touristy souvenirs as well as crafts, jewellery and art. Katherine thought about buying Claire or Mags something, but she wasn't inspired and they wouldn't be expecting anything anyway. She did spy a stall selling beachwear, and thankfully beach towels. If she couldn't find anything plainer she'd return and pick up one of the garishly patterned ones on her way back.

The smell of freshly baked bread stopped Katherine in her tracks. There was a lengthy queue at the stall. A boy replenished the stocks from a transit van parked around the corner. Katherine had hoped to pick up a sandwich, but there were no other food stalls that she could see. Presumably there would be something available in the kitchen at The Retreat.

On the side of the square closest to the church a row of stalls were all selling the lace that one the Scottish women spoke about. The breeze danced with the large pieces draped over the frames of the stalls. The whole row looked like a great ship about to set sail. Making her way towards it Katherine passed a group of street performers, one of whom, a mime artist, handed her a flower. A little embarrassed she dropped a euro into his hat.

The two Scottish women, Morag and Louise were at one of the stalls. From behind they looked alike, similar height, hats, shorts and square ankles.

"Ah Katherine, you've found the lace, I'm stocking up as you can see." It was Morag who spoke, holding up two circles of lace. The cigarette dangling from her lip seemed to complete her. Katherine had a flash of what Morag's home would be like, lace doilies under vases, chintz, heavy curtains and no surface that didn't contain an ornament, memento or photograph, dust-catchers as Vincent called them.

"Beautiful isn't it, and so reasonable," Louise said. "My mother was a great lacemaker. I'm thinking this would be gorgeous on my dining room table, what do you think Morag?"

"Did you enjoy this morning?" Morag asked, stepping to one side, her potential purchases still in her hands.

"I loved Imelda's gratitude list," Katherine said, but the women were diverted by the stall owner revealing more lace creations.

"What did you think of Iam?" Morag asked.

"Sorry?"

"Iam, Neide's partner, the fella that came in."

"What's his name?"

"I–am." Morag emphasised two syllables.

"I thought it was Iwan?"

"No." An expression of animated glee lit up Morag's face. She took Katherine by the elbow. "No he changed his name to, wait for it, Iam Love."

"What?"

"Yes. He was at The Retreat when our friend Rosemary was here. She was telling us about him because she was copied in on some email he sent a few months ago. Colin something, Barton or Burton something like that, he's an accountant from Sunderland, but changed his name to Iam Love. Can you credit it?"

"Get away." Katherine couldn't help but laugh. She suspected Morag liked nothing better than a juicy piece of gossip and this was a story she would be dining out on for the rest of the week.

"Is that a mid-life crisis or what?" Morag chuckled.

"Bizarre."

"You couldn't make it up. And he has two teenage boys, I'm sure they're not telling their mates that their father has changed his name to Iam Love. He changed it by deed poll you know. He wanted to just be called Love, but the officials said he needed two names."

"So he added Iam." Katherine was still shaking her head.

"Imagine, he wanted to be called Love."

"I won't be able to look at him again without cracking up," Louise said joining their conversation having added the tablecloth to her purchases.

"You know Katherine, what is it with some men?" Morag shook her head.

"Well maybe he's happy."

"Maybe he's just released his inner hippy. He grows a beard, doesn't cut his hair, quits his job, out come the tie-dye t-shirts, the open toe sandals, though I shouldn't slag the sandals I'm wearing them myself. What's the betting he'll be strumming a guitar before the week is out."

"Morag you're dreadful."

"I know we're supposed to be non-judgemental, accepting, creative and all that, but sometimes you just have to laugh at the craziness of it all. Let me tell you if you want a really good laugh, make sure you do a re-birthing workshop. Rosemary dragged me to one a few months ago, do you remember me telling you Lou, I had to leave, I thought I was going to wet myself. We had to re-enact coming out of the womb."

"Now that's a bit much Morag," Katherine said allowing Morag to take a breath. She had a willing audience in Katherine and she was now in full flow.

"Hysterical. There was this big woman, though not as big as Tonya; I know I shouldn't be cruel, but there she was lying on the floor pretending she was seeing the world for the first time. An eighteen stone newborn baby. Everyone else was so serious, now maybe it was just my Scottish sensibility but I said hold on now this is mad. And when Rosemary starts to go, she just shakes; we had to get out before we were thrown out." Morag had a tight hold of Katherine's arm. "You just have to laugh sometimes Katherine. We all come to these places for spiritual enlightenment, but some people are so serious. If they just relaxed and had a laugh, at themselves if nothing else, they would be a whole lot better believe you me. Now, you didn't happen to see a stall selling dolls, I collect them, you know the ones in local costume?"

Katherine confessed she hadn't and leaving the two women debating over the mounds of lace she strolled back across the square, realising she hadn't laughed as much in weeks. It was then she noticed Corinne, the tall black woman who came in at the end of the workshop, walking ahead of her.

After she joined them in the Big Room, Corinne had introduced herself to the group. She lived in London and had recently retired from the hotel industry. Katherine was curious to know how she managed it, because the woman looked as if she was only in her mid-forties. Corinne had gone on to explain that she was house-sitting a villa on the coast for a friend and that she was anxious that she wouldn't disturb the dynamic of the group because she wasn't staying with them. Above anything Corinne had said, Katherine remembered her voice. It had a sensuous, velvety quality that made Katherine think about starting a twenty-a-day habit just to emulate the sexiness of it. Now watching Corinne cross the square, she envied her elegance.

Katherine wandered down a narrow side street after Corinne, but lost her in the crowd. There would be more opportunities to speak with this intriguing woman she thought.

Ahead on the left a sign indicated an art gallery. Katherine had read that there were several in Teguise. She stepped down into the small gallery, which she suspected was once someone's front room. A man in a cap sat on a low stool in the corner by the window reading a newspaper, *La Provincia*. He didn't even look up when she walked in; probably weary of the turnstile of tourists seeking respite from the sun.

The space was tiny and Katherine was careful not to collide with some delicate looking sculptures perilously balanced on stands. The paintings were an interesting mixture of modern and more contemporary scenes. Katherine sipped her water. She appreciated the cool air. She drank in the vibrancy of the bold colours and the confidence of the brushstrokes.

She checked her phone. She had sent Vincent a text message before leaving The Retreat, Imelda's gratitude list having prompted her to extend an olive branch. But her phone had remained stubbornly silent. She knew it was Sunday lunchtime and he was probably on the golf course, but a few words from him would at least keep the lines of communication open. She tried to focus on the paintings, but it was difficult not to let her mind wander.

***

The first rule of relationships and temptation is proximity. Mark Goodwin came into Katherine's life when he accompanied his sister Val to the book group that gathered in her friend Mags' cafe, in early February. Ever the matchmaker, Val had invited the newly single Mark to introduce him to the recently divorced Eve. In most of their eyes Mark was a minor celebrity, a dentist who appeared in an advert for toothpaste and he was the go to expert whenever a daytime TV show wanted to discuss dental hygiene.

There was no doubting Mark was a handsome man. For Katherine, it wasn't the fact that he was classically good-looking with wavy dark hair and the first hints of grey that would soon usher in the adjective distinguished, it was his ease of movement and quiet self-confidence that she found attractive. In many ways he was the complete opposite of Vincent whose drumming fingers and twitchy shoulders betrayed an underlying nervous energy. Eve left the book club early that night, knowing she was wasting her time staying.

At the Golf Club's captain's dinner the following night, where the masters of the universe still held dominion, Katherine knew when Vincent, the newly elected vice captain, put his arm on the back of her chair that several hours later he would be rolling over to her side of the bed. In recent years, sex with Vincent was like her infrequent but dutiful trips back home to Tramore. Katherine always hoped the journey would be more interesting and the destination less awkward. Her imagination usually brought either Russell Crowe in full Gladiator regalia, a dripping wet Colin Firth, or if she was being particularly louche, a smouldering Robert Pattison into her bed. That Friday night she surprised herself, because when she closed her eyes, it was Mark Goodwin she saw.

For some time, Katherine had the niggling feeling that something was missing in her life. Mark's attention reminded her in a very corporeal way, that not only were fun, passion and excitement absent from her life, but also that somehow she was missing too. She found herself paying just a little more attention to what she was wearing and she started to go for her morning walk that little bit earlier on the off chance that she would bump into Mark, knowing he usually did a few laps of the park before starting his surgery.

It had been all perfectly innocent until the book club gathering the following month. They had been in cahoots the entire evening, both trying to sound like they had read the book, Virginia Woolf's *Mrs Dalloway*. Mark offered to drive her home and like a giddy schoolgirl she'd accepted.

***

"Katherine."

Suzy and Declan walked in. Declan ducked just in time to avoid banging his head on the beam over the door.

"It's hot out there isn't it?"

"Did you buy anything in the market?" Suzy asked. A waft of perfume followed her in.

"No, I just pottered around." The three of them were taking up nearly all the available floor space.

"There's a lot of tat isn't there?" Declan said. "Oh that's nice." His eye caught a painting of a tall figure in silhouette on a blue background. "Two thousand, two hundred euros, you'd need to know the artist before forking out that."

"Did you hear the story about the guy that came into the workshop with Serendipity?"

"Neide's partner?" Declan's attention was now back with Katherine.

"Morag filled me in."

Katherine proceeded to tell the story as told to her. Their gasps and laughter were enough to stir the gallery owner from his newspaper.

"That could be you next year Dec, what do you think?" Suzy slapped her friend's shoulder. Declan just grimaced at the thought. "Sure you might even discover you're straight by the end of the week."

"Suzy, I can't even drive straight."

"You should tell Katherine about what happened to your parents last Christmas."

"Now that's a story and a half, told best over a glass of something I think. Why don't we find somewhere nice for lunch? Katherine you'll join us won't you?" Declan was already halfway out the door.

"If you're sure."

"Of course and didn't you say something Dec about a great tapas bar nearby?"

"There's supposed to be a good place off the square near the church." Declan led the way, side-stepping the throngs of people that still filled the narrow streets.

Katherine complimented Suzy on her sunglasses, secretly hoping Suzy would notice that hers had interlocking Cs as well.

"We're not due back till three, so loads of time for a glass of vino," Suzy said.

"Everywhere will probably be jammed," Katherine said looking at the crowd in the square.

"Don't forget this is Lanzarote, lunch is much later here."

"And most of these people will be heading for their buses and their picture menus of burgers and chips," Declan added.

They passed the church. Katherine wondered if Imelda was inside.

"This must be it," Declan said stopping by an archway with black barrels and tall shrubs on either side. A chalk board propped against the wall had the word 'open' written on it. Above the archway hung a wooden sign reading 'Palacio del Marques'.

It was like walking into a dark cave. It took a moment for Katherine's eyes to adjust. Three pairs of sunglasses were pushed up. Katherine could hear the sounds of a restaurant but couldn't see any people. Ahead what initially looked like a mosaic was on closer inspection a wall of wine bottles.

"They're not going to run out any time soon," Declan said.

A red arrow directed them to the right. They were walking around the edge of a courtyard. Now the people came into view. It wasn't a large restaurant; perhaps seating for fifty, but it was a hive of activity. Waiters all dressed in black weaved between closely spaced tables, plates and glasses pirouetting above diners' heads. The aroma of garlic stimulated Katherine's taste buds. Great clusters of flowers, bougainvillea and roses tumbled into the restaurant from the over-hanging roof. It was a space Katherine would gladly just sit in, even if food wasn't served.

They waited to be seated. Katherine rubbed the leaves of a purple basil plant thriving in the sunshine. She doubted if Vincent would keep an eye on her herbs and vegetable garden this week. A row of old wine bottles their sides sculpted with hardened candle wax, and several lanterns of different sizes lined the wall behind them. Spread around the courtyard they would create a magical atmosphere. Already Katherine wanted to return one evening.

"And no unruly children," Declan said scanning the restaurant.

"Dec tell Katherine now about your parents last Christmas. This will make you laugh."

"Well." Declan gathered himself for a performance as the witty raconteur. "My parents have a place in France, they spend most of their time there now." His tone was serious.

"Stunning house in the Loire."

"Suzy, who's telling this story? Anyway, there is an ex-pat community, mainly retired English couples, you can imagine the whole scene. Well, last Boxing Day my parents were invited to friends of theirs, Max and Sheila, a couple in their sixties. So picture the scene: my folks ringing their doorbell, father in his military tie, bottle of wine in hand. The door opens and Max is standing there, dressed as a woman."

"Get away."

"Now this is a man approaching seventy, married for forty odd years."

"I couldn't believe it when Dec told me."

"Now Mum had said she always found him a little strange. He's balding and has a bit of a comb over, but here he was in a blouse, his hair combed back tied in a bow, wearing a black leather skirt and high heels."

"Oh no." Katherine was laughing again.

"It's the thought of the black leather skirt that gets me

every time." Suzy had her hand across her mouth to contain her laughter.

"What did your parents do?" Katherine asked.

"This is the funny bit. They said nothing."

"I wouldn't know where to look."

"They sat through dinner and behaved as if everything was normal."

"But how did they not just burst out laughing?"

"You have to remember Katherine, my parents are stiff upper lip Brits, keep calm and carry on."

"But surely your mother spoke with his wife?"

"She rang my mother the next day, saying that that was something Max had done for years, he wanted to express that part of his personality and apparently he felt safe doing so with my parents."

"He should have warned them though. Your poor parents, they must have been mortified."

"And do you know what my mum, bless her, said to Sheila?"

"What?"

"He had great legs."

The three of them burst into laughter. Suzy grabbed Katherine for support. Declan just looked to the skies knowing he had delivered the punchline perfectly.

A young Spanish waiter showed them to a table at the far end of the courtyard that thankfully was in the shade. The table had a beautifully patterned tiled surface. It wobbled slightly, but the waiter quickly secured a piece of card under one leg. Suzy nudged Katherine as Declan hung on the waiter's every word. Before leaving them, the waiter said there was no menu, only a set lunch for fifteen euros and they only serve wine. Katherine loved the idea of a menu-less restaurant.

"Oh, chilled white I think would be nice, what do you think Katherine?" Suzy asked.

"I don't know, I want to be alert this afternoon."

"You're on your holidays!"

Five minutes later they were toasting The Bliss Retreat, gratitude lists and hot sunny weather. The platter of tapas looked like a painting. Pieces of chicken, thin slices of local cheese, a small meat patty, salmon, salad, something unidentifiable but delicious wrapped in filo pastry and a range of dips delighted their senses of taste and smell. It didn't take long for a second bottle of wine to be ordered.

"This beats the food at The Retreat," Declan said.

"I'll be back here again before the week is out," Katherine said pointing out the line of small birds perched on the roof ready to dive and retrieve any discarded crumbs.

"It's always such a treat to eat lunch in the sunshine with a glass of wine," Suzy said moving her chair back into the sun.

"So what have we got at three? Do we need another bottle of wine?" Declan said.

"I think it's a continuation of this morning. Neide is only easing us in."

"If Iam Love is there, I'll struggle to keep the laughing in, you know what I'm like." Suzy smiled refilling her glass. Katherine felt that these two would happily stay where they were all afternoon.

"So Katherine you left your husband at home?" Declan enquired.

"I escaped for the week."

"And you have two children you said?" Suzy asked, leaning in.

"Yes, Thom and Claire. Claire's studying in Manchester, well she's just finished her first year, she'll be going back in September."

"What's she studying?"

"Physiotherapy."

"And what does Thom do?"

"I think he's still trying to figure that out."

"Aren't we all?" Declan said.

"He talks a lot about photography, he has a blog and works part-time in a department store. In fairness he's never idle." Katherine paused. "Oh and what's the phrase he used, he's a friend of Dorothy."

Declan nearly spat out his wine. "Now that's a phrase I haven't heard in a while." He laughed.

"What do you both do?" Katherine asked, trying to steer the conversation.

"Advertising, for my sins," Declan said.

"I've my own interior design business." Suzy rummaged for a business card and handed it to Katherine. "I made the leap two years ago, when I took a redundancy package from a bank in the city."

"I like your card," Katherine said feeling the weight of it.

"I love it, doesn't feel like work half the time."

"Plumping cushions and spending other people's money, isn't that it Suze?"

"You're only jealous, because I was brave enough to follow my passion."

"Passion?" Suzy gave Declan another dig in the ribs as he stared at the young waiter passing their table.

If they were returning to a traditional classroom in the afternoon, she suspected Suzy and Declan would be the two at the back, passing notes to each other. Katherine had noticed Suzy's habit of running her fingers through her hair, piling it on her head then letting it fall down during the workshop. Here in the sunshine she did it continuously, as if starring in her own shampoo advert.

"Of course Katherine now that I've got the work life sorted, I'm hoping this week to sort out the love life issues." Suzy was beginning to slur the odd word.

"Well unless you fancy that guy Bruce, I wouldn't hold your breath." Declan chirped. "But of course he is single and that makes a change for you." Declan winked at Katherine.

"Bitch." Suzy slapped his arm. Katherine couldn't help thinking that these two were performing life, rather than living it.

"Well at least you know your pattern now Suze." Declan rubbed the front of his head, causing his dark hair to stand on end. "You're attracted to unavailable men."

"That may be, at least it is not boys in men's bodies," Suzy said turning her back to Declan. "But you know Katherine I'm more annoyed at myself. The last guy, Nick, he had me at his beck and call. At first it was fun, you know when you're swept off your feet. But do you know he even bought a separate mobile phone to use to contact me. I knew he was still living with his wife and I suppose I knew he was never going to leave her."

"But you loved him." Declan touched her arm.

"Yes, I loved him and I got hurt."

"I've said it before Suze we're the sort of people who fall in love with love. We get so caught up in the craziness of it all that we project all the qualities we want to see on to the man. It's never really real."

Katherine thought of Mark. Perhaps emboldened by the wine, the sunshine and the easy conversation she pictured Mark sitting in the unoccupied fourth chair at the table. She imagined what it would be like if she were to allow Mark to sweep her off her feet.

"Oh, there's no fool like an old fool."

Suzy looked so smart, together and happy, but the exterior hid a secret. Behind the glamour was a woman at the junction of mid-life, nursing a wound because she loved a man who didn't love her in the way she wanted to be loved. Although their circumstances were totally different and Katherine was a good ten years older, they had more in common than Chanel sunglasses.

"And do you know what's funny Katherine?" Declan asked.

"I run the same pattern as Suzy's men."

"Maybe that's why we get on," Suzy said. "Remember you're my fall back guy."

"Suzy says I shy away from commitment. Or as Paul, my ex, put it, I never invest in relationships. We were together nine months."

"Which is the equivalent of what, nine years in the gay world?" Suzy's high spirits were returning.

"Is that like dog years?" Katherine chipped in.

"Dog is right." Suzy was laughing again.

"Whatever. But anyway, Paul wanted us to live together. It was all very serious, all too grown up."

"You were just scared, admit it," Suzy said.

"Maybe."

"Afraid of giving yourself one hundred per cent to a relationship for fear of being hurt."

"Anyway you can see Katherine why we're here. We will be front row centre at the relationship workshop."

"That should be an interesting one alright."

"You know deep down we all just want to be loved don't we?" Declan said motioning for the bill. "We want to be loved for who we are not who we think we should be."

"Sometimes he comes up with something quite profound, doesn't he?" Suzy said. "It's a pity we have to listen to drivel the rest of the time."

Katherine excused herself to visit the bathroom. Declan's off the cuff remark had gone to the core of her recent troubles. She no longer felt loved by Vincent and maybe above and beyond anything else, that was all she wanted, to feel loved. And it wasn't just Vincent. Thom had moved out and now Claire was at college, she wasn't needed anymore. No one really depended on her. Everyone was getting on with their lives and she felt she was standing still on the sidelines.

Checking she hadn't crushed the flower she had dropped

into her bag, she remembered she had her new notebook with her. Sitting on the loo, she scribbled two more lessons into her journal. Like Morag said, *don't get too serious, remember to laugh, especially at yourself.* Below that she added *we all just want to be loved, for who we are, not who we think we should be.* There was something else she couldn't quite sculpt into a succinct one-liner. Something to do with love or being in love with love. In the end she wrote *'I am Love'* but added a string of question marks.

Returning to the table she contemplated sharing her story. The temptation of marvellous Mark and vile Vincent. But speaking about it she felt would somehow trivialise it, and besides she didn't know how to tell the story because she didn't know the punchline.

"Now I have to pick up a towel on the way back, I forgot to pack one."

"Same with us," Suzy said linking her arm through Katherine's as they left the restaurant. "We're used to bathrooms stocked with fluffy towels and toiletries to pinch. But just ask for some, that's what we did yesterday and Serendipity, fab name that isn't it, dropped some into our rooms."

It was almost three. They would be a few minutes late for the afternoon workshop.

Declan linked Katherine's other arm and the three of them, slightly tipsy, half-walked, half-skipped back through the labyrinthine side streets of the old town, no one quite sure where they were going.

Katherine was too busy chatting to hear her phone ring.

CHAPTER 4

Katherine, Suzy and Declan tiptoed into the Big Room, mouthing their apologies to Neide. Katherine felt like the bold girl in school. Giddy spirits and maze-like streets meant they had probably taken the most circuitous route possible back to The Retreat. If it wasn't for the fact that Katherine had recognised the street with a tree in the middle of it, they would still be wandering around the old town.

All heads turned to inspect the latecomers. Bruce clicked his tongue in what Katherine hoped was mock disapproval, especially as she now had no option but to take the empty seat between him and Tonya; Declan and Suzy having made a beeline for the two other vacant spots.

"If we could try to be back on time, out of courtesy to everyone else," Neide said. Tardiness was something she was probably well used to Katherine thought. "As you see, most people have changed seats. As I was saying, if you sit in a different spot you will have a different perspective."

Bruce and Tonya occupied the same seats as they had that morning, and being wedged between them for the afternoon was, Katherine believed, her punishment for being late. Pushing her bag under her seat brought her too close to Bruce's exposed feet. She swallowed hard. Tonya looked straight ahead, oblivious of her new neighbour.

"You haven't missed anything, we were discussing the morning session and bargains found in the market," Neide smiled.

Katherine checked to see if there was garlic on her breath by coughing into her hand. The breeze had retreated and the sun was mounting an attack, creeping ever closer to the semicircle of students. Katherine could feel herself sweating. A thin line of scented smoke rose from the sage stick. Beneath the acrid tang there was a note of staleness, perhaps body odour. Katherine hoped it didn't emanate from her.

"We have a wonderful brainstorming exercise planned for this afternoon. It's probably my favourite." Neide rubbed her hands. "And it's all about inspiration."

"Can't wait," Imelda said from the centre of the semicircle. She was sitting next to Corinne. Katherine cursed herself for not getting back on time.

"This exercise sets us up for the workshops ahead and people always say they enjoy it."

Sounds of rustling and crunching came from the far end of the row. Morag had opened a bag of nuts and seeds and began passing them down the line.

"Bird seed," Bruce whispered.

"Let's get started by dividing into groups of two or three. Serendipity will you be joining in?"

Katherine hadn't noticed that Serendipity was sitting on a beanbag in the corner, sucking a lollipop.

"I might just hover, if that's ok."

People began to stand and form groups. The packet of nuts was passed back without reaching Katherine.

"Maybe work with people you have yet to connect with. Morag and Louise maybe split up for this one."

Katherine wanted to get up and form a group with Imelda and Corinne, but she stayed where she was thinking it would be rude to just move away from Bruce and Tonya.

"I suppose it's us three then?" Bruce spoke, sharing his attention between the two women.

"Looks like it." Tonya added.

Tonya was a big mound of a woman. She totally consumed the chair beneath her. Ten dainty toes with dots of pink varnish peeped out beneath a floor length black dress. Her hair, which

Katherine thought could do with a good wash was pulled into two pigtails, secured with pink ties that Katherine could now see were shaped liked poodles.

"I want you to chat about how do you know when you are inspired and how do you feel when you are inspired," Neide said to Imelda and Corinne who were working together and to Morag who had buddied up with Suzy.

"Fantastic." Imelda was practically bouncing up and down.

"I presume Neide we can leave the room?" Corinne asked.

"As long as you're back here for four." The four of them stepped into the courtyard and headed for the tree by the cactus garden. She knew she was just being silly, but Katherine felt left out.

The other groups moved outside too. Declan gave her a wink as he wandered out behind Louise to discuss how inspiration differs from motivation. Marie the life coach from Belfast and Sophie were handed armfuls of old magazines, their task, the one Katherine would have loved, was to cut out images they found inspiring.

"Bruce, Katherine and Tonya, great, I want you to discuss what inspires you. Now you don't have to agree on everything, what inspires one of you may not inspire someone else, but note everything that comes up. If you need any help I'll be in the kitchen and Serendipity will be around."

"We might as well stay here," Tonya said rolling her eyes to the heavens.

Katherine felt like she was the last one being picked for the hockey team.

***

"So." Bruce moved his chair to face the two women. "What inspires you Katherine?"

Put on the spot she couldn't think of anything. Bruce's glasses hung from his beard. His gimlet eyes reminded Katherine of Dr Clarebourne the psychiatrist she saw at the hospital.

"Any ideas Tonya?" Bruce asked, releasing Katherine from her growing discomfort.

Tonya just shook her head and started texting.

"Let me throw a few ideas out there?" Bruce twisted his pen. Men of a certain age really shouldn't wear shorts Katherine thought. "Books inspire me; I read a lot. And I know this probably makes me sound sad, but I enjoy going through the Law Review every month. As a barrister Tonya that's probably the same for you."

"I can't stand the Law Review." Tonya remained focused on her phone.

Awkward silence became the fourth member of their group.

"Well I think you should jot down reading as a source of inspiration Bruce. I'll pick up a gardening magazine every so often which I always enjoy," Katherine said. This was going to be a challenging exercise, not just because inspiration was a topic she had never really contemplated before, but because she suspected they were going to have to walk on eggshells with Tonya.

"You're getting started?" Serendipity knelt beside them.

"Just about. It's a tough one," Bruce said.

"Think about times when you have felt inspired and what you were doing or what made you feel that way." Serendipity's hair was also in pigtails but the two young women could not be more different. Enthusiastic about everything, innocent, perhaps a little naive would be how Katherine would describe Serendipity. Surly, bordering on rude and obese would be the picture she would paint of Tonya. Katherine seized the moment to ask Serendipity for a towel for her room.

Tonya shook her head. Katherine didn't know what the young woman's problem was, but it was behaviour she wouldn't tolerate in one of her own children.

Bruce pulled over one of the flipcharts and wrote the words 'reading', and 'books'. Katherine suggested art as a source of inspiration and Bruce readily agreed. Bruce added travel and nature. Beautiful scenery was another of Katherine's which led to photography being added to their list.

"Painting." The word erupted from Katherine. "I used to love painting and I appreciate good painting, which I suppose is art, but for me anyway add painting to the list."

"Great, making art, not just viewing it, I see where you're coming from. You must be excited about Ran Kaplan's workshop then? Not a bad list so far." Bruce tapped the marker on the flipchart.

"Tonya, anything you think we should add?" Katherine asked, aware that the woman with the phone glued to her hand hadn't yet contributed to the exercise.

"I don't see the point of this." She dropped the phone onto her lap.

"I suppose it's to help us be more aware of the things that inspire us, that make us feel good."

"I don't see why we couldn't do it individually."

"To help us get to know each other perhaps?" Bruce answered.

Tonya just shrugged.

"What about music?" Bruce suggested. "I love classical music."

"That should definitely go on the list." Katherine compensated for Tonya's lethargy by being more animated.

"What do you think Tonya, would you be happy if we added music to our list?" Bruce asked. Reaching for his bottle of water on the table behind her, he inadvertently brushed Tonya's shoulder.

"I'd appreciate it if you didn't touch me. Don't invade my personal space." She glared at both of them.

"I didn't mean anything by it." Bruce was clearly taken aback.

"We are all just trying get along," Katherine said in an attempt to defuse the situation. The role of peacemaker came easily to her.

Without uttering another word, Tonya stood up and stomped out. Katherine and Bruce just stared at each other.

"My God what's up with her?" Bruce asked sitting down, clearly deflated.

"She's just incredibly rude. I don't know what her problem is."

"Should I go after her?"

"No let her stew."

"What?"

"Let her stew. As my mother used to say, let her stew in her own juices. Let's just keep going with this exercise. We're not going to let her spoil the afternoon."

Distracted by Tonya's antics, their ideas slowed. Katherine couldn't fathom how someone so huffy and irritable and clearly having many issues would come on a holiday like this. She could tell Bruce wasn't used to such irrational behaviour. Behind the beard and the persona of a distinguished legal boffin, she sensed a kind heart.

They were stirred from their deliberation by roars of laughter from the courtyard. Katherine stood to investigate. Corinne and Imelda sat in the shade by the cactus garden were clearly enjoying themselves. Imelda's face was red from laughing. There was plenty of banter between them and the others spread around the long table outside the kitchen.

"People are inspiring." Katherine took the marker from Bruce.

"Those who have overcome challenges." Bruce nodded.

"Take Imelda, a woman in her seventies, who has made some dramatic changes in her life. You know she travelled around Asia last year by herself."

"Good for her. So yes, jot down 'people'. Maybe it isn't in

the same category, but when I was teaching, I used to love when students were really interested in what I was teaching. Seeing them develop their thinking, their critical reasoning, I always found that inspiring."

"Sure we'll add that one as well – 'seeing people develop.'"

"And seeing ourselves develop?"

"I'll buy that." Katherine was enjoying writing on the flipchart.

"Your writing is better than mine." Bruce put his hands behind his head. Before Katherine thought it was a pose of arrogance, but now she could see it was what he did when he relaxed. "You know Katherine, I had a reputation for being tough when I was teaching, but I was only tough because that's how my students really learnt. I wanted them to argue their points, to challenge me just as I challenged them."

"I'm sure they respected you for that."

"Hearing a student argue their point, making their case, that's what I really enjoyed, seeing them grow I suppose, that was the inspiring part of it. Now that I think of it, I suppose that lesson applies outside college too."

"The classroom of life." Katherine recalled the phrase.

They had managed to fill the page. Katherine excused herself as she needed to visit to bathroom before the group reconvened. The toilet off the kitchen was closer, but she preferred the privacy of her room.

She got a big wave from Imelda as she passed the cactus garden. There was no sign of Tonya.

A green and white striped towel was folded neatly at the end of her bed. She must remember to thank Serendipity. Lifting her blouse she sprayed deodorant under her arms. The floral freshness enlivened her.

It was only when she took her hairbrush from her bag that she saw she had missed a call from Vincent. He hadn't left a message, which was typical of him. She contemplated phoning back but she didn't want to be late again for the workshop. The compromise was a brief text saying she would phone later.

She held the phone in her hand as she re-crossed the courtyard, just in case he sent her a quick 'ok', but no message appeared. In the Big Room everyone was retaking their seats. Katherine was relieved that Tonya's chair remained empty.

It was time for the groups to share their findings. Katherine was ready, pen in hand. She hoped when it was their turn that Bruce would be happy to read out what they had noted. Declan spoke first. He said his group had decided that motivation could be positive or negative, the carrot or the stick, whilst inspiration was always positive. Katherine suspected they were all Declan's points, they had a business-like tone to them. Louise just nodded along.

"Now I always think the clue to motivation is in the word." Neide moved to the flipchart and started writing. "If we add the letter 'e' into the first part of the word 'motivation', we have the word 'motive'. Motive meaning why; why something is important to us. If something is not important to us we are not going to do anything about it, we are not going to be motivated. Now if we add in the letter 'c' to the second part of the word 'motivation' we get 'action'. It's very difficult to be motivated if we're just sitting still. Action means movement and energy."

All heads were nodding. Katherine scribbled in her journal.

Marie the life coach held up a collage of images she and Sophie had collated. Words of approval and admiration flowed from the group. Trees, people exercising, the faces of children, a designer handbag, a sleek looking car and a turquoise sea were some of the images making up the colourful montage.

"You know you will all have a chance to do something similar later in the week, when we discuss vision boards and goal-setting," Neide said. Katherine felt excited about the prospect of working with the images. Katherine could see Sophie in particular light up with the positive feedback. "That's a great exercise in creativity and of course that's the topic for tomorrow."

"Inspiration and creativity go hand in hand, don't they?" Marie spoke still exhibiting her creation. In her four inch heels and short skirt Katherine thought she looked like a hostess on a game show.

"For sure, it's difficult to be creative unless you're inspired." Neide motioned for her to retake her seat.

Morag spoke on behalf of herself and Suzy. She reported how they all loved the feeling of inspiration and that they would like to be able to experience more of it more often.

"When I'm inspired I make the best decisions." Corinne said, her silky voice a joy to listen to. "I feel like I'm the best of myself. I don't second guess myself, my thinking is clear. I feel congruent."

"In the zone." Suzy added.

"Fantastic," Neide said. "Sounds like there was some great conversation under that tree."

"And laughter." Imelda added.

"Like motivation I think the clue to inspiration is in the word." Neide started writing on the flipchart again. "If we split the word and drop a few letters we have 'in spirit', being connected to spirit."

"Or allowing spirit to flow into us," Imelda added, grinning from ear to ear.

Katherine wrote the words 'in spirit' beneath the words 'motive' and 'action' in her journal. She wasn't sure what she would do with them, but she felt they were worth recording.

"I remember reading a beautiful phrase in something a while back." Corinne was speaking again. "It was something like, God's love will always shine on us, but it is up to us whether we let it shine through us."

"Beautiful, and true," Imelda said.

"I feel inspiration is something similar." Corinne continued.

47

"Inspiration is always available to us, but it is up to us whether we connect with it or act on it."

As she wrote what Corinne had said, Katherine also jotted down the point Bruce had made about growing when we are challenged. Katherine wondered if she was growing. If the logic of Bruce's point was valid, she had to be growing more now than she had been in years. Looking at the faces in the room and the notes already filling the first few pages of her journal, it felt like she was in the right place for some serious growth.

When it came to their turn to share, thankfully Bruce took the lead. There were plenty of nods and murmurs of approval when he finished going through their list. Katherine felt relieved that they had done the exercise properly, then proud when Neide said they had come up with more points than the group had the previous week.

"Now we are all going to think for a few minutes about what inspires us. Bruce and Katherine maybe you can add to your list, but this is a question that's useful for us all to reflect on." Neide circled the group as she spoke.

Katherine copied down the words from their flipchart page. Her mind wandered to what the group might be doing for dinner. She then realised that food was something she always found inspiring – cooking it, eating it, shopping for ingredients, going to restaurants, reading reviews. Whether enjoyable was the same as inspirational, she wasn't sure, but she added food to her inspiration list.

Neide then invited everyone to share one thing they had written, starting at the far end of the line.

Louise who still had her bag of lace under her chair and an almost empty packet of nuts and seeds said she found her children inspiring. Katherine felt guilty for not having Thom and Claire on her list.

Marie said it was her clients, seeing them progress.

Sophie spoke softly but again her words struck a chord with

48

Katherine. "I love to dance, to move to music."

Suzy said fashion and design inspired her and that she was fortunate to now be working in the area of design.

"If we can harness our inspirations, our passions and create our profession around them, well that's the ideal," Neide said.

"Like you've done here, with The Bliss Retreat," Suzy stated.

"That's was the plan, for sure."

Declan was next. He and Suzy had been chuckling whilst doing the exercise and Katherine could imagine some of the comments they were sharing. She suspected when Declan said he was inspired by travelling to new places and meeting new people, he was sharing one of the less risqué ones the two of them had been whispering.

Imelda was next and after her powerful gratitude list from the morning session, Katherine was expecting some more profound words.

"I completely agree with what you said about inspiration being 'in spirit' Neide so all I wrote is knowing that wherever I am I can connect with spirit, with God, whenever I take a moment to breathe and relax. I don't know if that was doing the exercise properly, but I'm inspired when I allow myself to be inspired, when I get out of my own way. I suppose that's the point I'm making."

"You know Imelda I've not really thought about it that way before, so thank you," Neide said.

Katherine noticed Corinne place her hand on Imelda's arm.

"I wrote many things, I've found this a really useful exercise." It was now Corinne's turn. "I agree with everything that's been mentioned and I love what Imelda just said about allowing myself to be inspired. So if I choose just one item from my list, it would have to be my granddaughter Nenah. She's nineteen and just heading out into the world. I'm inspired by her spirit, her energy, her enthusiasm for life, despite some recent knocks she has had."

49

"How can you have a nineteen-year-old granddaughter?" Suzy voiced what everyone else was thinking.

"In the same way I've a forty-two-year-old son." Corinne laughed.

"No way," Marie said.

"I'll be sixty-three in November," Corinne said matter-of-factly.

"I don't believe you." Suzy shook her head.

Katherine looked at a slightly embarrassed Corinne. She couldn't believe that this poised woman was over ten years older than her.

"You'll have to tell us your secret." Marie joked, readjusting a bra strap.

"Bottle your secret and you'd make a fortune," Suzy said. "Katherine you should add Corinne's name to the list on the flipchart as sources of inspiration."

Just for fun Katherine wrote Corinne's name at the bottom of the page. Corinne smiled at her, shaking her head. It was the first time they made eye contact.

It was then Morag's turn and in an effort to come up with something different she said that she loved motorbikes. She said she was inspired by everything about them, the smell of burning rubber on the roads, the excitement of the races, even the leather gear. She said she tried to get to the Isle of Man races each year, but that it had been ages since she was actually on a bike.

Suzy made some comment to Declan that resulted in him digging his elbow into her arm.

There was no mention of Tonya and her empty chair was not queried by the group. The fact that Neide didn't enquire after her suggested she had already spoken with Tonya, or what was probably more likely that Tonya had found Neide and complained about the exercise and Bruce's so called invasion of her space.

Katherine decided to share that she was inspired by food and Bruce mentioned his love of hillwalking.

Neide invited them all to give themselves a round of applause and resumed her position at the front of the group.

"We don't often spend time thinking or reflecting on those things that inspire us. But as you said Morag, we all like to be inspired. It's a feeling of connection, or being in spirit Imelda." Katherine loved the way Neide linked back to the comments people had shared. "If we are more aware of the things or situations that inspire us then surely it makes sense to connect with them more purposefully. If you know you are inspired and enjoy hillwalking Bruce then how can you make sure you go hillwalking regularly. Or Corinne how can you visit with or stay in touch with your granddaughter? I'm sure there are things you have all written down that you haven't done in a while? Maybe it would be a good idea to plan to do one thing from your list when you return home."

Katherine couldn't remember the last time she had visited an art gallery in Ireland, but when she did, she always enjoyed it. Everything Neide was saying was making sense.

"And most of the pursuits you all mentioned don't cost a lot. We can get books from the library, walking in nature is free, most art galleries are free, being still and allowing inspiration to settle on us is certainly free, isn't it Imelda?"

"Absolutely."

"Perhaps travel has an expense to it Declan?"

"Trust me and my expensive tastes."

"But of course travel is about new experiences, relaxing, exploring and learning, and maybe you could do some of that without actually going on a physical journey. How can you connect with the holiday spirit more frequently? How can you be curious and try new things even when you are at home?"

"That's an interesting point." It was Bruce who spoke. "But difficult to do on a wet November day in London?"

"But it's a different way of viewing a situation." Neide glanced at her watch, prompting others to do likewise. It was just after five. "So tomorrow, for those who are interested, there is a yoga session, at seven."

"Oh count me in for that," Imelda said.

"Iam runs it, just some gentle exercises to start the day. We have enough yoga mats for everyone."

The idea of early morning yoga in the sunshine was appealing, but Katherine suspected it wouldn't be as appealing at five to seven when she would have to haul herself out of bed.

"And we're kicking off in here at nine thirty. As you know we are fortunate to have the artist Ran Kaplan lead the morning session. He'll be speaking about his art and creativity in general. I can't wait. And then there's a change in plans tomorrow afternoon. Pamela who facilitates the relationship workshop has to go to the UK later in the week, so we've brought her slot forward."

Katherine smiled at Suzy and Declan, who gave her the thumbs up.

"Now for the men in the group, you can decide whether you want to stay in the workshop with Pamela or you can do a separate session with Iam on relationships from a male perspective."

"I'd sooner go hillwalking," Bruce whispered to Katherine.

"What about the gay perspective?" Declan asked.

"Have a chat with Pamela tomorrow and decide what would work best for you."

Katherine felt Declan would never be backwards in coming forwards on issues of equality.

"So, I hope you've enjoyed your first day?"

"Fantastic," Imelda said, a sentiment echoed by the room.

***

"Oh Katherine could I have a quick word before you go?" Neide said, extinguishing the sage. "Enjoy the day?"

"I certainly did. And apologies for being late back from lunch, we lost track of time."

"Don't worry about it, it happens quite a bit." Neide tucked her hair behind her ears and gave Katherine her full attention. "I wouldn't normally ask you this, but when you mentioned your love of food earlier an idea popped into my head and if I've learnt anything over the last few years it is to act on those ideas, the flashes of clarity as I call them."

"You were inspired?"

"Feel free to say no, but I was wondering if you would like to put together a meal for the group one of the evenings later in the week. Carlos who does the cooking needs to take Wednesday off for a family wedding and my standby chef has let me down. Myself and Iam would normally cope, but we've been invited to Carlos's niece's wedding too and I don't know if Serendipity is up to it to be honest. It might just be an opportunity for you. You don't mind me asking?"

"I'm not sure Neide."

"It doesn't have to be anything fancy. Speak with Carlos and I'm sure you will be able to rope in all the help you need. I was just thinking it might be an opportunity for you to enjoy yourself in a way you didn't expect. Don't feel pressurised though, there's no obligation."

"I have to say it is tempting. A little scary but tempting."

"Sleep on it and let me know tomorrow."

Katherine wasn't quite sure what to think. Deep down she was intrigued by the idea and would like to give it a go. The thoughts of planning a menu and seeing people enjoy her food in the evening sunshine was exciting, but what if they didn't like what she cooked, or what if she prepared too much or too little food?

Possibilities battled with concerns as Katherine crossed the courtyard to her room. She sat down on her bed and looked up at the majestic picture of the bird-like figure. Part of her wanted to accept Neide's offer, the other part couldn't banish images of a burning kitchen and food poisoning from her mind. But when she contemplated declining Neide's offer, she felt her stomach sink.

The conversation with Neide had been a brief but welcome distraction. She pushed it to the back of her mind having resolved to chat with Imelda or Suzy about it later. Then the all too familiar quandary weighed in. Vincent.

She retrieved her phone from her bag and began pacing the room. She kicked off her shoes and crunched her toes on the mat beside the bed. What mood would he be in? What would they talk about? Should she apologise? What did she want him to say anyway?

Taking a deep breath she rang him. This time he answered.

Chapter 5

"Well, how's it going?" Vincent sounded normal enough Katherine thought.

"Great, I'm enjoying it so far. The place is charming and the people are nice. Everything okay at home?"

"Fine. How's the weather?"

"Nearly too hot. Could do with proper air conditioning in my room, but I'm getting by." Katherine plugged in the fan beside the bed which wheezed into action.

"Well, there's no heatwave here. The wind was right in our faces on the fourteenth yesterday, we had to wear jackets."

"Did you play well?"

"Good enough, went round with Gerry, he was asking after you."

It was a superficial conversation, they were following a familiar script, but at least they were talking. Perhaps it was the residue of the way things were before she left, or the retreat from the battleground that gave her a different perspective, but Katherine felt that the barrier of stilted politeness between them was more tangible than ever. She craved honest conversation, a clearing of the air. Unasked questions burned in her throat.

"You probably ate at the club?" Katherine said. "Don't forget there are a few dinners in the freezer."

"Don't worry about me; you just concentrate on getting better."

"I'm not sick Vincent."

"Well you know what I mean."

Katherine was afraid of what she might say, so she remained silent. She picked at the edge of the pillow case.

"Oh, whilst I think of it, Joan rang, left a message on the

machine; she wants you to ring her back."

It was probably something to do with their mother's will. She had spoken with her sister Joan more on that topic in the last six months, than they had done on any topic in the last six years. Katherine didn't have the headspace to think about Joan now.

"So where are you now Vincent? Sounds quiet?"

"At home, why?"

"Just wondering, I didn't know if you were still at the golf club. Were Thom or Claire on?"

"No, but sure you know what they're like."

"No other news?"

"Nothing I can think of." Nothing I'm willing to share with you was the more accurate response Katherine thought.

"Oh, Neide the woman who runs the retreat asked if I'd be interested in organising a meal for the group on Wednesday."

"I thought you were there for a rest."

"We were discussing things we enjoyed doing this afternoon and I mentioned cooking." Katherine knew she couldn't use the word inspiring with Vincent.

"Well it sounds like cheap labour; don't let them take advantage of you."

"It's not like that Vincent."

"Well you know yourself."

You know yourself – it was one of Vincent's common expressions. He said it to detach, to wash his hands of a situation. Now it taunted her. At fifty-one, she felt she didn't know herself at all.

"I'm not sure if I'll do it yet, but it was nice to be asked." Katherine was sorry she had mentioned it; she had known exactly how Vincent would respond. Tears of frustration welled in her eyes. She stood up and paced the room. "No other news then?"

"Not offhand."

"I'll let you go then, I'll text later in the week."

"Enjoy the rest of your time."

"I'll do my best."

"Bye Kay."

What was normally a term of endearment that reminded Katherine of her aunt, now just seemed patronising. She didn't know what she had expected from speaking with Vincent, but after just a few minutes of awkward conversation she felt aggravated. The buzz from the workshops and the beautiful lunch had vanished. She felt like screaming. The leather bound journal on the bed mocked her. She pushed it away and stretched out.

Her eyes followed a tiny spider crossing the ceiling. She could hear Morag in the courtyard. She would have loved to have told Vincent about the exercises in the workshops, the lunch, the people she was getting to know, but she knew that if she did, her enthusiasm would be devoured by his nonchalance and very soon she would be justifying being here.

Life for Katherine always seemed more real when she was recounting her experiences to someone else. Even as a child she had loved reporting the day's news. Back then, she would stand by the fireplace in the kitchen and regale her mother with the tales from school and on Saturdays when helping her aunt Kay with the weekly bake she would describe the week's events and get another round of pleasure from them. In recent times it was the twice weekly phone calls with her mother, but they ceased at the beginning of the year with that inevitable call from Joan.

Gone too were the days when Thom and Claire would climb on to the kitchen stools, talk over each other and almost forget to breathe with excitement as they shared their news. Now she had to scan Facebook or Twitter to see what they were up to. Of course they had to live their own lives, but Katherine desperately wanted to play more than just a cameo role, a once significant figure now reduced to a walk-on part.

Katherine couldn't remember the last meaningful

conversation with Vincent, a conversation that went beyond confirming arrangements, sharing inconsequential gossip, or repeating preferences. It was a long time since he rubbed her shoulder whilst propped up in bed and said that together they could solve any problem, overcome any challenge.

She thought about phoning Joan, but wasn't up to another tetchy exchange. Instead Katherine replayed the conversation with Vincent. A thought gnawed at her. He had said he was at home. She could always say she had meant to phone Joan. She scrolled her contacts until 'home' appeared on the screen. She pressed call.

It started to ring. She didn't know whether she wanted him to answer or not. She began counting the rings. After six, she could feel her heart sink. After nine, she knew he had been lying. On the twelfth ring the answering machine clicked in. She was listening to her own voice. Was she just another gullible middle-aged woman whose husband was cheating on her?

Battalions of emotions jostled for expression. She felt stupid and naive. It was anger that made her bounce the phone off the bed, but sadness was the ultimate victor. It gripped her heart and wouldn't let go. Deep down she had desperately wanted him to pick up. She couldn't control the tears; it was like something inside her had torn.

***

At first she wasn't sure if she heard knocking, but when her name was called she knew someone was at her door. Hauling herself from the bed Katherine peeped out the window. Serendipity was standing outside shifting from one foot to the other. Katherine opened the door an inch or two.

"Ah Katherine, I'm not disturbing you am I? Are you okay?"

"I'm fine." Katherine's head was pounding. She squinted in the bright evening sunshine that was now in a full on assault against her side of the courtyard.

"I was just checking if your towel was okay or if there was anything else you needed?"

"No, I'm fine, thanks."

"Are you sure?" Serendipity was full of youthful concern, but Katherine only saw interference and chirpy annoyance. She wanted to be left alone.

"I'm fine." She abruptly closed the door. If only she could lock it.

The room was like an oven. She pulled the curtains and flipped the damp pillow before coiling into a ball on the bed.

For several months Katherine had felt she had been drifting further and further from the shore of all that was familiar and stable in her life. Now she was lost. There was nothing to hold on to, nothing to anchor her. She had run away, forgetting that at the end of the week she had to go home. She could taste the loneliness that was consuming her. She pulled the cover over her to silence her sobs. Despite the heat, she was shivering.

Images scurried in and out of her head. Memories; her wedding day, the children, Vincent's PA Nicola standing in her kitchen that day she came home from the hospital. And the imagined scenes; Vincent dropping his wedding ring into his pocket, Vincent and Nicola in bed laughing. She grasped at the soothing memories that were all too fleeting, her mother sitting at the edge of her bed, the rattle of her father's van pulling into the yard, her aunt Kay in her apron hands covered in flour. For the first time in her life she had no one to console her, no one to tell her that everything would be alright.

***

The rap on the door was louder this time. She decided to ignore it. She could pretend to be asleep?

"Cooee, Katherine." It was Imelda. If it had been anyone

else she would have stayed where she was.

Taking the blanket with her, Katherine peeped around the door.

"I was thinking of going for a stroll, fancy joining me?" Imelda took a step closer. "Oh, what's up?"

"I've just woken up."

"Oh, I'm sorry, everything okay?"

"Fine."

"I can tell you're not."

"I just need some time by myself." Katherine moved to close the door. She had too many of her own emotions to deal with to concern herself with niceties.

"Maybe I can help?" There was a kindness in Imelda's tone that made Katherine pause. She stepped back from the door and retreated to her spot on the bed. Imelda followed her. Shame prevented Katherine from looking up.

"What's happened, you were in great form this afternoon?"

"You don't need to be burdened with my problems Imelda." Pride was just about damming her tears.

"Problems shared and all that. If nothing else I'm a good listener." Imelda sat beside her and gently rubbed Katherine's arm. "Come on, what's happened?"

"Oh I don't know. Sometimes I think I'm going mad."

"You're far from mad Katherine."

Katherine just shrugged. She couldn't look at Imelda in case she lost control completely.

"I wish I hadn't come here. It doesn't solve anything, it's made things worse."

"Maybe you need this week to gather yourself, a bit of time so you can go back home feeling stronger?"

"I feel like such a fool." The word 'home' had triggered Katherine's tears.

"We usually only feel that way when someone we trusted let us down." Imelda sighed.

"You might as well know Imelda, my husband is cheating on me and I don't know what to do." Katherine spat out the words. Unexpressed they were toxic; out of her mouth they formed a new entity, a new reality that she hoped would stop devouring her from the inside. She held Imelda's eye defiantly, but the compassion reflected back at her shattered her fragile resolve.

"Ah my poor dear. I'm so sorry." Imelda put her arm around her.

Between weighty sobs the two women rocked back and forth. The bedside fan rattled and whined.

***

"I know what you need; I'll be back in a jiffy." Imelda darted from the room, leaving the door open. Sunlight advanced as far as the bathroom.

Katherine wiped the tears that had run down her neck. She was embarrassed that she had broken down in front of Imelda, proof that perhaps fragments of her dignity remained.

"Now my dear, here you go." Imelda displayed a flagon of brandy and two plastic cups. Katherine chuckled at the idea. Two large measures were poured. "It's the best heart medicine I know," Imelda said.

Katherine swished the dark amber liquid around the cup. The pungent woody aroma pinched the back of her nose. She sipped the liquid fire.

"I shouldn't be drinking this, I've a splitting headache."

"You've had a shock Katherine." Imelda knocked hers back then poured them both some more. "Besides it's cocktail hour."

Katherine took a few more gulps. She could feel a delicious warmth settle on her stomach. Her shoulders began to drop.

"Why don't you tell me what's happened?" Imelda kicked off her sandals and pulled her feet beneath her on the bed.

"I don't know where to start."

"Start at the start. We're in no hurry."

Katherine related everything that had happened in recent weeks. How she had spent a few days in hospital, just to get checked out, to have a rest, as her doctor had phrased it and how she had discharged herself only to arrive home and to find Nicola, someone who worked for Vincent, someone she never liked, standing in her kitchen. Vincent, she soon discovered was upstairs pulling up his trousers. He claimed he had spilt milk on them at a meeting and had to pop home to change. He denied cheating, but there was other evidence. Three weeks earlier she had noticed he wasn't wearing his wedding ring. He said he lost it, but after twenty-six years, a ring just doesn't fall off a finger, it is purposefully removed. And then there was this evening's lie about where he was. Katherine was making the case for the prosecution. She didn't mention Mark Goodwin.

"Oh my dear, you've had a rough few weeks." Imelda rubbed her arm. Katherine could feel tears approaching, but she blinked them away. More brandy was sloshed into her cup.

The worries that had wrapped themselves tight inside her, now spewed from her in a torrent of semi-coherent babble. Katherine knew these worries and woes intimately – her mother's death and the awkward situation with Joan, the empty nest and the fact that Thom was gay, how she was a bad mother and a dreadful wife and lastly the wound that sliced the deepest, the fact she felt lost and that her life was purposeless.

It felt to Katherine like she was unpacking a suitcase of worries and losses, placing each item in a pile on the floor between them, where they would be judged. But she knew too that any relief gained from voicing her troubles would only be temporary, because as soon as Imelda left she would have to pick each one up and carry them again.

"I'm so embarrassed Imelda. I hate being like this." When the flow of words ceased the tears began again.

"Now don't be silly. You're only human. And never be

ashamed of tears. Tears are just emotions leaving the body, tears of frustration, tears of anger, tears of sadness, believe me I've cried them all."

"I feel so stupid."

"Keep sipping." Imelda winked. The bottle in her hand was now more than half empty. "You know I've never been married, unless you count the forty years I was a nun, married to Christ as they say, but I've been around long enough to know that personal relationships contain the highest highs and the lowest lows."

"I've never been this low Imelda."

"All I can say to you is this, if your husband is having an affair, you are not the first woman to go through it, nor will you be the last. It's easy to take things personally, but there's little point in blaming yourself. Everything is raw right now; it is only human to be feeling what you are feeling, don't be ashamed of your emotions. You're hurting and that's okay. You know some people try to brush emotions under the carpet, it's been my experience that the only way to deal with stuff like this, is to look at it head on. Have a good cry if you feel like crying, swear if you want to swear, scream if you feel like screaming, get it out."

"Believe me there are times I want to scream."

"Do it, you know to be human is to be emotional, our emotions tell us we're alive. God in all his wisdom allows us to experience every emotion under the sun. Of course there are some that aren't pleasant, but maybe without sadness we would never have compassion, without shame we would never have trust, without anger we would never have resolve, without despair we would never have hope."

"There's one thing I didn't tell you Imelda. I'm not completely innocent myself. I almost cheated on Vincent myself a few weeks ago."

"How can you almost cheat?"

"There was this guy Mark, we got friendly. He gave me a lift home from our book club and made his intentions known. He kissed me. I jumped out of the car, but he just sat there. I didn't go into the house. I stood in the driveway looking at him. When he opened the passenger door again I walked back to the car." Katherine drained her cup. "I knew what I was doing Imelda but ironically it was Vincent who stopped me. I'd just got back in when he opened the front door. I got back out. We never spoke about it. But you see Imelda I knew exactly what I was doing and this is my punishment. So you see I'm just as bad as Vincent. I don't deserve any sympathy."

"Oh, child, who am I to judge. I walked out of a forty year marriage to the son of God." Imelda laughed.

"I've brought all this on myself, haven't I?"

"Katherine I'm sure those questions have been swirling around your little head for weeks and you may never know the answer. But for what it's worth here's my take on it. You did something or were about to do something that deep down you knew you would regret, that went against who you truly are, so as a result you feel bad. When we violate our true natures that gentle, compassionate, loving core of ourselves we suffer for it."

"Maybe."

"You know the tradition of confession, the sacrament of confession in the Catholic faith?"

"I haven't been in years."

"Let me tell you what I think about confession. It's not about seeking absolution from God; it's about forgiving ourselves. Katherine you need to forgive yourself for getting back into that car because until you do, no matter what's going on with Vincent, you will never think clearly or more importantly you'll never feel any better."

"It's driven me mad; they even sent me to a shrink in the hospital. He was a quack; you're making much more sense."

"And I don't even charge for the hooch. So here's what you

do, where's that journal of yours, the fancy leather one?"

Katherine retrieved it and her phone from the floor on the far side of the bed. Sitting up she felt light-headed.

"Write out the phrase 'I forgive myself for' and dump onto the page everything you have beaten yourself up about. Fill three or four pages if you have to. Get it all out. Forgive yourself for not spending more time with your mother, forgive yourself for the fact your son is gay, forgive yourself for skipping classes at school, whatever it is. Forgive yourself for getting back into the car with what's his name. Hear your own confession and forgive yourself. And remember it's not what you did or didn't do that eats away at you, it's the judgement, the fact that you have judged yourself continuously and harshly about decisions and events that probably no one else even remembers."

"But what about Vincent?"

"Look after you first Katherine. Vincent is round two. Besides you can only deal with the here and now."

"I don't know."

"Katherine you can't do anything about Vincent right now. You can only deal with where you are in the present moment. All of your stress and upset is a result of dwelling on the past or dreading the future, but we can only act in the present. Promise me you'll give that forgiveness exercise a go, it will help heal your past and you will be better equipped to deal with the future."

"Whatever that will bring."

"You know what I think; you are absolutely in the right place. Being here this week can only help. I'm a great believer in fate Katherine. For some reason I felt I needed to check in on you this evening, isn't that funny."

"I'm glad you did."

"Can I play angel's advocate here for a moment?"

Katherine nodded cautiously.

"You can't be completely sure he's cheating on you, maybe there are innocent explanations for everything you mentioned.

What is it they say in those legal dramas; could it all be just circumstantial evidence?"

"I don't think so, I know Vincent."

"Well even if it's what you expect, you'll get through it Katherine. Call me a silly old woman, but I believe that life unfolds as it's meant to unfold; there is always a bigger picture. That doesn't mean life is easy, but it's always evolving. Sometimes we have to say goodbye to say hello to something even better. Sometimes change is trying to take place in our lives, a change that leads to something tremendous, that doesn't mean the change isn't chaotic or painful or bloody scary, believe me I know. And maybe that's why you're here Katherine, because change is trying to take place in your life."

"You might be right." Beneath the layers of confusion and hurt, Imelda's words struck a chord in Katherine.

"And the more we resist that change the more painful it is." Imelda got to her feet. "My rusty hinges." Imelda rubbed her knees. "Now I'll open these curtains and let this gorgeous evening in and there's no point in me bringing this back." Imelda dangled the almost empty bottle of brandy. "Sip on it when you're doing your homework, your self-forgiveness list." Imelda drained the bottle into Katherine's cup.

"I shouldn't, I've had too much already."

"I won't tell if you won't, besides it's medicinal."

"Neide asked me if I would be interested in preparing the evening meal on Wednesday. I don't know what to say to her? I'm not sure about a vegetarian menu."

"It's up to you. If you think you'll enjoy it, do it, if you think you won't, say no. But between you and me, there's a few people here who could do with a good feed. Take poor Serendipity, a juicy steak would do her the world of good. And I'm sure Bruce is a meat eater."

"You think I should do it."

"Your choice, but sure it'll be nothing you've not done

before. You've put three meals on the table for your family every day for years, haven't you? The mothers of the world all run restaurants; they're just all called the kitchen. You could do it with your eyes closed. It'll be fun. I'll be your, what do you call it, sous-chef and we'll see if we can rope Corinne in, get her to stay that evening. We'll have a blast. Now it's time I left you in peace." Imelda opened the door, concealing the empty bottle under her arm.

"Imelda thank you, I mean it."

"You're welcome dear. I'll see you later."

Katherine couldn't help smile at the sight of Imelda crossing the courtyard. Her room was directly opposite, but her route was not quite straight.

***

The fierce sun that had cooked the courtyard all day was now in retreat. Katherine opened the small window in her bathroom, hoping to entice the breeze to chase the heat from her room.

Imelda had left her journal open on the bed. The blank pages stared at her defiantly. Katherine lifted it onto her lap and wrote the words as Imelda had instructed her – '*I forgive myself for...*'

The empty pages were intimidating. She twisted the stubborn pen in her hand. Katherine looked around the room for inspiration. Her eyes rested on the painting of the angel-like figure that hung over her bed. She remembered Serendipity saying it was the Angel of Freedom, painted by a previous guest. The blend of bold colours and how the figure in the centre emerged from the background was pleasant to the eye. With a bit of practice Katherine thought she could probably paint something as good.

She began to doodle at the bottom of the page, the head of a flower with drooping petals. Frustration grew, why couldn't she write anything? She took another sip from the plastic cup then opened a bottle of water. Her headache had eased, but now she felt groggy. A shower was needed, now that she had a towel.

Katherine picked up the pen again.

'*I forgive myself for the fact I can't do this exercise.*'

***

The water from the shower head was sporadic, but the temperature was constant. Katherine kept her face in the water, something she loved doing even as a child. Her eucalyptus-scented shower gel slowly began to deliver on its promise of invigoration. The herbal mentholly scent cleared her head.

Lathering her hair, a thought shot through her mind like an arrow – *I forgive myself for getting old.* Where did that come from she thought? Then another arrow and another. *I forgive myself for being too tough on myself. I forgive myself for letting Mark turn my head.* Katherine was afraid she wouldn't remember these shots from the unconscious. She quickly rinsed her hair and still dripping, wrapped the towel around her and grabbed the journal and pen. Not wanting to get the bed wet, she perched herself on the toilet and rapidly inscribed the sentiment that came to her in the shower. And the salvoes kept coming.

I forgive myself for not spending more time with Mam.
I forgive myself for the fact I never really had a career.
I forgive myself for being rude to Serendipity
earlier – I'll apologise later.
I forgive myself for being too extravagant with money in the past.
I forgive myself for boasting to others about my lifestyle.

Katherine wasn't totally sure about the next one, but she wrote it anyway.

*I forgive myself for thinking about cheating on
Vincent with Mark – I am only human.
I forgive myself for being only human and far from perfect.
I forgive myself for not being perfect.
I forgive myself for wanting to feel attractive and loved.
I forgive myself for not being a better friend to my children.
I forgive myself for not being a better wife to Vincent.*

Katherine pondered the last sentence. It didn't sit right with her. She drew a line through it and wrote – *Screw that, I've been a great wife.*

*I forgive myself for not speaking my mind when I should have.
I forgive myself for wishing I was happier.
I forgive myself for not continuing to paint.
I forgive myself for forgetting I had dreams.
I forgive myself for worrying – it just means I care.
I forgive myself for not being as wise as Imelda.*

Katherine paused to allow her pen to catch up with her mind.

*I forgive myself for not being the best sister
to Joan – though I have tried.
I forgive myself because I've a gay son – but
as long as he's happy, I'm happy.
I forgive myself for no longer going to Mass and for
not having some sort of spiritual practice.
I forgive myself for getting into that car with Mark.*

Katherine looked at the last sentence she wrote. She wrote it again. Every time she replayed that scene she would cringe, but now it was like she was watching someone else.

I forgive myself because I've always done my best.

Before she had finished writing it, warm tears were streaming down her face. Her body wasn't heaving as it had done earlier. It was like a vial had been broken and the contents were draining away. Imelda had mentioned the different types of tears; Katherine knew she wasn't just crying, she was purging.

> *I forgive myself for crying.*
> *I forgive myself.*
> *I forgive myself.*
> *I forgive myself.*

Not having dried herself properly a small puddle had formed around the base of the toilet. Katherine mopped it up. If the plumbing was better Katherine would have ripped out the pages and symbolically flushed them away. Putting them into the waste basket would not be the same. She was proud of her list, though she suspected there was probably more she could have written. Washing the tears from her face, she smiled at the thought of adding another one to the list – *I forgive myself because there is so much to forgive.*

She certainly felt fresher, inside and out. She stepped into a brightly patterned summer dress, one of several that only saw the light of day overseas. A spritz of perfume and her favourite lipstick revived her spirits even more.

A crash made her jump. The frame of the painting that hung over the bed lay in pieces on the floor. It had taken the fan and the cup of brandy with it. Katherine got to her knees and began to pick up the pieces. Thankfully the painting itself didn't appear to be damaged. She wondered why the painting fell, because the nail was still in the wall above the bed. Perhaps the vibrantly painted Angel of Freedom was trying to send her a message.

CHAPTER 6

Ten years ago Ran Kaplan could have walked straight out of the pages of a Ralph Lauren catalogue. Middle-age had loosened his tautness, but he was and probably always would be a strikingly handsome man. Suzy had whispered to Katherine that she thought he resembled a long-haired, shabbier version of George Clooney. His barely-buttoned white shirt with panels of multi-coloured embroidery would have, on any less rugged a man, seemed girly, but with his dark tan, his attire could be described as ethnic. Everyone in the creativity workshop was hanging on his every word and more than just Katherine admired his chest.

True to her word Imelda had reserved seats either side of her for Katherine and Corinne. Charlie's Angels, Imelda labelled the three of them. Bruce had attempted to sit beside Katherine but gallantly withdrew to his usual seat on the left so Serendipity could sit beside Sophie. Neide and Iam were also participating in the morning's workshop and Tonya had returned, so Ran Kaplan was playing to a full house.

"Who would describe themselves as creative?" Ran asked, pushing up his sleeves.

Iam's hand shot up and was followed by Neide's and a little reluctantly Serendipity's. Keeping their side in the game Declan raised his and he encouraged Suzy to do likewise. That was fair Katherine thought, they both worked in creative industries.

"Okay, now put up your hand if you're human?" An embarrassed chuckle escaped most lips. All hands were raised. "That's it, anything above the ear counts." Ran scratched the stubble on his chin. "To be human is to be creative. Everyone is creative."

The most studious participants, Serendipity, Louise and

Marie the life coach were noting his every word. Katherine just looked at him and drank in his rich, lyrical accent, a mix of romantic French or Italian with a hint of the exotic Middle East. She could easily imagine him on horseback crossing a desert.

"Being creative is not just for artists, we're creative when we put a meal together, when we seek new ways to engage with our children or grandchildren, when we tell stories. I'm sure some of you work in business. The most successful business people are creative."

"Unless they're accountants." Bruce interrupted. His attempt at humour fell flat. Katherine felt uncomfortable for him.

"Yes, I don't recommend creative accounting, but the best sales people are creative when they are seeking new leads or want to close a deal."

"That's true; I'm always trying to think of new ways of attracting more clients," Marie said, perched at the edge of her seat.

"Perfect example. My point is we are all creative and the beauty of it is that we can all be creative in our own unique ways." Ran sat down on the table behind him. "Here's a little challenge for you. Just for a moment look around this room, and excluding the people in it, excluding us, note four or five things you see."

All heads swivelled. When Katherine leant a little to her right she could feel the cool air from the fan, a welcome addition to the room. On the far right of the row of chairs, Tonya was enjoying its full force. Again she was dressed head to toe in black, but the pink accessories from yesterday were gone. Her hair looked as if it still hadn't been washed. If there was group work today Katherine resolved that she would latch on to Imelda and Corinne.

"So everything you've noted, the walls, the paint on the walls, the cabinet, the fan, the posters, the chairs, the clothes you're wearing, the seats you're sitting on, the pens in your hands, everything in this room, including the room itself, began as an idea in someone's mind. The artist, the designer, the creative person, the craftsman, the builder, the architect; what we are witnessing and enjoying are the fruits of their creative labour. And Neide of course you had a big role to play. Wouldn't it be true to say that this wonderful retreat started with an idea?"

"For sure, many years ago." The owner of the retreat straightened her skirt. Katherine felt Neide could have sat in a more appropriate way. The last time Katherine's legs were that far apart she was giving birth.

"And think how much poorer our lives would be if Neide hadn't acted on her idea, or if all the writers, painters, designers, songwriters, film-makers, photographers in the world didn't act on theirs?

"That's very true," Iam said. "But tell me Ran have you ever come across someone who wasn't creative?"

"I've come across people who have lost touch with their creativity sure, but everyone is creative."

Iam launched into another question. He really just liked the sound of his own voice Katherine thought. She found herself mentally turning down the volume when Iam, aka Colin the ex-accountant spoke, his nasal tone irritated her.

Katherine hadn't made it to the dawn yoga class as it was called. Imelda informed her at breakfast that she didn't think Iam was a great yoga teacher. He more or less ignored her and gave Marie and Sophie, the only others who had escaped from their beds by seven, scant attention either. She felt their purpose in attending the class was to admire his flexibility. She did say that the location for the yoga, just outside the walls of The Retreat was stunning. The view over the island was spectacular and seeing the morning sun pour into the valley was the best thing about being up at that time.

Katherine had slept better than she had expected. When her head touched the pillow she couldn't avoid revisiting the situation with Vincent and the probability that he was having an affair. In her mind it was no longer a possibility. Whether it was the self-forgiveness exercise, the tears she had shed, or simply acknowledging the reality of the situation, she didn't feel as raw. A new fan in her room helped too. It actually cooled the air rather than just spin it around and when she woke to go to the loo in the early hours, she had the brainwave to shove cotton wool into her ears to quieten the metallic hum.

Katherine had dreamt that she was walking by the sea on an unfamiliar beach. Massive waves were crashing at her feet. She was able to scramble to higher ground, but the raging black sea frightened her. The grass around her was soft and when she buried her face into it she couldn't see or hear anything. At one point in her dream she could feel massive arms around her. She recounted her dream to Imelda at breakfast, who pointed out that in dreams the sea always symbolises emotions. Katherine liked Imelda's interpretation that the arms around her meant she was protected.

"Now I'll be setting you all a little challenge shortly, a practical exercise. Listen, we can have a discussion on creativity all day long, but the real learning is in the doing, so you are all going to have an opportunity to exercise your creativity in a fun way." Ran played with the straps and bangles on his wrists.

Some of the group rubbed their hands in anticipation. Escaping from the pit of her stomach, anxiousness climbed up Katherine's body. What if she wasn't creative, what if she couldn't do the exercise. Needless to say Imelda couldn't wait to get started.

"You were saying earlier Neide that you explored the topic of inspiration yesterday? Great timing because knowing what inspires us allows us to connect with our creativity. So to get into that space again maybe someone could share what they took from yesterday?"

Marie jumped up and displayed the collage of images that

rested against the wall. Katherine admired her commitment to her stilettos. Neide prompted Katherine to talk through the points she and Bruce had noted on the flipchart. Nervous at first Katherine enjoyed being able to make a contribution and even had the group laughing again when she mentioned why Corinne's name had been added to the list. She avoided making eye contact with Tonya whose leaden expression hung over the group like a cloud ready to unleash a downpour.

"I love the Einstein quote – creativity is intelligence having fun. So we are going to exercise our intelligence, connect with our sense of inspiration and let our creativity flow." Ran pushed his sleeves up to his biceps. Katherine noticed the start of a tattoo. "Okay, so ready for some fun?"

"Bring it on," Iam said.

"Is it a group or individual task?" Neide asked.

"Individual, I guess, but if people want to work in small groups, two or three maximum that's fine too. Each of you has until twelve, so that's what, an hour and twenty, to produce a piece of art, to exercise your creativity."

"Oh I don't know what to do," Sophie said, the loudest voice in a chorus of concern.

"Now don't worry, remember this is a fun exercise."

"I thought we were going to have a discussion on creativity, you make it sound like playtime in nursery school," Tonya said, the first roll of thunder Katherine had feared.

"Play is exactly what it is and isn't that wonderful." Perceptive to Tonya's scowl, Ran took a different approach. "From my experience there's no substitute for doing. It's no different than say trying to improve your listening skills. You could attend a lecture on how to listen, but you will only become a better listener by actually practising listening."

"That makes sense," Bruce said, backing up Ran.

"But before we get started I want to speak about the two

P's, the two big blocks to creativity. Anyone want to guess what they are?"

"Procrastination." It was Marie who spoke.

"That's one, well done. And the other one?"

"Professionalism?" Suzy offered.

"I see where you're coming from, but no. The 'P' I have in mind is perfectionism. Most people are afraid to tap into their creativity because they immediately make an assessment that there is no point in attempting anything because it will never be good enough."

"So true," Corinne said.

"They think there's no point in lifting a paintbrush because they'll never be a Van Gogh or a Jackson Pollock. There is no point in writing; they'll never be a Hemingway. There's no point in picking up a camera they'll never be a Bailey or a Mario Testino, or who am I to design a shirt, I'll never be a Lagerfeld." Most of the room were nodding in unison. "We forget that it's not about the result, it is about enjoying the process. If you focus on the result you will never get started. So to go back to your point." Ran turned to Tonya. "The one lesson I want you all to take from this workshop is this – get started, do something."

Perhaps Ran expected a response from Tonya but none came.

"And what about procrastination, I think that's where I struggle?" Corinne asked.

"The two are related. We will procrastinate, avoid getting started because we are questioning whether what we are attempting will be good enough and of course that's really what perfectionism is about too. It took me years to realise that perfectionism is never about high standards it's really lack of worthiness in disguise."

The last comment had most people in the room reaching for their pens and notebooks.

"Listen, I still struggle with perfectionism and procrastination, it's like: Hello, I'm Ran and I'm a re-forming perfectionist."

"Do we have to paint?" Tonya asked with the same amount of enthusiasm as she might ask, do I have to slice off my fingers?

"Not at all. Painting is my main medium for expression and I've been fortunate that I've been able to align my passion with my profession, but over the next, what hour and a quarter, you can do anything you like. Write a short story, a poem, draw, take some photos, write a song, there are no rules."

"It's bit scary," Sophie said.

"That's only because you're not used to letting your imagination run wild. As children we were tremendously creative. As adults we forget that learning is just as much about expression from the inside as it is packing in information from the outside."

"But what will I do?" Sophie asked, moving ever closer to panic.

"Anything you want. You know you could use two socks and perform a puppet act, a group I worked with a few weeks back did a little play with their shoes as the main characters. Remember, you are absolutely avoiding being perfect, go into this exercise thinking the sillier it is, the better."

Katherine could see Tonya follow the same route she followed yesterday. The phone was now out and she was busy texting. Of all the people in the room she was the one who needed an injection of silliness.

"I came across a phrase once that I think might be useful here," Neide said. "We resist what we need the most."

"I agree," Ran said. "The greater our resistance to this exercise, the bigger the gift that awaits us."

"I like that," Declan said, getting to his feet and stretching. "Let's get started."

"Great, so I'll be here if anyone needs to bounce anything

off me. Neide you said earlier that people can make use of whatever materials are in the cabinet."

Katherine looked to Imelda and Corinne. "What are you thinking, ladies?"

"You know I think I might try to compose a song," Imelda said beginning to 'la la' away to herself.

"Maybe a few lines of poetry. It's something I dabble with now and then." Corinne smiled. "What about you Katherine?"

"I'm going to pick up a paintbrush for the first time in years."

***

Katherine and Louise rummaged through the painting supplies in the cabinet. After some debate about where to set up Katherine suggested the yoga deck with the great view that Imelda had mentioned. Ran led the way having offered to carry their easels. The two women followed him through the kitchen area and the common room, past the noticeboard heavy with postcards and the apt sign for the baggage room 'physical and emotional baggage only' down a narrow corridor, until they emerged again in bright sunlight.

A strong wind raced around the walls of The Retreat as if trying to find a way in. They found the most sheltered spot and pulling her hat down tight, Katherine hoped the amazing view would inspire her. Stretched below them was the heart of the island of Lanzarote. The landscape was bleak, barren lava fields with little greenery. An azure sea was just visible beyond the folds of extinct volcanoes. The road Katherine travelled from the airport bisected the scene. If she was going to paint what she saw she would be reaching for the reds, browns, greys and plenty of blue.

"Now I think you've got everything you need. Have fun ladies and remember it's about enjoying this hour, not about the end result," Ran said. The wind was having fun with his shirt.

Katherine loved the clean woody scent of his aftershave. She was nervous in his company and fiddled with her bracelet. She could have been seventeen again, hovering by the swingboats in the carnival that Jim Corr used to operate many summers ago.

"The view that way is not great," Katherine said, turning her back on the two cars, an old TV aerial propped against the wall and a large bin. "But this is stunning isn't it? We can see for miles. Have you painted much Louise?"

"I joined a class last September, did twenty weeks, only finished in May. It was mainly still life though."

"You'll be more of an expert than I will."

"Hardly, I did it to get out of the house. Morag kept at me to do something, now that I'm on my own again."

Even when she was enjoying herself, deep in conversation or doing a workshop exercise, like a spectre, the situation with Vincent would creep up on her, tap her on the shoulder and whisper in her ear, you're going to have to dance with me sometime.

"Did I hear you say you were married twenty-five years?" Katherine said, mixing some blue and grey; she wasn't ready to put the brush to the page just yet.

"Twenty-six."

"Same as me and Vincent."

"It's funny now, what nine months after the divorce, I'm remembering more and more of the good times, not just the bad," Louise said, sketching away with a pencil.

"Great that you're getting on with your life though."

"That's what people say, but it's not that simple, not for me anyway. Myself and Martin were a team for twenty-six years. We've three children."

"We've a boy and girl."

"Being married that length of time you see each other at their best and worst, don't you?"

"Absolutely."

"I'd lived with Martin practically all my adult life. A piece of paper might say we're divorced, but you know when we separated it was like amputating an arm and a leg."

"I can imagine."

"But I suppose we've just got to get on with things don't we? Now I think I need some white for these walls." Louise rummaged in the box of paints.

"I might be heading that way myself. I suspect my husband is cheating." Katherine felt Louise was being honest, so she should be honest too.

"Oh no, Katherine I'm sorry to hear that. That's tough. At least I didn't have to go through that. Maybe it would've made things easier if Martin had strayed, but he's not that sort of guy. With me and him it just fizzled out. You know we were married at twenty, and you see it so much don't you, if you don't grow together you grow apart. The children were our focus, but when they left home there was nothing holding us together."

"There's no one to spoil anymore."

"Until the grandkids come along."

"I don't see that for a while, but you're right, Claire our youngest moved to Manchester last September to study, so it's only us now."

"You run out of conversation don't you. You know I was only saying this to Morag last night, I think Martin and I both thought that the marriage certificate and the wedding ring meant grand, we don't have to make an effort any more, we're settled. Now I can see that emotionally Martin and I both left our marriage years before we did physically. You know I can remember the exact time I opened the door and put a foot out of my marriage, it was nearly twenty years ago and I started to say things about Martin to my friends, I started to betray our marriage by speaking to others about stuff I should have been saying to him. That's when I started to repress my feelings, you know when the word 'fine' becomes your standard response when you're supposed to be discussing feelings and let's face it if we're not discussing feelings we can't expect the man to."

"True." Katherine couldn't remember the last time Vincent spoke about his feelings. Conversations were only real when feelings were discussed openly and honestly. But how could she get Vincent to open up about his feelings when she could barely articulate her own.

"And another thing, I think it's the exception rather than the rule if you find your match, your soulmate at age twenty. I don't know about you, but I could barely match clothes at that age. Of course Morag keeps saying I just need a new man, but I'm not sure if I'd be any wiser choosing one now."

Katherine stared at the pad propped in front of her. She was reluctant to place the brush on the page, to soil the pristine whiteness. She took a deep breath.

The tip of the brush touched the page. And there it was, the feeling was back, a feeling she hadn't experienced in years. The nervousness of the first touch, the fear of committing to the first stroke mixed with layers of excitement that would unfold as each caress of the canvas brought something new into creation. A line like a raised eyebrow was born.

Katherine loved the feel of the brush in her hand and the fine lines left in its wake. Twenty years had passed since she last stood by an easel. An old pleasure was emerging from a lengthy sleep. She had intended to paint the row of hills on the horizon, but the brush just wanted to have fun. She loosened her wrist, ignored the scene in front of her and stepped closer to the page. She let the brush rise and fall. Thicker and thicker amounts of paint were applied, the colours didn't matter. She was painting and she loved it.

"How are you getting on?" Louise asked.

"I'm not sure what I'm painting, but I have to say I'm enjoying it."

Katherine didn't want to talk. Her page demanded her

attention. Her brush strokes had become circular; a spiral of colour had formed, a whirlpool of red, purple and lilac. She was being sucked into the page.

***

Both Katherine and Louise were unaware of the time when Iam stuck his head out the door and said the group were getting back together in a few minutes.

Katherine stood back from her work. She didn't think it was finished, but it would do for now. Someone else looking at it would probably just see a multi-coloured circle, a swirling mess. But for Katherine, she was looking at a memory of freedom.

"Do you see much of your husband now Louise, if you don't mind me asking?" Katherine began to tidy up.

"Now don't dare repeat this to anyone else." Louise stepped away from her easel and took Katherine's forearm. "I didn't even tell Morag this, but sometimes I still do his washing."

"What?"

"I know I'm crazy, but Martin never washed so much as a sock in his life. He didn't have a clue and I felt sorry for him. I had to show him how to use his washing machine and he's learnt to cook a bit, though I know he's in the chippy at least twice a week."

"You never think of all those practical things, do you?"

"I've learnt to change fuses." Louise laughed. "I suppose we are fortunate in that we're still friends. I know come Karen's wedding, that's our youngest, she's getting married at Christmas, I'll be ironing his good shirt that morning."

"He must be living close by."

"Just up the road."

"He's not met anyone else I take it."

"Who'd have him? It would be strange to think of Martin with anyone else." Louise shook her head.

Katherine wondered what her life would be like without Vincent. Despite their occasional fumbles, the passion had gone from their marriage, but what about the love. She hated the thought of him cheating, but was that the same as hating him? She must love him if she was so upset at the thought of him being with another woman. Or maybe that was just the terror of looking into the darkness of an unforeseen future.

She looked over at Louise who was adding the final flourishes to her creation. Katherine couldn't help thinking that if she and her husband could only have talked to each other, they wouldn't have separated. When the timing was right she had to have a series of honest conversations with Vincent, conversations that dealt with feelings and fears. If there were problems in their marriage, they were the ones who had to sort them out. If they did separate would it be possible for her and Vincent to remain on good terms? It struck Katherine as they headed back that just as there wasn't a blueprint for marriage, there wasn't one for divorce either. She remembered Declan's words from the restaurant, deep down we all just want to be loved.

***

There was a palpable sense of excitement in the Big Room. Serendipity and Sophie were dressed like avant-garde fashion models. Sophie wore a white shirt that had been attacked with a box of felt-tip markers. She had the tanned slender legs that only a twenty-year-old could have and although a little self-conscious, as she was wearing the shirt as a dress, Katherine could see that the young Belgian girl was having fun.

With encouragement from Ran, the two young women paraded their creations like models on the catwalk. Serendipity had taken the scissors to a t-shirt, exposing her shoulders and one side. They got a big cheer from the group and even a wolf whistle from Declan.

Ran parked himself on the table and invited the group to share their works of art. Bruce was first to his feet. He read a short story he had written. The dialogue was a little wooden Katherine thought, but the idea of a man putting on his suit every morning, even though he had retired, struck her as a poignant insight into the mind of the recently retired law professor. It was only when Bruce sat down that Katherine noticed Tonya hadn't returned.

Marie volunteered to go next. She lined up a load of paper fortune tellers, just like the ones Katherine used to make and play with in primary school. Back then they would tell you what sort of house you would live in, or what occupation you would have when you grew up. Marie had used the simple structure as a way of concealing what she labelled powerful coaching questions. She had made one for everyone and invited the group to come forward and select theirs.

Katherine tried to remember the rhyme she used to sing whilst using her thumbs and forefingers to move the paper. The four categories on the top of Katherine's were 'Career', 'Living environment', 'Finances' and 'Relationships'. She chose the latter. When she opened the lip of paper her question read – what do you want?

A myriad of questions had consumed Katherine's mind over the last few weeks, but not once had she asked herself the question 'what do I want?'

"Oh, great question Katherine." Marie was tottering up and down the row observing how everyone was getting on. "You know when I'm not sure what to do or say, or even when I'm working with a client, the question I always revert to is what do you want? Nothing focuses the mind quicker. It gets us from problem to potential solution."

"What if you don't know what you want?" Katherine asked.

"Well maybe you start by figuring out what it is you don't want?"

"That can be a daunting question Katherine. I've found that some people know exactly what they want; others can spend years trying to figure it out," Corinne said, leaning across Imelda who was having great fun with her puzzle.

"And most people never even ask themselves the question," Marie said.

"Perhaps for now just allow yourself to get curious as to the possibilities." Corinne added.

"Sometimes I'll ask clients, how will you know when you know what you want?" Marie said, running her hands through her hair.

"Oh hold on now that's a bit head wrecking." Katherine's brain contorted to get itself around Marie's words. She distracted herself by asking Imelda what question she got.

"What are you learning?" Imelda said. "I'd have a lengthy answer to that one. Corinne, what about you?"

"If I were more courageous, what would I do?"

"Oh, that's a good one," Katherine said.

"How would you answer that one Corinne?" Imelda asked.

"If I were more courageous?" Corinne pursed her lips. Tiny wrinkles appeared at the corners of her mouth. "You know I'd set up a place something like this, but by the sea."

Katherine wondered how she would answer Corinne's question. If she was more courageous she'd probably phone Vincent. She would need courage to ask the questions she needed to ask and even more courage to listen to the answers.

"Great questions and a great exercise," Neide said to Marie who was basking in the attention. "What question did you get Ran?"

"A really timely one – how can I cherish my gifts even more?" Ran had kicked off his shoes. The tufts of hair on his toes looked like spiders were attacking his feet.

"I've always found with these types of exercises that the questions or the quotes, whatever it is you select, are the perfect ones for you right now," Neide said.

"Great creativity Marie," Ran said, jumping down from the table. "Well done, now who's next? Where are my painters?"

Louise and Katherine looked at each other. Katherine's heart was pounding. She never liked displaying her work. She nodded for Louise to go first.

"Now it's not quite finished but it's the start of a scene, a landscape." Louise held up her pad.

"Ah it's the view over the valley," Neide said. Louise had painted the wall of The Retreat, the purple bougainvillea in the corner, the red door and the lemon trees and then off to the left, the outline of the hills and valley floor. She got a well-deserved round of applause.

"And Katherine what about you?" Ran invited her to step forward.

"Mine's more abstract, well that's my excuse and not nearly as good." Katherine reluctantly held her up pad with the purple blob in the centre. There were one or two 'ahs' from the group, a quizzical or pitying tone Katherine wasn't sure. "I started painting the scene but then I just found myself putting paint on the page and I drew something a little more free-form."

"I like it. We can be inspired by something, like a landscape but we don't always have to reproduce it. You might see a colour in the landscape and you work with that to create something else."

"I suppose that's where I got this mauve colour from, I think. I saw it at the base of the hills. But I remember what you said about enjoying the process and that's what I went for."

"And we had a good chat," Louise added.

"You've painted before haven't you?" Ran asked.

"A long time ago."

"I can tell by the brushstrokes." Ran took the page from Katherine for a closer inspection. "It's like an eye, the eye of your soul perhaps."

"I don't know about that."

"What would you call it?"

"I hadn't thought about it." Katherine took back her picture.

"If it had a name what would it be?"

Katherine looked at her work again. The room was silent.

"I'd call it freedom."

"I love that. I did a series of paintings a while back called Freedom I must show them to you, they're on the website," Ran said. Katherine could feel herself blush. "Some advice if I may, never apologise for your work, this has real merit, be proud of it."

There was a round of applause when she returned to her seat. Katherine's heart was still beating fast. She held her painting tight. Ran's words of encouragement had lit a beacon of pride inside her. She could feel tears behind her eyes.

The group had a good laugh when Morag performed a short play she'd written. Playing a teenage girl late home from a dance. Katherine could see the punchlines coming, but somehow that only added to the enjoyment. Morag went for it one hundred per cent, there was no doubt she could be on the stage in her own one woman show. She got a loud cheer when she took her bow and darted back to her chair.

Suzy shared a short story she wrote about a girl locked in her room by overbearing parents. It had a cliffhanger ending because the room caught fire and you weren't sure if the girl escaped. Declan had taken some photographs around The Retreat and had printed them off using Neide's computer. Everything was taken at odd angles and it made for an interesting and thoughtful collage.

Neide and Iam had participated in the exercise as well. Katherine didn't know where to look when they started a cringe inducing duet. They must have practised because they had co-ordinated their moves. The chorus had the line 'fear you can leave here' and when they sung it they pointed to their hearts.

Katherine was squirming and the whole row twisted in their chairs. Suzy and Declan's heads were hung low. She avoided looking at them for fear unstoppable laughter would erupt. How Ran kept a straight face at the top of the room she didn't know. When they finished Katherine felt the group were applauding themselves for having endured the spectacle.

That just left Imelda and Corinne. Imelda also sang. She had composed a song on the theme of gratitude. What she lacked in harmony she made up for with commitment. The chorus was 'Blessed Am I' and the melody, a lament, had a familiar ring to it.

"So that just leaves you." Ran invited Corinne to step forward.

"I put a few lines of a poem together. I've called it wisdom."

Corinne cleared her throat and in a slow purposeful way began to read.

> "Wisdom speaks when we don't,
> Its voice kind and clear.
> Wisdom is remembering
> What we thought we had forgotten.
>
> Wisdom's voice is of the past
> Inherited in the now.
> Wisdom always feels right,
> Though it may not feel good.
>
> Wisdom is present, even when we are not.
> Wisdom is of the heart
> And sings when we sit in quiet solitude.
>
> Wisdom is the cloak of common sense seldom worn.
> Wisdom is knowing what to do,
> When we don't know what to do."

There was a long pause.

"Wow," Ran said, starting a round of applause, the most sincere of the session.

"You have to read that again," Imelda said. Corinne repeated her poem this time with the courage to look up from the page and just speak the words she had written. There was a second round of applause. Neide offered to type out the poem and give everyone a copy.

Katherine wrote the last two lines of the poem into her journal. She smiled at Corinne as she took her seat, slightly embarrassed by the impact her words had had on the group. It was only the start of what Katherine would learn from the elegant black woman.

CHAPTER 7

It was almost too hot to eat lunch outdoors. A lazy breeze pushed the heat around the courtyard. Corinne and Imelda had retreated to the cool of the common room. Because eating outdoors was a rarity in Ireland, Katherine helped Declan erect two parasols to shade the dining table before taking a spot beside Suzy.

In pride of place at the centre of the table was a colourful concoction of fruit. Hands reached for the slices of melon, mango and papaya, whilst more hands waved away persistent flies. It didn't take long for the platter to be reduced to a scattering of rinds and pips and a puddle of juice.

Katherine loved the crusty sourdough bread at The Retreat. She drizzled it with olive oil then liberally applied slices of cheese and ripe tomatoes. She always loved the muskiness of tomatoes, especially when gnarled and misshapen, unlike the perfectly formed, but perfectly bland ones that lined the supermarket shelves at home. A few basil leaves crowned her king of open sandwiches. Katherine promised herself she would cut back on the carbohydrates, but she was hungry and savoured every mouthful.

Halfway through lunch Tonya entered the courtyard, a two-litre bottle of coke in her arms. She ignored the lunch table and headed straight for her room. No one at the table passed comment. Following her, a slender and smartly dressed woman, the antithesis of Tonya entered. The heads at the table turned in unison.

"That must be who we have in the afternoon?" Katherine said to Suzy. All eyes followed the tanned woman in a white shift dress and platform shoes.

"I'm feeling inadequate already," Suzy replied, reaching for one of the remaining fans of melon.

"She looks like she's stepped off the stage at Miss World," Declan said. "I need to speak to her, don't I?"

"Pamela Lorne, that's her name." Morag had retrieved the workshop schedule from her bag. "*Attracting the man of your dreams, creating the relationship your heart desires* – that's what's in store for us this afternoon."

"That's what you need Declan." Suzy poked his arm.

"Like you're the expert my dear," Declan retorted.

The conversation at the table turned to the fact that most of them missed having a glass of wine with lunch and how they lamented the lack of a good coffee machine in the kitchen. When Pamela Lorne re-emerged with Iam in pursuit she was carrying a large bouquet of flowers. They watched him replace the chairs in the Big Room with beanbags and cushions.

"If I get into one of those beanbags I won't get up," Morag said having spun around to get a full view of what was going on.

"I might as well have that word with her now." Declan got up as soon as he saw Iam leave.

"You know I think he'll really find this afternoon useful Katherine," Suzy said. "He said to me last night that he knows he has issues when it comes to relationships."

"Don't we all," Katherine said.

"He's such a good person, but he always has to be in control and not that I'm an expert by any means but I've learnt enough to know that control and relationships don't mix."

Suzy and Katherine watched Declan shift from one foot to another, his hands gesticulating as he spoke. Katherine thought of her own relationship with Vincent. She didn't think she wanted to control him, but she knew Vincent well enough to know that he liked to be in control. Maybe control was just what men did. As a wife and mother Katherine's role was to hold everything together. She had long since given up on the idea of being in control.

"I don't think he's too pleased." Suzy tapped Katherine's arm. Declan was crossing the courtyard shaking his head.

"Now I'm pissed off." He sat down on the bench with his back to the table. "I don't think that woman realises there are actually gay people in the world."

"What's goin' on?" Suzy asked. Katherine picked at the crumbs of bread on her plate.

"I asked if I should sit in this afternoon," Declan said, eyes flashing. "And she said it's usually only women who attend her workshop because her main theme is female sexuality. So I said to her what about gay people. She looked at me as if I'd two heads. She then started going on about core energies and did I consider myself male or female sexually?"

"The cheek of her, what sort of a question is that." Suzy covered her ears as if a bomb was going to explode.

"You know me I'm not usually stuck for words, but I was gobsmacked. Eventually I said asking a gay person a question like that is like asking a chopstick whether it's a knife or fork."

"Great comeback." Suzy gave her mate a high five.

"I don't think she had a clue what I was trying to say. She just looked at me with a Valley of the Dolls' smile. She said I could sit in if I wanted, but there's no way I'm going to that this afternoon. I want to be celebrated, not tolerated."

"Look at you." Suzy laughed.

"What will you do?" Katherine asked.

"Soak up some rays. If only there was a swimming pool around here." Declan pushed up the sleeves of his t-shirt.

"You could always meet with Iam?" Suzy said, winking at Katherine.

"I'd rather stick pins in my eyes. There must be a bar around here somewhere?"

"I don't think you will find any of the bars you're used to,"

Suzy said, laughing.

"One that sells booze is all I'm looking for." Declan stood, grabbing the last few grapes from the fruit platter and headed back towards his room.

"That's a pity," Suzy said. "He puts on a front, but he's a sensitive soul, he'll spend the afternoon brooding."

"You can always fill him in later on any useful stuff." Katherine offered.

"I better check on him before we kick off. I presume we're starting at two."

Katherine checked her watch; they had fifteen minutes before they were due back.

***

With everyone else around the table locked in their own conversations, Katherine decided to head back to her room to freshen up. She heard Neide's voice in the kitchen, this was her chance to speak with her about preparing the meal on Wednesday evening. Imelda had encouraged her to do it, so had Suzy. Corinne had asked her whether she would feel better or worse if she said no. She knew that if she said no she would regret it. The sooner she spoke with Neide, the sooner she could make the commitment and that would mean following through no matter what new misgivings surfaced.

"About Wednesday evening, I'll give it a go if it's still okay with you."

"Oh, the meal, yes, great. I'm delighted."

"Now I'm not sure about sticking with a vegetarian menu, I'd be more comfortable cooking what I know."

"Oh, that might be a problem. It's what people expect, it's what we advertise."

"That's not my forte." The thought had entered Katherine's mind several times over the last few days that it was unlikely

Neide restricted herself to a vegetarian diet. She was a sizeable woman, with the elasticated waistbands to prove it. Morag even went as far to say that because she never ate with the group Neide probably gorged on pizzas and chips behind the scenes.

"I tell you what, if the others are happy for you to cook your own menu, then we can make the exception this one time."

Neide called to Carlos the chef who was tidying up after lunch. Switching between English and Spanish Neide explained the situation. The more Neide talked the more he nodded. Carlos towered over Neide. He was a big man with broad shoulders and a bulbous nose. His chef's tunic had seen better days. Declan said he wasn't really a chef because he did more assembling and mixing than actually cooking, but Katherine liked Carlos; he was a gentle giant, always happy to exchange pleasantries. For someone working with food he was a little liberal with his aftershave and in the confines of the small dining room, his scent was overpowering.

"Ah Katherine, I show you everything," Carlos said, beaming.

"Maybe tomorrow, I don't want to be late back for class."

"Very good, later, I show you my kitchen, I show you everything later."

Through the archway to the kitchen Katherine could see a large oven and another long wooden table that could do with a good clean down. Large jars filled with beans, nuts and pulses lined a shelf that ran the length of the room. Several baskets where filled with fruit and vegetables.

"Great, so you can speak with Carlos when it suits you. That's a weight off my mind, I appreciate that Katherine," Neide said.

"Just as long as I don't poison everyone." Katherine nodded her goodbye to Carlos who stood motionless staring at her.

"Oh Katherine, another small favour if you don't mind. Would you mind keeping an eye out for Tonya?" Neide's expression changed to one of concern.

"Tonya?"

"She's not in a good place at the moment; she's finding it difficult to fit into the group. You might just ensure she's included."

"She needs to make the effort too Neide, I thought she was quite rude to Bruce yesterday. She just walked out during an exercise we were doing."

"I know. We all have our own challenges and ways of coping. But like all of us she's doing her best." Katherine didn't say anything. She wasn't going to babysit a grown woman who should know how to behave. "If I rub your arm like this, may I?" Neide gently rubbed Katherine's forearm. "This might irritate you a bit, but it doesn't really bother you, does it? But suppose you had a big wound or a bruise on your arm and I touched it, what would you do?"

"It would hurt."

"Yes, you would scream and push me away." Neide raised her eyebrows.

Katherine nodded slowly.

"Tonya has a few wounds, a few challenges. When we are hurting we do what we have to do to stop hurting. Some people lash out, others run away."

"Fight or flight. I hear what you are saying Neide."

***

The others were assembling in the Big Room. Pamela Lorne was perched on the table beside the flower arrangement. She looked like a different species of human. There was something doll-like about her. Her make-up was perfect, her figure was perfect, she had a beautiful deep honey-coloured tan, the ideal foil for the diamond encrusted watch on her arm and the large diamond on her wedding finger. Easy to attract the man of your dreams when you looked like that Katherine thought.

Katherine manoeuvred herself as gracefully as she could into one of the beanbags beside Suzy, grabbing a spare cushion for extra back support. The scent from the lilies in the bouquet hung heavy in the air.

"Enjoy your afternoon ladies," Bruce called out as he passed. He had changed into hiking boots and carried a small rucksack. Iam was going to have the afternoon off.

"Where's Imelda?" Katherine asked Suzy.

"She's giving this one a miss." Corinne responded from the next beanbag over. "She said that at this stage in life the only relationship she was interested in was the one with herself and with her maker."

Somehow Corinne managed to still look elegant whilst seated on the floor. With her legs curled beside her Katherine was reminded of the posture of her aunt Kay in the black and white photo she kept in her bedroom at home.

Just as they were settling, Tonya walked in. Obviously under instruction from Neide a crossed-legged Serendipity beckoned for her to sit with her at the front of the room. Katherine decided she would give Tonya a second chance. She would be pleasant, but if she felt Tonya wasn't making an effort, neither would she.

"Well ladies, are you ready for some fun this afternoon?" Pamela re-crossed her legs. "This is our time to celebrate our femininity and this afternoon we're going to explore personal relationships from the female perspective. So a quick show of hands first, who here is in a relationship?"

Marie's hand shot up. Sophie raised hers sheepishly, as did Katherine.

"Wonderful ladies," Pamela said getting down from the table and smoothing the side of her dress. "Now would I be right in saying that there is always room for improvement in relationships?" The room was silent, even Marie, normally one of the more assertive voices was looking at the floor.

"Sure," Katherine said, feeling she probably had more reason than most for responding.

"The rest of you ladies, I take it you're temporarily single and are seeking a relationship?"

"Absolutely." Without Imelda to rouse the group's enthusiasm, it fell to Serendipity to be the cheerleader.

Corinne raised her hand. "I can only speak for myself, but I was married for over forty years and I've been a widow for three. At this stage in my life I'm not looking for a relationship." Corinne spoke with a certainty that Katherine admired. She had noticed the wide wedding band Corinne wore, but she had no idea she had been widowed.

"I appreciate where you're coming from," Pamela said. "But never say never, eh?" Katherine wondered whether the incessant preening by the woman at the top of the room was as much nervousness as it was vanity.

"We're definitely seeking a relationship. We want to be swept off our feet." Serendipity spoke on behalf of herself and Tonya. The enthusiasm of youth made Katherine smile.

Pamela launched into a well-rehearsed introduction. Her story managed to be both long-winded yet vague. She was born in Spain to a Spanish father and English mother. She had a business on the island but didn't expand on the nature of it. When she announced she got engaged last Christmas, Serendipity actually clapped. The diamond ring was displayed like a trophy, tangible evidence of a deal secured. Katherine glanced at her own engagement ring; just as well she didn't suffer from carat envy. Pamela told the story of how she met her fiancé Richard at a boat show where he was buying a yacht.

"She's a hooker and she runs a brothel," Suzy whispered to Katherine, who tried to remain poker-faced. "I bet she earned that ring."

"I'm going to share with you ladies the rules I followed to secure the man of my dreams and for those of you already in relationships, these rules can be used to enhance an existing relationship."

Katherine's legs were going numb. Corinne shifted position too, but from her expression, she suspected Corinne was more uncomfortable with the tone of the workshop than the seating arrangements.

"Now we're going to start with a little introduction exercise. As you can probably tell, I love flowers, so we're going to introduce ourselves by saying which flower we most closely resemble and why?" The assembled women began looking at each other. "Take a few moments to think about it."

"Venus fly trap?" Suzy whispered.

Hydrangea was Katherine's favourite flower, but she couldn't think what flower symbolised her. If she could choose a tree, she felt a weeping willow would be the most accurate.

"I'll start shall I?" Pamela stepped out of her nude coloured platform shoes and sat down on a cushion. Her toenails had been French polished. "I would describe myself as an orchid. The orchid has long been a symbol for love and that's what I'm all about. It's also an elegant flower with many varieties, the different aspects of my personality and I would like to think it requires careful handling."

"And bloody high maintenance?" Suzy whispered. "Those shoes must have cost five hundred quid."

If the goal was for Pamela to discover more about the people in the room, the exercise failed. People just listed their favourite flowers, with a rose being the most popular. Up to now, Katherine would have selected poison ivy for Tonya, but she was surprised that Tonya actually compared herself to baby's breath. She said she chose it because it's usually used to fill in the gaps in bouquets and sometimes she feels like she doesn't fit in. Katherine admired her honesty and when she looked at the large woman swathed in black she could see a gentleness in her face that she hadn't noticed before.

Because she couldn't think of anything else, Katherine compared herself to the hydrangea. It doesn't require much upkeep, has big flowers, and can change colour depending on the type of soil it's in. It was as good an answer as anyone else had come up with.

Curiously Corinne bent the rules and chose bamboo. It just grows and grows she said emphasising that the more she learns the more she realises she doesn't know. Insightful Katherine thought, scribbling the phrase into her journal.

"Now ladies, for the next little while we're going to focus on what sort of relationship we want. Has anyone here sat down and listed out the qualities they're looking for in their ideal partner or in their ideal relationship?"

There was much rustling of beanbags and cushions.

"I've thought about it," Serendipity offered.

"I'm sure some of you write out goals and create vision boards, but most of the time we don't get clear as to what it is we want as regards our relationships."

"That's true. I'm a great believer in the power of goal setting, it's fundamental in my business as a life coach," Marie said. "But I've never really applied a goal-focused mindset to relationships."

"Well it's the same principle. How will we know if we're on the right track unless we know our destination?"

"But what if you're already in a relationship?" Marie asked.

"It's the same thing; we need to be clear as to what it is we want. So up to break time we're going to think about the qualities, the characteristics, the values we're seeking in our relationships."

"Is it worth my while doing this exercise Pamela? As I said I'm not looking for a relationship," Corinne asked.

"Perhaps instead of a romantic relationship, you can look at qualities in a platonic relationship?"

Corinne nodded and retrieved her pad and pen from her bag.

"So for those of you not in a relationship I want you to do the following." Pamela moved to the flipchart. "I want you to start describing your ideal partner. What qualities do you want him to possess. List everything you're looking for, physical description, financial status, personality, his hobbies. Have fun with it. When I last did this exercise I listed over seventy qualities."

"Isn't that just being fussy?" Suzy asked.

"Far from it. You're getting clear as to what it is you want. This is only step one. Now for those of you in a relationship I want you to start by writing out what's great about your current partner."

It was a question Katherine didn't expect. She opened her journal and stared at the blank page. It had been a long time since she'd focused on Vincent's good qualities. She could rhyme off his annoying ones without taking a breath.

The words were slow in coming. *Provider – good father – focused – hard-worker.* Katherine could see the others writing vigorously. She felt like the slow girl in class. She could see Suzy was having fun describing her ideal man. Katherine thought about whispering to her to make sure she included the word 'single' in her list, but she kept the thought to herself.

Over Suzy's shoulder, Marie was writing at speed. She could make out the words loyal, loving and passionate on her page. They were words Katherine would love to be able to write. Instead she wrote '*organised, professional, good businessman*'. Katherine thought of Ran. If only traits like creative, artistic, relaxed and rugged could be transplanted into Vincent. She used to think Vincent was handsome, but what was slim in his thirties and slender in his forties was now just wiry in his fifties. She thought of Mark as well – suave, confident, smart dresser. At least she could add those last two traits to her list.

"Anything strike you when you review your lists ladies?" Pamela asked, once again perched on the table.

Katherine looked at the nine sad qualities on her page. She could be writing the job description of a tax collector.

"There are many qualities I really admire in my partner John," Marie said. "But I often take them for granted."

"That's a good observation, isn't it?"

Katherine feared that if she was asked to list the qualities she admired in her husband she would have to lie.

"Now are you ready for step two? Those of you not in a relationship I want you to list the qualities or characteristics you want to avoid. In other words describe your partner from hell."

"I've dated him and his brother," Suzy said making the group laugh.

"Marie, Katherine and Sophie I want you to list the qualities or characteristics you do not want in your relationship. We are not talking about aspects of your partner you don't like, but characteristics of your relationship. When we are in a relationship we have to remember we each do fifty per cent of the relating."

Katherine took a deep breath. She was putting her relationship under the microscope. She had done this in a haphazard way in her head many times, but jotting down the undesirable characteristics of her relationship was scary. Actually writing them out was an acknowledgement that her marriage was in serious trouble.

I don't want a lack of trust or openness.

I don't want awkward silences and being afraid to say what's on my mind.

I don't want to be made to feel stupid.

I don't want to be patronised.

I don't want to feel bored, stuck in a routine.

Katherine thought there would be more. She had only written five sentences, but they were five big ones.

"Any comments or thoughts on that exercise?" Pamela asked when she saw most of the women had stopped writing.

"I must have learnt something from my disastrous relationships," Suzy said. "At least I know now what to avoid."

"Makes us more aware of the early warning signals perhaps," Pamela said.

Katherine wanted to ask what she could do to turn her relationship around, but she felt that was too personal. Maybe she could speak with Pamela later. She wondered what Louise had been writing. Her painting partner from that morning was transfixed by her notebook.

"Okay ladies are you ready for the key insights for this first part of our workshop? You might want to jot these down. To attract the man of our dreams we have to be attractive and to transform a relationship we have to transform ourselves."

"What do you mean attractive?" Tonya asked.

"When I say attractive we have to look at the qualities we are displaying or need to display to attract the man of our dreams into our lives. So when I say attractive, I mean attractive in the magnetic sense of the word." Tonya nodded, placated.

"Say that again please about transforming ourselves?" Katherine asked.

"To transform a relationship we have to transform ourselves."

Katherine wrote it in capitals in her journal and then underlined it.

"Remember ladies that we cannot change other people, wouldn't life be simple if we could, we can only change how we relate and interact with other people. So if we are seeking to enhance our relationships, we have to start by looking in the mirror and enhance or transform ourselves."

Katherine found herself sitting up straight.

"Now for you single ladies, I want you to review what you've written, especially your first list, describing your ideal man. The question you must now answer is – to attract this man into my life, what qualities do I need to display?"

Katherine noticed Marie was busy writing everything Pamela was saying. No doubt relationship coaching would soon be offered in the Belfast area.

"My three spoken-for women, you have two follow up questions. Firstly, review your list from the last exercise, the characteristics you don't want in your relationship, if what you wrote is currently present in your relationship, what do you need to do differently, remembering that you are part of that relationship dynamic. Your second question is: for your relationship to flourish what qualities do you need to display?"

"I'm not sure I follow the first part Pamela," Katherine asked.

"Shout out one of the relationship traits you want to avoid Katherine?" Pamela asked walking over to where Katherine was seated.

Katherine scanned her list to select the least pathetic answer. "I don't want to be patronised."

"Okay, so to ensure you are not patronised, how do you need to show up in your relationship?" Still seeing a look of confusion on Katherine's face, Pamela spoke again. "If you don't want to be patronised what do you want?"

"I want to be trusted, treated with respect, know my opinion matters."

"So what qualities do you need to display, what qualities do you need to bring into the relationship?"

"I need to stand up for myself, be more assertive."

"Right. And what about trust and respect?"

"But I don't trust him that's the problem." Katherine just blurted it out, regretting that she had opened her mouth in the first place.

"We're not talking about him, we're talking about you. If you want to be trusted and respected what do you need to do?"

Katherine sat in silence. There was an answer she felt Pamela wanted her to say, but she didn't know it. All the eyes in the room were on her. She could see Marie raise her hand, but Pamela ignored her.

After what seemed like an age but in reality was only a few seconds, Katherine could feel a response emerge from deep within her. "I need to trust and respect myself."

"That's it, isn't it?" Pamela was nodding and the other faces in the room were now smiling. "So you capture that Katherine, and then think about what else is needed for your relationship to flourish, for it to thrive."

Something had shifted in Katherine. She began to write rapidly.

I need to trust and respect myself.

I need to listen to my own wisdom and what feels right.

I need to be independent and know I can stand on my own two feet.

I need to have the open honest conversation with Vincent – so I need to be brave.

I need to be strong and know my own mind.

I need to know exactly what I want.

I need to take risks to save my marriage.

But then her pen stopped. She found herself writing – *do I want to save my marriage?*

The internal voice that had released the awareness that she needed to trust and respect herself had stirred something else. Marie's question from the adapted fortune-teller exercise that morning spun in her head. What do I want? For the first time she realised that maybe she didn't want to save her twenty-six-year marriage. Maybe she knew this all along. Was she the catalyst for the state her relationship was in? After all she was the one who had got into the car with Mark. She could feel tears hover in the background.

Katherine didn't want to be seen crying. She got to her feet and excused herself from the group.

***

104

The heat in the courtyard hit her like a blow to the head. There wasn't a breath of air. She crossed to the kitchen to get some water.

"Katherine, you want me to show you everything now?" Carlos stepped through the archway flinging a dishcloth over his shoulder.

"Oh Carlos, I'm just getting some water, I'll have to get back."

"Ah you're sad."

Katherine tried to smile away the tears.

"Come sit, I make you some tea." Carlos rubbed her arm. The compassion in his eyes made her feel even worse. He was looking at her in a way Vincent hadn't looked at her in years.

"I must get back."

"Only take a minute."

Katherine followed the chef through the archway into the heart of his kitchen. He pulled out a chair for her. The kettle was soon boiling.

"I see it every week, many people cry here, but they feel better later."

"You're very kind."

"You like my kitchen?" He waved his arms displaying the double oven and a six-ring hob.

As Katherine cradled the mug of hot tea, Carlos pointed out everything she might need on Wednesday night. The shelves on the dresser contained enough plates, bowls and serving dishes to cater for an army. A variety of pots, pans and utensils dangled over her head. She laughed when Carlos pointed out the microwave, the ping ping as he called it. He said he never used it, he hated the thing.

"So what you going to cook on Wednesday?"

"Maybe some chicken, I'll have to ask the others," Katherine said.

"Ah chicken and chorizo my favourite, proper Spanish food, I show you."

Dropping to all fours Carlos began rummaging under the table. One by one cookery books with titles in Spanish, German and English all relating to vegetarian, vegan and macrobiotic food were stacked on the table. Eventually Carlos found what he was seeking, an old Spanish book, a thick tome with a torn dust jacket.

"You take."

Katherine ran her fingers over the cover. The author's name in bold print was Simone Ortega. She opened one of the many dog-eared pages. From the pictures she scanned a recipe for some type of fish maybe bass with tomatoes, and another for green beans with bacon and garlic. "I won't be able to follow the recipes Carlos, I don't speak Spanish."

"I help you."

"I'll have a look through it. Maybe I could bring it back tomorrow?" Katherine loved old cookery books. She had quite a collection herself. From the typeface and pictures, the book in her hands must be at least thirty years old. Katherine relished the thought of flicking through all nine hundred odd pages whilst propped up in bed.

"I wish I cook these, but Neide say no, only vegetarian, only macrobiotic."

Katherine stood but every time she took a step towards the door Carlos would find something else to show her. From a drawer in the table came garlic crushers and vegetable peelers. From a cupboard on the far wall, tin foil and plastic wrap. A large colander came from another press and he took great pleasure in demonstrating the sharpness of his knives. Ten minutes later Katherine could hear voices in the courtyard.

"Katherine we wondered where you went." Morag stuck her head through the archway.

"I popped out for water, but got chatting to Carlos. I'm going to be cooking the meal Wednesday evening."

"Good for you and please do something I can sink my teeth into." Morag grabbed her arm. "We were only saying how all this salad and fruit is getting boring. I need a bit of stodge. Now, Corinne's not happy."

"What happened?"

"Well Pamela started to speak about connecting with our Inner Princess, the girl inside us who wants to be nurtured or wooed or something like that. And then she was saying that if you want to meet a rich man you have to go to the places rich men go to. I was only half paying attention because Suzy had whispered to me that she thought her boobs were fake and I was paying more attention to them, they didn't seem to move that much, but anyway Corinne said her days of being a Princess were behind her. The atmosphere got a little tense. Just as well it was break time."

Crossing the courtyard Katherine could see Corinne and Pamela were still talking.

"I'm sorry Pamela, but you're speaking as if the goal for everyone here is to get themselves a rich husband. You seem to think that marrying a man of means and having him treat you like a Princess is what a relationship is about. My husband never treated me like a Princess and I wouldn't have wanted him to. He treated me like a Queen, his equal, not like some child who needs to be indulged," Corinne said.

"It's about having the best in life isn't it and being treated and valued as a woman? That's what we'll be getting into after break."

"I just think your picture of relationships is quite one dimensional."

"I appreciate your perspective." Pamela stood with arms akimbo. From across the room Katherine could tell from her tone and expression she was far from appreciative.

107

"You know I might just pass," Corinne said reaching for her bag.

Pamela's smile broadened as her eyes narrowed. She said nothing. Corinne turned and with her head held high she walked slowly from the room, every inch of her a Queen.

Katherine contemplated seeking Pamela's advice on her situation, but she was preoccupied adjusting her dress and hair. Seeing Corinne heading for the door of the compound, Katherine grabbed her bag and journal and with the weighty cookbook still under her arm went after her.

"Corinne, wait a second."

"That woman makes my blood boil. I've had enough for today."

"Don't rush off."

"I feel sorry for the naive young girls in there. You know the other workshops have been so grounded and real, she's all image and little substance."

"I thought some of her questions were good, got me thinking."

"Granted she had some useful insights, but that stuff about being treated like a princess and spending time where wealthy men congregate, it was like a throwback to the fifties. Tell me Katherine in all honesty what can a girl like that teach you and me about being a woman or about relationships? But you know what's annoying me even more, when someone makes my blood boil like that; it usually means there's something for me to learn."

"She's just pushed one of your buttons Corinne, that's all."

"Yes, but they're my buttons. You know the thinking; we learn the most from those that annoy us."

"How about there are times when people just piss us off, full stop."

Corinne laughed. "Fancy playing truant? We'll go for a spin, find a nice spot to eat and I'll drop you back later," Corinne asked, her facing lighting up.

Katherine knew immediately that a few hours out of The Retreat, a change of scenery and a chance to get to know Corinne was just what she needed.

"Should I say something to Neide?"

"It's not boarding school Katherine; we can come and go as we please."

"Well then, what are we waiting for?"

Katherine held the gate open for Corinne then followed her down the alley to where her little white car was parked in the shade of a tree.

It would be twenty-four hours before Katherine would return.

CHAPTER 8

"Isn't this breeze delicious?" Corinne said, rolling down the windows banishing the sauna-like heat from the car.

Katherine felt guilty just walking out of The Retreat, but she was excited about spending time with Corinne. A change of scenery would do her good. As the town of Teguise grew smaller in the wing mirror, Katherine sat back allowing the wind to play havoc with her hair.

"You can't beat old-fashioned air conditioning, can you?" Corinne said rubbing her cropped white hair. "I'm still kicking myself though for actually going to that relationship workshop."

"The others won't think us rude just walking out like that?"

"Let them think what they think. I remember someone saying to me once that if you think about the amount of time you spend worrying about what other people think of you and if everyone is doing that, then other people have no space in their heads to be thinking about you."

"That's another one for my journal." Katherine laughed, patting the journal that lay on her lap.

"I'm glad we have a chance to get to know each other. That's what I like best about a week like this, meeting like-minded people."

"Imelda is great, isn't she? Should we have asked her to join us?"

"I think she is happy doing her own thing."

"Incredible landscape," Katherine said, her eyes drinking in the barren scenery. It seemed more than two days since she travelled this road in the taxi from the airport. "Where are we heading?"

"I thought we'd dump our stuff where I'm staying in Playa

Blanca, it's only forty minutes or so away. There's a lovely prom along the coast. A bit of sea air will do us good and I don't know about you, but I get stiff sitting all day and those beanbags were dreadful. If we get hungry maybe we could grab a bite to eat. I got a recommendation for a fish restaurant that I've been dying to try."

"Sounds like a plan to me."

Corinne turned up the volume of the classical CD that had been drowned out by the wind. Katherine recognised the aria but couldn't name it. Her eyes followed the shadow of a cloud on the mountain slopes; it was like an unseen hand was drawing a curtain. The painter in her wondered how she could capture the desolate beauty of the scene.

Corinne took a right at a large roundabout following the sign to Playa Blanca. Seeing a sign for the airport stirred feelings of dread in Katherine. She was trying her best to do what Imelda had said, park the situation with Vincent and focus on enjoying her time here, but the airport sign was a stark reminder of the reality that awaited her at home. She rubbed the leather cover of the journal that sat in her lap. She still couldn't believe that she had actually written the words, 'do I want to save my marriage?'

"Not too long now, I'm beginning to get used to travelling this route."

As the road swung to the left the landscape widened. A gash of deep blue sea separated the land from the sky.

"You're great at driving on the opposite side of the road. I've never been brave enough. Vincent always does the driving when we're away."

"Well, needs must. I only started driving a few years ago."

"Really?"

"Terry forced me to get lessons. He said I needed to be independent."

"How long is it since Terry died?"

111

"Three years and three months. Cancer, died within the year of being told."

"That's awful."

"It was, but you know what he kept saying – we're all gonna die girl, I just know when."

"My mother died in January and as tough as that was and is, it's easier to accept, it's part of the cycle of life, but it's scary when you're now the older generation, when there's no one left ahead of you."

"Savour the time we have, it's all we can do. It's a cliché but you only realise what you have, what you take for granted, when it's taken from you."

Katherine knew she would be devastated if Vincent were to die suddenly, but a tiny part of her, a part she was ashamed to even acknowledge, knew it would be an escape route. "It sounds as if you are doing well though?"

"It's weird looking back I can see that I went through all the stages of grief Katherine, disbelief, anger, acceptance. I remember after the shock of the diagnosis I was so angry at everyone and everything. I was even angry with Terry for getting cancer. I was furious that I'd be cheated out of all the plans we had made. God forgive me but I remember shouting at Terry that I wanted him to die straightaway, because I just wanted to get the pain over with. Can you believe he was the one who ended up consoling me?"

"I'm sure I would've been exactly the same."

"I can still remember it, he sat me down in our front room and he said to me girl, that's what he always called me, girl, for the next nine months, or however long we have together we're going to make the most of it. We're going to laugh every day, we're through with crying. We have our faith and our savings and now's the time to use both. And that's what we did, we laughed and we prayed and we spent our rainy day money. Now I did my crying too, but I was going to uphold my part of the bargain. If that brave man never complained once, I wasn't going to either."

"He sounds quite a character."

"Married forty-one years and it seems like an odd thing to say but those last few months were probably our happiest."

"The best of times, the worst of times."

"True, the age of wisdom and foolishness too, if I can remember my Dickens. I was only saying to Imelda at lunchtime, I've got so many good memories of our time together. We made our bucket list of all the things we wanted to do or experience and we packed them in whilst Terry was still able to travel. Now believe me there are still days when I bawl my eyes out, when I feel abandoned and lonely but I've learnt to think of the good memories, the great times we had together and to celebrate those, rather than mourn the loss of unmet expectations. It could have been worse, he could've been knocked down by a bus and we wouldn't have had those last few months."

"We do the best we can."

"Just get on with the business of living. You might think I'm mad Katherine but I still talk to Terry every day. I ask him for advice and when I'm lying in bed at night I tell him about everything that's happened that day."

"That's not mad at all."

"That's why I'll never be interested in another relationship. Terry is still my husband and I still feel so close to him. A friend of mine asked a few weeks after he died was I going to take my wedding ring off, now that I'm single again. Well, I nearly threw her out of the house; I'm still married in my head."

Katherine toyed with her wedding ring.

"Now you'll definitely think I'm mad because sometimes I think he's playing a joke on me, he's up there still yanking my strings. He was an awful prankster."

"Why's that?"

"Funny coincidences, that sort of thing. Last week I went

with Nenah, that's my granddaughter, to this modelling agency. This guy had stopped her in the street and gave her a card, asked her if she ever considered being a model that sort of thing."

"She must be a stunner."

"Takes after me." Corinne pursed her lips then winked. "Anyway Nenah's mother couldn't get time off work, so I went with her to make sure it was legit, I wasn't having her getting mixed up in anything seedy."

"You did right."

"Anyway, it was all above board, a proper model agency, a busy office. So there I am sitting in the reception flicking through magazines waiting for Nenah and this guy keeps staring at me. Then another woman joins him. In the end I dropped my magazine and asked them what they were doing. And get this; they wanted to know if I would be interested in doing some modelling work."

"What?"

"Yes, the man kept saying I had a great look, and what did he call it, a luminous quality and would I be interested in being part of some ad campaign they were working on."

"And what did you say?"

"When I stopped laughing, I said my granddaughter was the model and who would want an old woman like me. But he said they were looking for women of different ages and sizes for a campaign for some brand of soap and they thought their client would really like me."

"Oooh Corinne, I can see you in the pages of a magazine already."

"Right, me and Naomi Campbell."

"What did you say?"

"I said I'd think about it, it was only last week. Anyway he gave me his card. But's here's the freaky bit. Guess what his name was? Terry Peters."

"Terry, same as your husband."

"It wasn't just that, Terry's second name was Peter, Terence Peter Stanley."

"Now that is a coincidence."

"All I thought was there's my Terry having a bit of fun with me, getting me to think that I could be a model. Could you imagine?"

"I wouldn't be too quick to discount it, it might be fun and they'd be paying you I presume."

"Well they must be keen because Nenah texted me yesterday saying that guy Terry was trying to contact me."

"You should get back to him."

"Well, we'll see."

"I'd jump at it, though I think they'd only want me for the before picture for some make-over show."

"Oh, get outta here." The two women laughed.

Corinne's little white hire car approached the outskirts of Playa Blanca. Rows of unfinished villas lined both sides of the road.

"They've their ghost estates here too, I see," Katherine said.

"Now the villa is about a mile from the old town," Corinne said, taking a right turn. The flags at the entrance to a hotel fluttered in the strong breeze. A sprawling development of single storey villas stretched off to the right, only the ones closest to the road looked lived in. The view ahead was dominated by a rust-coloured mountain. Large villas nestled on its slopes.

"You'd have some view from up there," Katherine said, leaning forward in an attempt to see the summit.

"Montana Roja, the red mountain, stunning isn't it? Now Katherine, there's a buzzer for the gate in the glove compartment."

Corinne pulled up in front of a large gate that jolted open as soon as Katherine pressed the buzzer. A high boundary wall of volcanic stone surrounded the development, its blackness the perfect foil for the pristine white villas, each one on its own spacious and well-maintained plot.

"We're right at the front." They drove straight ahead down the slope towards the sea. Some of the villas had roof terraces and from what Katherine could make out behind the walls and plants, their own pools. Corinne swung left at a small roundabout with an ornate lamppost and pulled into a shallow driveway. "Here we are, Casa Castille." Bronze lanterns stood on either side of the entrance. The villa itself was concealed behind an outer wall that was covered in a magnificent white flowering plant. Katherine thought she recognised the delicate petals and as soon as she stepped out of the car, the rich exotic scent of jasmine was unmistakeable.

"I love jasmine." Katherine took one of the flowers and rubbed it in her fingers. "No oil or perfume can ever match Mother Nature."

"We'll go around the side." Corinne opened a side gate and invited Katherine to step through. She ducked under the flapping leaves of a palm tree that rattled in the wind, the sound of the tropics. Scattered throughout the garden of yucca plants, palm trees and cacti were unusual metal sculptures.

"Jean, the owner, is a fantastic artist; all these sculptures and figures are hers."

But Katherine didn't hear Corinne; the view ahead consumed all her senses. Spellbound Katherine was pulled towards a one hundred and eighty degree view of sparkling azure sea. On the horizon the dome-like mountains of Fuerteventura, shrouded in a heat haze, were mysterious and inviting.

"Now that's what I call a sea view Corinne."

"Stunning isn't it?"

"I could stare at it all day."

The two women sat on the wall at the front.

"That's the coastal path you were talking about?" Katherine leant forward. About fifteen feet below them a promenade

116

stretched off to the right and left. A few souls, braving the afternoon sun sauntered by.

"It runs all the way from that lighthouse to the marina beyond Playa Blanca."

To the right Katherine could clearly see the tall lighthouse. In the other direction at the top of a slope stood a large hotel, its domes and cupolas playing homage to North Africa only four hundred miles away.

"That hotel is gorgeous lit up at night. Playa Blanca is about a mile or so in that direction and it's a lovely walk. Do you want to leave your books inside and we'll freshen up."

Reluctantly Katherine turned her back on the view. For the first time she surveyed the villa. A protective blue plastic cover concealed an oval swimming pool. Removing one shoe she dipped her toes in. As expected it was like bath water. Purple bougainvillea cascaded over one wall of the villa and across an awning crowning the outdoor dining area. Teak sunloungers were arranged in pairs around the pool. On the far side of the villa a lush garden provided the backdrop for a row of tall warrior-like bronze sculptures.

Katherine followed Corinne inside. The walls were covered with modern art. Katherine was intrigued by the experimental paintings of misshapen heads and landscapes that seemed to lack any perspective. Wooden and metallic sculptures were propped in most corners. Heavy looking furniture and inviting cushions filled the main living area. A massive skylight flooded the dining room and kitchen with natural light.

"It must cost a pretty penny to stay here."

"Mike and Jean, the owners, stay here quite a bit themselves. They only really let it to friends or people they know. Cousins of theirs were due to be here for two weeks, but they cancelled at the last minute. Mike offered it to me when I told them I was going to The Retreat. So here I am in a fab four-bedroom villa for a week and it isn't costing me a penny. If that isn't abundance I don't know what is."

"I'm not sure I'd be able to drag myself away, retreat or no retreat."

"Listen, why don't you stay here tonight Katherine, there are plenty of bedrooms?"

"Oh I couldn't."

"What's stopping you?" Corinne handed Katherine a glass of iced water.

"Sure they'll think I'm missing."

"There's a wardrobe full of towels and sheets and if you need anything else there's a supermarket just down the way."

"I'll have to ring and let Neide know."

"If you like."

"Are you sure Corinne?"

"Of course, it means we're not under pressure, we can take our time getting something to eat. I can have a glass of wine."

"Well I was thinking I could get a taxi back anyway, no point in you making another trip."

"Nonsense, you're staying here."

"Well if you are sure, then I'd love to."

***

Her room was far more luxurious than her cell at The Retreat. Leaving her journal on what would now be her bed, Katherine returned to her spot on the wall to wait for Corinne who said she wanted to make a call. The sea below was choppy. A strong breeze hurtled down the mountain and skimmed the surface of the water as it raced towards Fuerteventura. Katherine closed her eyes. The hypnotic clacking of the palm trees and the hollow grind of the sea were to her the sounds of paradise.

She was nudged from her reverie by a flock of sparrows darting from the shrubbery to bathe at the edge of the pool. She kept as still as she could so as not to disturb them. Katherine regretted not having a swimsuit.

Her phone rang. The birds scattered. Katherine didn't recognise the number. It was Serendipity letting her know that there was a change in the schedule. Ran's painting workshop, scheduled for the morning, was being pushed back to the afternoon. Iam was arranging an excursion to the citadel, but most people were planning to do their own thing. Relieved that there was no hint of disappointment or rebuke in Serendipity's voice, Katherine told her of her plans to stay with Corinne. She now had permission to enjoy the evening guilt free and if they didn't have to be back until the following afternoon, they could spend a lazy morning by the pool.

***

"You know I've been to too many workshops and courses that start off with the premise that there's something wrong with me, but that's not been the case with Neide's classes," Corinne said, pulling the door of the villa shut behind her. Katherine had told Corinne about the change in the schedule and they were discussing what they thought of The Retreat. "There's a path down to the prom this way."

Framed by a wrought iron gate, the mesmerising sea pulled them like a magnet down a narrow shaded path. Emerging onto the promenade Katherine was aware of the curious looks they were getting from two older couples who had watched them come through the gate with the sign *'Residencia Private'*.

Thankfully Corinne had located some sun lotion on a shelf in one of the bathrooms. It would have been too easy for Katherine to get sunburnt; the strong sun was deceptively tempered by the ever-present breeze. Corinne added a wide brimmed hat to her ensemble, the only sun care she said she needed.

"What a stunning villa and as for location, literally a stone's throw from the sea," Katherine said, looking up at the high black stone wall, the roof of the villa just visible above it and the red mountain beyond it again. Katherine leant on the back of a bench, one of several she could see dotted along the prom. The sea lapped at the shoreline just a few feet away.

"We'll head towards Playa Blanca, what do you think?" Corinne asked.

"Lead the way. It sounds like you're a pro when it comes to retreats Corinne?"

"I was at one this time last year in Greece, although that was more of a creative writing workshop. Actually Bruno Reye who's doing one of the talks here this week was at it. He's an interesting character."

"I wonder will he remember you."

"Maybe. And I went to a three-day course in Somerset in March, that was a bit too hippy for me though. I've always had an interest in personal development work and spirituality, but it's only really since Terry died that I felt I really needed to do something for me, if you know what I mean. A woman I met in Greece raved about The Bliss Retreat. When you're travelling by yourself it's easier to mix with people when you are all involved in an activity or in a class together."

"This is the first time I've ever been away by myself."

"Really?"

"Well I'm either with Vincent or I'll head away with some friends maybe for a weekend."

"And how did you end up here then?"

As they sauntered towards Playa Blanca Katherine told Corinne the story of how Rhona had broken her leg. She contemplated divulging more about Vincent and the state of her marriage, but she had to concentrate on breathing as they ascended a steep incline.

At the summit, tourists caught their breath and posed for

photos beside the ruin of a lookout tower. The crumbling structure reminded Katherine of the Martello towers in Dublin. Ahead of them an arc of golden sand was backed by a line of shops and restaurants. Then it hit them, a rank smell that suggested a blocked, or worse, a burst sewage pipe. In the heat, the rancid odour clung to them. They picked up their pace.

"If you need anything for tonight Katherine, there's a supermarket we could stop in on the way back," Corinne said. Passing the store Katherine was delighted to see swimwear in the window.

The path hugged the coastline, following every hill and inlet. Katherine could see it stretch before them, up another incline and past another hotel.

The two women continued to share their stories. Katherine was reticent about revealing her marriage woes, but she spoke of her mother's death, her empty nest and financial concerns. She found Corinne's story inspiring.

Corinne's parents were one of the first to emigrate to England from Jamaica in the early fifties. Family folklore said her mother descended from West African royalty. Perhaps that explained Corinne's regal demeanour. Corinne had been told that she had been conceived on the boat on the way over. Her parents wanted their first child to be born in Britain.

Corinne left school without qualifications and worked for years as a chambermaid in a hotel. Terry was her first boyfriend. As so often happens, restraint and a strict religious upbringing only fuelled their passion and she found herself pregnant at twenty. Under pressure from their families they got married and thankfully made a go of it. When their son George started school Corinne did a night course to get her O levels. It was only then she said she discovered her love of learning. Her parents had always wanted her to have a college education and even though Terry couldn't see the point of it, she persevered and went on to get a degree in hospitality management.

There was no way a chambermaid would ever end up front of house, so she left and got a job on the switchboard at another hotel. She must have had her sultry rich voice even as a young woman, Katherine thought. In time she moved to the front desk and worked as a receptionist. From what she was told, she was one of the first black women to have such a role in an upmarket London establishment. It was a job she loved and she stayed front of house for the rest of her career turning down several opportunities for promotion. Until she took early retirement when Terry got sick, she was a senior receptionist in a hotel on Park Lane. A position she viewed as being the pinnacle of her profession.

The coastal path had led them to the harbour in Playa Blanca. A large ferry was docked and rows of cars and vans queued to board. Corinne took Katherine's arm as they crossed the broken tarmac of the harbour car park and climbed the stone steps to the seafront prom in Playa Blanca.

"Let's walk along the front rather than up the main street, what do you think?" Corinne suggested.

The front in Playa Blanca was busy. Katherine loved the scent of floral perfume mixed with sun lotion that lingered outside a row of identical looking perfumery shops all promising the best prices in town. People of all nationalities, ages, sizes and states of undress weaved amongst the souvenir stores, the ice cream parlours, bars and restaurants. Katherine and Corinne paused only to browse the windows of the odd shop selling local crafts or jewellery.

"Are you hungry Katherine?"

"I could certainly eat a bit, some of these aromas have my taste buds tingling."

"We can always nibble on something, have a drink then order later."

The narrow beach in the centre of the town was packed. A few boisterous teenagers were diving off a pontoon moored in the centre of the bay, their screams just audible over the thump of music from an arcade.

"I think that's it with the green awning." Corinne pointed ahead.

The restaurant was bigger than Katherine expected. Usually restaurant recommendations are for tiny places in back streets, but this restaurant stood proud in the middle of the town. There were similar looking restaurants all with outdoor seating on either side, but this one was the busiest. Word had obviously got out.

Most of the wicker tables at the edge were taken, but there were plenty of vacant tables under the awning.

"I think we're having a late lunch rather than an early dinner. What do you think? It sounds more decadent," Corinne said, leading the way. A waiter gestured towards a table for four in the shade. The roof was covered with baskets of ferns. A fine mist was sprayed in spurts, evaporating before it ever reached their heads. "Now that's novel air conditioning."

"Keeps us cool and we get a facial at the same time. I like this place already."

A mature waiter handed them two menus. The heavy leather cover reminded Katherine of her journal. The laminated pages inside contained the same menu in several languages.

"I have to say I'm hungry, I didn't eat much at lunchtime," Corinne said.

"You have to tell me your secret Corinne, how do you keep your figure?" Katherine had admired how the sandy-coloured linen dress hung on Corinne.

"It's no secret, I try to keep active, I drink plenty of water, but I suppose if there's one thing I've learnt is that I listen to my body. I eat when I'm hungry and I eat what I want, within reason of course."

"That's a common sense diet."

"I wouldn't call it a diet; it's just what people did years ago.

You know, who says we need breakfast at eight or lunch at one or dinner at six. Some days will go by and I'll hardly eat a thing, because my body is saying it's not hungry. Other times I'll spend the day grazing at whatever is in front of me. I'm a firm believer in the wisdom of our bodies, the old wisdom that we seemed to have lost. Right now my body is telling me it would like some fish."

"Some omega-three oils."

"Yes, and a nice glass of wine, what do you think?"

"You could twist my arm."

"There are a few dishes for two, fancy sharing the fish platter or maybe paella, that was the dish Mike and Jean recommended and it says it takes twenty-five minutes, so they must cook it fresh. It will give us time to nibble on a few olives."

Katherine sat back. Fine water hissed onto the ferns above them. She turned her face to it and could just about feel the gentle mist descend.

"Look how fast it's going." Corinne pointed at the massive catamaran that seemed to be steaming straight towards them. At the last minute, the engines roared into reverse and it backed into the harbour. The wake from the large vessel created waves that crashed against the seawall and pummelled the swimmers at the water's edge, who were loving every minute of it. The teenagers swimming in from the pontoon were trying to body surf.

"That's not a sight I like though. I think it's cruel," Katherine remarked, pointing at two parrots their wings obviously clipped perched under a parasol on the sea wall.

"I'd say they're connected with this place. It gets people to stop. Look there's a waiter approaching them with a menu. Clever marketing."

Further along the wall a large black woman in a colourful robe had set up a stall and was braiding a child's hair. Beside her a man with an easel was sketching caricatures.

A big man with his arm around a much younger woman strolled towards them. Katherine's eyes followed them into the restaurant. Removing what looked like a cowboy hat, the man was bald. He was easily old enough to be the girl's father, if not her grandfather.

Corinne placed their order and Katherine sat back. Vincent, financial worries, even The Retreat seemed a world away.

CHAPTER 9

"Why is it that it's always the fattest men who wear the smallest swimming trunks? Look what's going to walk by." Katherine nodded towards a large middle-aged man wearing tiny yellow swimming briefs, barely visible beneath his expansive stomach. The two women casually glanced towards the sea as he waddled into view.

"Budgie smugglers, isn't that what they call them," Corinne said, her hand to her mouth.

"I've not heard that one." Katherine laughed.

"It's never the twenty-year-olds, that's for sure." The two women sipped their wine.

"He could be arrested for indecent exposure. This wine's delicious, isn't it?" Katherine took the blue bottle with the elongated neck from the ice bucket. She was glad they settled on a local wine. "We'll need to be careful or we'll be on a second bottle before the food arrives," Katherine said, topping up both their glasses. "Oh look at the tattoos on them, now that's too much." Katherine's eyes followed a young couple pushing a buggy. Both the man's arms and one leg were covered in a mass of ink. The woman had a large Celtic design on her back and shoulders.

"It used to be people got tattoos to stand out, now I think they get them to fit in," Corinne said.

"I have to say I prefer my art on my walls."

"Myself and Terry got tattoos."

"Really?" Katherine was surprised at Corinne's admission.

"A moment of madness. It was when he was sick. We were passing this tattoo parlour in New York, spur of the moment thing."

"What did you get?"

"A small butterfly, in a place that's not visible." Corinne winked; a fond memory brought a smile to her face.

Warm bread rolls arrived.

"I'm getting hungry now," Corinne said, picking at the end of one of the rolls. "I try not to eat too much bread. I bake my own when I can."

"It's getting popular again, isn't it, people going back to basics, making their own bread, baking. My mother and aunt were great bakers, every Saturday afternoon that was the routine."

"When my son was young I used to love making his birthday cake, nothing fancy a basic sponge, maybe chocolate, I'd cover it with cream and hundreds and thousands or thousands and millions as he called them. Now you see all these cartoon cakes or cakes based on computer games, and the colouring in them."

"Don't talk to me about kids' parties. A family in our cul de sac not only had the bouncy castle, they hired a mobile zoo. I thought I was hallucinating watching a llama and a goat being led up their drive."

"No."

"And I remember the mother saying to me that she was so stressed about the whole thing, she didn't know what to put in the kids' goody bags."

"What's that teaching youngsters? It's that adage of people spending money they don't have, to buy things they don't need, to impress people they don't like."

"I'm sure myself and Vincent have been guilty of that too. We over extended ourselves. We just never thought the boom times would end."

"A friend of mine was absolutely in bits a few weeks ago, she rang me after she discovered her husband hadn't paid any income tax for the last four years, hadn't declared a penny. They ran their own business; he looked after the finances or said he did; now she thinks they might lose the house."

"Oh God love her."

"And her husband is a decent man, but you know men, they don't like to show vulnerability or that they are not in control. I'm sure it's the same with Vincent, he'd hate to let you down."

Katherine didn't say anything. Her eyes looked down at the table and she began fingering the bread roll.

"Did I say something I shouldn't have?"

"We're not in a great place. I think he might be having an affair." Katherine's tongue had been loosened by the second glass of wine.

"Oh I'm sorry to hear that Katherine."

Katherine contemplated what she would share with Corinne, but in the end she felt Corinne was a kind-hearted woman, a clear thinker and she felt comfortable in her company. Katherine took a deep breath and told Corinne about how she found Nicola in her kitchen when she came home from the hospital and how she was convinced that Vincent took off his wedding ring at different times and how he lied when he said he was at home when they spoke on the phone.

Corinne listened attentively, nodding and empathising as Katherine placed the evidence of Vincent's infidelity on the table. When Katherine concluded her case, Corinne sat back, her eyes drifting up to the baskets of ferns above them. Katherine anxiously awaited Corinne's response, when it came it wasn't what she expected.

"Do you love him?" Corinne leant forward.

Katherine didn't know how to respond.

"Right now, if I'm honest Corinne, I don't know. I'm too hurt and unsure to know what I'm feeling."

"But you did love him."

"Of course, I've known him thirty odd years, we have two children, we had, I mean we have, a very good life."

"What was he like when you first met him?" Another question Katherine didn't expect. The quizzical look on her face prompted Corinne to add, "I just want to give you another perspective."

"Full of energy and ideas; he was big into his music and politics. It sounds so old-fashioned now, but he was my first serious boyfriend."

"In challenging times we tend to forget the better ones. Inside Vincent there's still that young man with his dreams of music or politics who fell in love with you. Now we don't know whether he's cheating or not, but if you're not happy Katherine in your marriage, Vincent cannot be happy either. Now it's not my place to judge anyone, I don't know the man and we're only getting to know each other, but when I hear of marriage difficulties or challenges of any kind, I always find it useful to remember that inside all of us, Vincent included, is a little child, innocent and maybe hurt who is looking for love and safety and validation. And whatever we do or don't do, at some level, we are making the best choices available to us. We all do what we have to do to be seen."

The thought of seeing Vincent like a little boy stirred a forgotten emotion in Katherine. She could see the picture of him in the old album sitting on his grandmother's knee dressed for his first day at school. She certainly didn't feel sorry for Vincent, but she did miss the good times. A familiar sadness resurfaced when she thought of the college girl, not long in Dublin, meeting Vincent for the first time in that nightclub all those years ago.

"It's so easy when we're hurt to lash out and make judgments, and that's probably only human nature, but I find judgement, jumping to conclusions just prevents us from thinking clearly. When we judge someone whether it's that large man in the swimming trunks or those kids with the tattoos or Vincent, or even ourselves, opinion hardens inside us, we've labelled the other person; we've made them a one dimensional caricature, just like the ones that man is drawing over there. And of course when we judge and label someone all we do then is seek evidence to support our judgement. Think of it this way, if you weren't suspicious of Vincent, you may have thought nothing of it when you rang back and he didn't answer. Maybe he stepped out into the garden or was even in the bathroom when you called, who knows."

"I hear what you are saying, but what am I supposed to do."

"There's no easy answer to that one, but here's what I do when I'm unsure of anything. I ask myself three questions. First, what does your head tell you to do?"

Katherine thought for a moment.

"Have a conversation with him, bring everything out into the open, one way or the other, the finances, if he is cheating, the lot."

"Okay, and what does your heart tell you?"

"My heart?"

"Yes the wisdom in your heart."

"I don't know."

"Try this, put your hand on your heart and close your eyes for a second and take a few nice deep breaths."

Katherine glanced around her. A group of local men had just sat at the table across from them and were shaking hands with the waiters. A few tables down, the big bald man and the young woman were engrossed in their own conversation. Somewhat self-consciously Katherine did as Corinne suggested.

"So what does your heart tell you?" Corinne asked again.

Katherine was silent allowing her breath to slow. "To figure out what it is I want?"

"Okay, anything else?"

Katherine kept her eyes closed. She could feel her shoulders relax.

"To be really honest with myself and Vincent." Somehow

Katherine felt these words were coming from a different place inside her, a wiser place.

"Great, anything else?"

"To be honest with you as well Corinne, there's one bit I didn't tell you."

Katherine opened her eyes and took another gulp of wine. She told Corinne about meeting Mark at the book club, about getting back in the car with him and how in her head she was the one who may not have physically cheated, but who had betrayed her marriage in every other way.

"Good old guilt."

"Now you're going to think I've brought all this on myself. That I'm judging Vincent by my own standards."

"Hardly, what was I just saying about judgement. I believe that we are always doing our best. Vincent is doing his best. You're doing your best all the time; you've been doing your best every day Katherine."

"Oh I don't know about that."

"Sure you are, now your best today may not be the same as your best tomorrow, but you are doing your best. You were doing your best when you tried to speak with Vincent and he stormed upstairs. You've made the best decisions you could. You were even doing your best when you got into the car with what's his name, Mark. Now that doesn't mean with hindsight there were other choices, maybe better choices you could have made, but you were always doing your best. When we remember that, I think it helps to lessen the guilt, because feeling guilty doesn't achieve much."

"I suppose not."

"Guilt just alerts us to the fact that we've been unfair to someone, or we've acted against our values or betrayed our true authentic self."

"It just eats away, doesn't it?"

"We can beat ourselves up with guilt. Believe me I've learnt this lesson, I felt guilty that Terry was sick and not me, but all I was doing was punishing myself, locking myself in a cycle of despair and judgement that robbed me of clarity about what I wanted. You know Katherine we are only human, we're not perfect, we're never going to be perfect, there is no such thing as being sorted. We are going to make mistakes, we are going to stray off course, we are going to cock things up, but it's what we do afterwards that counts. Sometimes all we can do is forgive ourselves for not being perfect and do our best not to make the same mistake again."

"Imelda got me to do a self forgiveness exercise; I listed in my journal everything I needed to forgive myself for."

"Great idea, was it useful?"

"It was hard, but I did feel better afterwards."

"And remember Katherine, there's no final destination, well apart from the obvious one. All this stuff is just life."

Two waiters approached their table. The first, the more junior of the two, laid out plates and cleared some space. The second waiter then placed a steaming skillet of paella between them.

Katherine inhaled the enticing aroma. Five or six whole prawns were spaced around the dish and several large mussels were half submerged in the golden rice.

"Now this looks as if it has been worth waiting for," Corinne said waving the steam towards her face. "You serve yourself first."

Katherine picked up a large prawn that had been cooked whole. Two heaped spoonfuls of rice and seafood joined the prawn on her plate. After a generous squeeze of lemon from one of the many wedges in the skillet she was ready for her first forkful. The warm honey-like saffron scented rice, enlivened by the zing of lemon, danced on her tongue. The rice was smooth and sticky and the pieces of seafood succulent and juicy. After the salads and grains at The Retreat every taste bud in her mouth screamed 'thank you'.

"So you said there were three questions?" Katherine said halfway through her second helping.

"Oh yes, the first one is what does your head tell you, that's using the logical mind, then the heart question and the last one is the gut question – what does your gut tell you?"

"Right now it's saying this is delicious, but in relation to Vincent, what's my feeling?" Katherine chewed. "My gut is saying listen to me, pay attention to my instincts."

"That's always useful. I know the biggest regrets in my life have been when I didn't listen to my gut instinct. Terry had been complaining of stomach pains on and off for a few weeks and you know what men are like for going to doctors, but this nagging voice kept telling me to make an appointment for him. Of course I could have done it sooner. I beat myself up over that one for a long time."

"You know Corinne, maybe I'm just having my midlife crisis. Ten years too late mind you."

"I don't think crisis is the right word, maybe awakening is a better description."

"I'll take that," Katherine said, breaking off a prawn tail and sucking out the tender flesh.

"It's a reassessment of what's important to you and what you want for act two of your life. When we face tragedy or challenges, marriage breakdowns, deaths, a loss of a job, even a birthday ending with a zero, I always think it's a time to reconnect with what's really important to us. When Terry died I decided that right, this is not what I planned, I felt like I was starting from scratch, but it was an opportunity to live the life I wanted to live, not the life I thought I was going to live or was supposed to live. I counted my blessings, put one foot in front of the other and began to inhabit fully the new life I was building for myself. Maybe everything you're dealing with right now Katherine is your wake up call, your opportunity to let go once and for all who you think you should be and simply be yourself."

"It's not easy though Corinne."

"We just need a little bit of faith, faith in ourselves, faith in God and faith that everything will work out for the best."

"And courage."

"That too. Not being afraid of being afraid."

Katherine wanted to savour the paella so she rested her cutlery at the side of her plate.

"I remember Terry used to say to me, just be yourself girl. You know, when I was anxious about work or something, being yourself takes the pressure off and of course being loved for who you are, not who you pretend to be, is the essence of great relationships."

"Well that's brings us full circle back to Vincent."

"How's that."

"For a long time I've felt lost. It's hard to explain. I just don't feel like the real me, the real Katherine. I'm a wife, a mother, a sister, a friend, but it's like there's something missing."

"Now here's the question, where are you most yourself?"

"How do you mean?"

"When did you last feel like the real you? Just think, gut response."

"This morning when I was painting."

"There you go and when else?"

"When do I feel most myself?"

"Yes, most alive?"

"Getting stuck into a good conversation like this one, or when cooking, particularly trying out a new recipe."

"And what do painting and cooking have in common for you?"

"Well I just love them."

"We should always do the things that make us feel good. Just think of the joy you get from cooking and I'm really looking forward to Wednesday night by the way."

"I hope I haven't bitten off more than I can chew, literally."

"Just think of the pleasure you will be creating for others and the enjoyment you'll get from it. Have you ever thought about running your own restaurant?"

"I like going to them but running one, I could never."

"Why not?"

"Money for one thing."

"Oh forget money for a minute. You know I can see you in a lovely bistro type restaurant, good quality home style cooking, earthy, you know what I mean, and the walls covered with your own art."

Katherine laughed. "That's a nice dream alright." She emptied the remainder of the wine into her own glass as Corinne's was still full.

"A toast Katherine." Corinne raised her glass. "To being ourselves and not being afraid to dream."

"You know I have to laugh Corinne, you have me running my own restaurant and art gallery whilst I'm just trying to keep it together. After I put the phone down to Vincent yesterday I had a bit of a meltdown. Imelda was a real comfort though. People speak about breakthroughs, all I've had is a breakdown."

"Or a breakout?"

"It's like having lunch with my own guru Corinne, you should charge for your wisdom," Katherine said, smiling. "This lunch is going to be on me."

"We'll see about that. But listen Katherine we all have our challenges, I've had mine. Sometimes a bit of a breakdown is needed so we can begin again, a bit like how forest fires clear the earth for new growth. All we can really hope is to get through the tough times and come out the far side a little wiser and if I'm able to share some of the life lessons I've picked up, well and good."

"Well as my friend Rhona would say there's a lovely energy

around you, a real gentleness and you're a great listener."

"Thank you." Corinne placed her fork on the plate and put her hand on her heart in gratitude. "That means a lot to me. You know speaking about reassessing priorities and shaping our lives, one of my dreams is to have my own retreat something like Neide's but by the sea."

"You were saying that this morning. You've got the wisdom, a great personality and you've all those years in the hotel business, you could do it with your eyes shut." Katherine raised her glass.

"Cheers. You know I've a vision of the room where I'd deliver my workshops, probably so impractical, but it would be a big round room overlooking the sea."

"Somewhere hot?"

"Not necessarily, just by the sea."

"Well I think you should seriously consider it, you'd be a natural and I'd be your first guest."

"Did you ever see Steve Jobs' famous commencement address on YouTube, you know the founder of Apple?" Katherine shook her head. "You'll find it easily on the web. He gave a talk to graduates at a university, Stanford I think it was, a few years back. He spoke about joining the dots backwards and by dots he meant the clues as to what it is you are meant to be doing."

"What do you mean?"

"Well take me, what I loved most about working at the reception desk in the hotel was meeting people and helping them out. And I'd get such high praise from my manager, he'd say I had such great customer service skills but all I was doing was being myself. All my life, looking back I've been helping people, sharing my experiences, coaching, call it what you will."

"I helped my friend Mags set up her coffee shop."

"There you go, that's a dot."

"And I did art in college and a few evening classes a good few years ago."

"More dots."

"But sure that's just what I enjoy doing."

"Yes and maybe if you did more of it, designed a way to bring that front and centre in your life, you'd be beginning to find what you feel is missing. We find our true selves by doing what we love."

Katherine stretched her shoulders. She felt relaxed, but something inside her was unsettled. Somehow she knew that this conversation with Corinne was significant, that Corinne's words were going to be part of her forever.

***

The restaurant was the ideal spot for people watching. A never ending parade of people wandered by, either returning from a day's sunbathing or having a leisurely stroll before deciding where to eat. It was Katherine's favourite time of the day and she savoured the sensuous warmth of the evening sun.

"Fancy some dessert," Katherine suggested.

"I usually don't but a little sweetness might be nice. You know what I often do at home; if I'm heading out, I'll have a small bar of chocolate in my bag. You know the way after a meal when you fancy something sweet, well I'll just take a square of chocolate discreetly from my bag and my sweet tooth is satisfied."

"Now that's a handy tip. But as we don't have a piece of chocolate, fancy sharing a scoop or two of ice cream."

"Why not." Corinne excused herself to visit the bathroom.

Alone at the table Katherine looked around. The restaurant was filling up. The group of Spanish men dressed in shirts and ties were munching and gesticulating their way through a fish platter. It was a sight you'd never see back home. An old man sat at a table on the prom and looked out to sea, his dog at his feet. A regular she suspected. A waiter deposited a glass of what looked like sherry in front of him. A tall blonde woman had joined the big bald man and his ingénue but they were now leaving, or at least the two women were. Katherine watched him kiss both women on the lips and give them big hugs. He spoke English but with an accent. From the corner of her eye she watched him empty the bottle of red wine into his glass and order another one.

The sun was sinking behind the buildings. It wouldn't be too long before the lamps along the prom would announce nightfall. Katherine chuckled to herself. Imagine running my own restaurant, with my own art on the walls. She shook her head.

"Vanilla, chocolate and strawberry are the ice creams I think Corinne."

"Devine, thank you." Corinne resumed her seat and leant in conspiratorially. "That's Bruno Reye."

"Who?"

"The writer who'll be at The Retreat, the one I met in Greece."

"No way." Katherine looked over Corinne's shoulder at the big bald man now alone at his table. "He's looking at us. I think he's coming over."

CHAPTER 10

The sense of well-being that had settled on Katherine in the restaurant diminished with every step Bruno Reye took towards their table. She had been aware of him, not knowing who he was since he came into the restaurant with his arm around the woman who looked at least thirty years his junior. Even if he had dined alone, his loudly patterned shirt and gesticulating arms, not to mention the sheer size of him, would have made him difficult to ignore.

"Hello there." Bruno's voice reached them before he did.

"Bruno," Corinne said, twisting around in her chair.

"Ah so it is you, I thought I recognised a familiar face. Now the name will come to me. Was it Skyros or Italy?" He swallowed Corinne's hand in his and pulled out the chair beside her, his wine glass planted like a flag on the table.

"Skyros."

"I knew it."

"And it's Corinne."

"Of course, I knew that." Bruno kissed the back of Corinne's hand. In a bygone era it would have been a gallant gesture, but today Katherine felt it was just a sign that he had drunk too much.

"And this is my friend Katherine."

"Hello," Katherine said, extending her hand. When he released it, she had to massage her knuckles under the table.

"You're doing your creative writing workshop at The Bliss Retreat this week I see," Corinne said.

"Well you know what they say, those who can't teach and all that. You're there this week are you? Enjoying it?"

"So far," Katherine said. "We're playing hooky this afternoon though."

"Good for you. You don't want to overdose on that touchy feely stuff," Bruno said, his laugh revealing nearly every tooth in his head. Katherine could see he had at least two missing.

Entirely bald, well over six foot and barrel-chested, Bruno Reye reminded Katherine of a carnival strong man. The hair that once covered his head had migrated south. The wine glass looked almost dainty in his hand. He pushed his chair back so he could cross his trunk-like legs, a hairy arm resting on the back of Corinne's chair.

"Will your workshop be similar to the one on Skyros Bruno?" Corinne asked.

"Oh I'm sure a few new ideas will pop into my head. You know me I make it up as I go along."

Katherine wasn't sure if he was joking. She thought she could hear a slight American twang in his accent.

"Oh I remember now." Bruno sat forward. "You wrote a great poem in my workshop, something about loneliness, wasn't it?" Bruno said prodding Corinne's shoulder.

"You've a good memory."

"Well that stood out, believe me."

"And she wrote a lovely piece on wisdom today," Katherine added.

"I don't doubt it. You're a poet and you don't know it Corinne," Bruno said laughing at his own little rhyme.

"Oh I wouldn't say that," Corinne said her eyes dropping to the table.

"And you've written a few books Bruno. I was on your website," Katherine said.

"Eight and counting."

"I didn't know it was as many as that," Corinne said.

"Well only three have been published and two of those I published myself."

"Well that's the way the industry is going, isn't it?" Corinne said.

"That's what us self-published authors say anyway." Bruno emptied his wine glass.

A waiter brought the ice cream and coffee Katherine had ordered.

"Another spoon?" the waiter asked.

"I'm happy with my wine," Bruno said. "You don't mind me crashing in on you; I'm waiting for someone they should be along any minute."

"Not at all," Corinne said.

Bruno retrieved the wine from his table and refilled his glass.

Katherine took her first spoonful of vanilla ice cream and followed it with a sip of coffee. She loved the combination of hot and cold. Thankfully she never suffered from sensitive teeth.

"I read your book *Souled* Bruno, I got a copy from you in Greece. I loved the inscription you wrote – 'be your own inspiration.'"

"One of my better ones. Make sure you keep it; it might be worth something some day when I'm a famous author. I've brought a suitcase full with me and I'm hoping to shift them at The Retreat, though even then I'll probably only cover the cost of the damn excess baggage I had to pay."

"Is that an American accent I hear?" Katherine asked.

"New York born ma'am," Bruno said emphasising it. "But I haven't lived there since I joined the navy at seventeen."

"Bruno has travelled the world," Corinne said.

"A gypsy, that's me. I even lived in Ireland once upon a time." Katherine didn't think she had a strong Irish accent and was surprised Bruno picked up on it. "Spent eighteen months in Galway, but that must be twenty years ago now."

"Galway and Connemara are lovely," Katherine said.

"Always meant to go back."

"As a writer you can work from pretty much anywhere I suppose?" Katherine said.

"Oh, it's not as simple as that," Bruno said, spluttering his wine. "Now let's see, I've been a sailor, a builder, a carpenter, a waiter, a DJ, a property developer, a pool cleaner, a guide, what else, a librarian, a barman, a teacher of sorts. They've all been my trades but writing is my passion."

"A lovely way to put it," Corinne said.

"Writing doesn't pay the rent though, well not my rent, not yet anyway."

"That's true for so many creative professions," Corinne said.

"At least I've reached the point where it doesn't matter what other people think of my work. I do what I do for the pleasure of it. Well most of the time that's true. Sometimes writing makes me pull my hair out. That's what happened," Bruno said, slapping his head. "But if I wasn't writing, for me, I wouldn't be living, and if other people like my work great, if not, fuck them. Pardon my language."

Katherine's spoon had reached the bottom of the glass. Swirls of vanilla mixed with the remnants of the chocolate ice cream forming a pool of pure liquid heaven. Thankfully Corinne had indicated that Katherine could finish it.

The giant catamaran to Fuerteventura sounded its horn and sped out of the harbour as if it was a car pulling away from traffic lights. Across the straits another ferry was making its way towards them. Couples browsed the menu perched on one of the frontline tables where a young waiter tried to entice them inside.

Katherine was going to ask Bruno about his books, but she held back not wanting to admit she hadn't read any of them. She would ask Corinne what *Souled* was about later.

"Are you staying here in Playa Blanca?" Corinne asked.

"Yes, Lisa has a place here, so I'm staying with her and of course it's great to spend time with Zoe as well."

"Zoe?" Corinne asked.

"My daughter."

"Was that the young woman who was with you?" Katherine asked.

"That's my Zoe," Bruno said, his eyes bright with parental pride. "Ah here he is now?" Bruno stood up, almost knocking the table over. "Of course you know him; he's at The Bliss Retreat this week too. Ran." Bruno shouted down the restaurant.

Katherine's pulse quickened.

***

Katherine turned around to see the man who had run the creativity workshop that morning stride into the restaurant. Ran Kaplan looked even more handsome. The ethnic looking shirt had been replaced with a plain white one. Instead of jeans he wore grey linen trousers. His hair was slicked back. It was like he'd been on a TV makeover programme.

"Well, fancy seeing you two here. Bruno you're a fast mover," Ran said shaking Bruno's hand. Katherine figured Ran was searching his memory banks for their names.

"Sit down man, want a drink?" Bruno asked.

"A water would be good, I've the car."

Just when Katherine had thought her relaxing meal and chat with Corinne had been hijacked, she was thrilled that the day was taking another unforeseen twist. She found herself sitting more upright as she gestured for Ran to take the vacant seat beside her.

"Now this guy hasn't been bothering you, has he?" Ran said.

The two women shook their heads and laughed politely. Katherine could smell Ran's aftershave, the same spicy, citrusy scent she admired that morning. She inhaled deeply.

"You're all dressed up; you said this event was casual," Bruno said.

143

"There's casual and there's casual Bruno."

"Going somewhere nice?" Corinne asked.

"A new exhibition at the César Manrique Foundation."

"Oh I've heard of him," Katherine said. "Wasn't his house made out of lava?"

"That's where it's on," Ran said.

"And mister modesty here is one of the exhibitors," Bruno said.

"Really?" Katherine said, her opinion of Ran rising another notch.

"Just one piece and I'm only one of twelve artists. Not quite a retrospective yet."

"To the artist." Bruno raised his glass and everyone reached for theirs. Katherine found it curious that she was a little embarrassed when Ran made eye contact.

"You know you should come with us, we'll all easily fit into my car," Ran said.

"We haven't been invited," Katherine replied.

"I'm inviting you, there has to be some perks when you have a painting on show."

"Oh I don't know, I'm not really dressed for a swish reception," Katherine said, straightening her sunflower patterned dress that she'd been wearing all day.

"You look great. Besides with Bruno wearing that shirt everyone will be blinded," Ran said.

"It's my holiday shirt," Bruno replied, throwing his hands in the air.

Katherine took her final sip of coffee.

"Seriously Katherine, Corinne, you'd be more than welcome. It's only about half an hour away," Ran said. He has the brownest eyes, Katherine thought.

Katherine looked at Corinne who shrugged her shoulders. It wasn't the evening Katherine had planned, but then it wasn't a holiday she had planned either.

144

"Go on say yes, brighten up our evening," Bruno said. "If you don't people will think we're gay."

"Not in that shirt," Katherine said, continuing the joke Ran had started.

"Oooh." Bruno laughed. "Go on, haven't they taught you anything at The Retreat yet? Life opens up to you when you say yes."

"That's true," Corinne said. "Say yes more than you say no and life will say yes to you, isn't that the saying."

"Exactly," Bruno added.

"Well I suppose that decides it then," Katherine said. "It's a yes from me."

"Count me in too," Corinne said, winking at Katherine.

***

To Katherine's delight, Ran's car was a convertible. The two women slid onto the back seat. Bruno would never have fitted.

"I wish I was wearing something smarter Corinne. You look so elegant, you always do," Katherine said, kicking herself because back at The Retreat, a black shift dress lay in her suitcase for just such an eventuality.

"You look fine."

"Thank God I didn't throw on a top and shorts this morning."

"All set ladies?" Ran said, starting the engine.

Katherine sat back. She couldn't remember being in a convertible before and certainly not the back seat of one. She took the sunglasses from her head. She was going to arrive with windswept hair.

"What would Vincent think if he could see me now?" Katherine said to Corinne.

"Well he can't."

"This is fun, isn't it?" Katherine said, though she couldn't help thinking how would she explain being in a convertible with two men she hardly knew.

"We're saying yes," Corinne said, the wind trying to remove the scarf from her neck.

"Going with the flow." Katherine laughed. "I haven't been this spontaneous since I was a teenager. It's like a double date," she whispered to Corinne, squeezing her arm.

***

The low sun illuminated the volcanic peaks as they drove inland. The mountains glowed various shades of orange, pink and red. A scattering of amber-tinged clouds were set off by the darkening sky. Corinne asked the men in the front how long they had known each other and Ran recounted the story of how they had met on a kibbutz in Israel. Katherine was silently delighted when Ran praised her painting from that morning's class, which he made her promise to finish.

"Have you been to César Manrique's house before?" Ran asked, directing his question to the back of the car.

"No." Both women answered in unison.

"It's quite something. I was there yesterday when everything was being set up. It has a really cool vibe, built in the sixties I believe."

The sun had set by the time they reached the car park of the César Manrique Foundation. The house was now a stop on the tourist trail, an excursion for some of the more culturally curious visitors to the island. Tonight it was host to the artistic and social elite of Lanzarote. '*Twelve artists, Twelve countries*', was the title of the exhibition as advertised on the poster by the entrance.

"That's quite a sculpture," Katherine said looking up at the large iron structure that dominated the car park.

"One of Manrique's wind toys," Ran said helping Katherine from the car. "There's plenty more inside."

"Well there's no shortage of wind on this island," Katherine said.

They passed through an open barrier. No one seemed to be monitoring who was coming in. She felt Corinne and Ran blended in well with the other stylishly dressed guests as the four of them followed the path up to the main house. She felt herself and Bruno could pass for aged presenters on a children's TV programme.

Katherine couldn't compare César Manrique's house with any other building she'd ever been in. At any moment she expected a James Bond villain to be lurking in an alcove stroking a cat. The space was deceptive. She felt it wasn't a building that took itself seriously either. They walked through a small courtyard where the top of a tree poked out of a hole in the ground. Peeking in, Katherine could see people gathered in a cave-like room. To the left, music and voices floated up from a massive hole in the ground.

They walked into a traditional rectangular building that was the main exhibition space. It was heaving with people and it was a challenge to see the art on the walls. Even the waiters armed with drinks and canapés struggled to navigate the noisy crowd.

Katherine was drawn to the floor to ceiling windows. The floodlit lava field extended into dark nothingness. It really was an alien landscape. Looking down she had a perfect view of an enchanting turquoise pool fed by floodlit waterfalls. The area around the pool was all white. Trees and orange flowers filled the nooks and ledges. Invisible from the outside and framed by the black basalt rock it was a sunken oasis. Katherine felt she was looking into a lost magical world.

***

When Katherine looked up Ran was being dragged away by a woman who had obviously been searching for him.

"Let me get us some drinks," Bruno said, having to shout above the din.

It wasn't like any exhibition Katherine had attended before. Dance music was playing outside. She followed Corinne to the door at the far end of the room, passing a disturbing painting of a severed head. She hoped it wasn't Ran's.

"It's too warm for me in there," Corinne said when they stepped outside.

"There you are." Bruno handed them glasses of cava. "Now I'm going to improve my mind and ponder some art, coming with me?"

"We might just catch our breath and go in when things calm down a little," Corinne said.

"Don't do anything I wouldn't do," Bruno said, walking backwards into a very chic looking woman who looked more offended by his shirt than by the fact he nearly spilt her drink.

Katherine and Corinne surveyed the crowd from their vantage point at the top of the steps that were carved from the rock. The source of the music, a DJ, was set up beside the swimming pool. A band, all dressed in black suits and ties were unpacking instruments on a small stage beside a dance floor. Leaning forward Katherine could see several cave-like rooms fashioned from giant bubbles in the frozen lava flow.

In the car Ran had said that Lanzarote had experienced the world's longest volcanic eruption. For six years, starting in 1730 volcanoes spewed lava over a quarter of the island. Katherine tried to imagine the hellish scene. It was a testament to the vision of César Manrique that such a wondrous space could be created in the most desolate of landscapes.

"Now I want your honest opinion?" Ran said, tapping Katherine on the shoulder. "Come on. Corinne?"

"You two go ahead, I'm happy here for the moment,"

Corinne said, finding a spot on the edge of a flower bed hewn from a crevice in the rock.

Ran took Katherine's elbow and steered her through the packed gallery. She was excited that the artist himself was going to show her his work. She decided that whatever the painting was like she was going to praise it. Moving through the room, she couldn't help notice how Ran attracted attention. Did they know he was one of the artists or was it the way his white shirt fitted him, Katherine couldn't be sure.

"Well?" Ran said, leaning against the wall fully focused on Katherine's face.

Katherine's eyes darted between the four paintings, mounted squarely, two on two. She could make out what looked like parts of animals. She had to step forward to be sure. The plaque on the right informed her the piece was titled '*Hungry?*'

Ran continued to look at her, hand on chin. The smile on his face suggested seeing someone connect with his art was one of his true pleasures.

"I'm not sure what I'm looking at?" Katherine said, wishing she had a better understanding of modern art.

"Take all four in at the same time," Ran said, now looking between Katherine and his paintings. "Let your eye fill in the gaps."

"Oh I get it; they're different parts of a cow. There's the neck, is that the back?"

"I'll call them fillet, sirloin, brisket and rib."

"Oh." Katherine's instinct was to pull her hand to her mouth.

"Well that's a reaction," Ran said, rolling up his sleeves, a cartoon-like grin on his face.

"Sorry, but I get it now. You've painted the body parts those cuts come from. "Ah, '*Hungry?*' I get it. It's enough to turn me vegetarian, well almost."

"I tried to paint what remains after those parts are removed, hence the gaps." Ran laughed shaking his head.

"Sorry if that wasn't the right reaction."

"At least it was a reaction. The worst thing you could have said was it was nice or interesting."

"Thought-provoking, how's that?" Katherine said.

"I'll take that."

Four Spanish women, all in killer heels and all talking at once, edged in front of Ran's work.

"Look at Bruno, life and soul of the party as usual." Ran nodded towards Bruno who was impossible to camouflage.

"He must know loads of people?"

"Don't be fooled. He'll have just walked up to them and started chatting."

"Really?"

"Let me tell you what Bruno is like. A few years back we were waiting to board a flight that was delayed. Well next minute Bruno starts to sing, 'Always Look on the Bright Side of Life' you know the song, right there at the departure gate."

"Was he drunk?"

"Totally sober. He only knew the chorus and he's not a great singer believe me, but within a few minutes he had people laughing and chatting."

"I'd be cringing."

"Well there was some of that too, but you never know with Bruno. I've never met someone who takes themselves so lightly. He literally doesn't give a shit."

"Well maybe that's not a bad quality," Katherine said, looking at the bald man in the far corner. "And he's staying with his ex-wife, is it and his daughter? I wasn't sure back at the restaurant," Katherine said, moving towards the staircase.

"Yes, Lisa and Zoe. Nothing is ever conventional with Bruno."

Katherine was curious about Ran's marital status, but she didn't want to ask. She was well aware of the absence of a wedding band.

A booming laugh launched over the room. It wasn't just Katherine who turned to see a red-faced Bruno doubling over with laughter. Part of her admired, even envied his carefree attitude, but another part of her found the big man with the big personality just a little bit scary.

"Now I don't want to leave Corinne alone," Katherine said, fanning herself with a brochure she picked up on the way out.

"I'll hover here for a while; you never know I might manage to sell it," Ran said, brushing her arm.

Of course it was probably all in her mind and wishful thinking on her part, but Katherine allowed herself to indulge in the idea that Ran like her.

***

Corinne wasn't at the spot where Katherine had left her. She spied her on the lower level. Skirting the jewel-like pool Katherine couldn't resist bending to touch the water. She thought it might have been warmer. Corinne had found a seating area at the back of one of the volcanic chambers that housed the bar. A Santa's grotto for adults, Katherine thought.

Katherine drank the last of her cava which was now too warm to be refreshing. Glamorous women in gold jewellery and red-soled shoes weaved through the crowd. Katherine was happy to observe the scene from the back of the grotto.

"So what was Ran's painting like?" Corinne asked.

"I won't give anything away; you'll have to see for yourself. It's well..." Katherine was going to say interesting, but stopped herself.

"I'll wander up in a bit. Where did Bruno get to?"

"Oh he's in the gallery, life and soul of the place, or a heart attack waiting to happen."

"There's Ran now." Corinne nodded at the man descending the steps beyond the pool.

"I don't mind saying Corinne, if I was ten years younger and single – and that aftershave. No harm in window shopping is there?" Katherine laughed.

Katherine watched Ran hover by the edge of the pool. Was he looking for her? Hands wedged deep into the pockets of his trousers he looked effortlessly cool and relaxed. Two women approached him, glasses and mobile phones in their hands. They took turns posing with him. As one of the exhibiting artists he had the added allure of a hint of celebrity.

Suddenly Katherine felt like an impostor. She was far from being a hip young thing and felt dowdy in her summer dress and flat shoes.

"You know I might get a taxi back to The Retreat Corinne, we must be as close to Teguise here as Playa Blanca."

"I thought you were going to stay with me? And didn't Ran say he was going to drop us back?"

"I'm just a little tired."

"I'll get us some water," Corinne said.

Ran remained chatting to the two women who shifted from foot to foot, playing with their hair and hanging on his every word.

"That band is supposed to be good. I overheard someone say the singer is like a Latin Michael Bublé," Corinne said, placing two still waters in front of them. Five men of varying ages in matching black jackets were testing microphones.

"Sounds promising." Katherine tried to remain upbeat; she didn't want to put a damper on Corinne's evening.

Katherine wondered what Vincent was doing right now.

"I don't know what they're saying, but we can guess," Corinne said, nodding at a couple by the pool in the midst of a row. Hands gesticulated, voices were raised.

"She looks like she might throttle him. He could end up in the water."

"The Latin temperament."

"Comforting to know it's not just me and Vincent who have our problems."

"At least you're working on it. I feel sorry for those who go from one relationship to the next repeating the same mistakes over and over."

"Look, he's trying to make up to her." The black-haired woman was obviously not immune to her man's overtures. She brushed off his first touch, but the second time he reached for her, her shoulders relaxed. Corinne nudged Katherine when the man planted a kiss on the woman's cheek. Katherine wondered whether it was always the woman's role to forgive.

"Something else I've learnt in recent years Katherine, when we feel hurt, frustrated, angry, whatever, it usually means that life, that the situation we find ourselves in, doesn't match our expectations of how we wanted it to be. But of course we don't really have a say in the matter. Take me and Terry, that certainly didn't turn out as we had planned. Call me naive but I also believe that love always wants to manifest in our lives, but it often happens in ways we don't expect. Whatever happens when you go home always remember Katherine you have the second part of your life to live and you have all the wisdom from the first part to draw upon."

"That's a nice way of putting it."

"Girl you have an entire future to create. It might be different from what you thought it would be, but look at the life experience you have, the sense of possibility. You're a healthy, educated, talented woman of means. Do you know that the vast majority of the people on this planet would love your problems? Your life is already beyond the wildest dreams of millions of people."

"You're right."

"How many millions of people would love to be sitting here with a glass of clean water in their hands, not to mention listening to music on a sultry evening, in a beautiful setting, with some handsome men to distract us and the possibility of having a good boogie?"

"Well when you put it that way."

"Cheers." Corinne clinked Katherine's glass.

***

From their sofa at the back of the grotto Katherine could see the band and the dance floor as well as the main staircase to the upper level. At one point Ran caught Katherine's eye and waved. She was embarrassed that he had caught her looking at him.

The band started playing an easy instrumental. A few women poised by the edge of the dance floor started to sway with the rhythm. It would take a few more drinks and a livelier beat before the urge to move to music would take hold.

Katherine made the decision to make the most of the night. Corinne as ever spoke real sense and Katherine was pleased to have someone beside her who said things she really needed to hear.

"Another water Corinne, or fancy something stronger?" Katherine asked.

"Water's good."

Katherine took another glass of white wine from the bar for herself.

'The Girl from Ipanema' was the band's first number. The lead singer was a man in his thirties with slicked-back hair, a narrow moustache and a real crooner's voice. Katherine stood by the bar to get a better view.

The young guitar player caught Katherine's attention. No more than twenty and with a mop of dark hair, he had obviously inherited his ill-fitting suit. He looked nervous. He started a guitar solo. Katherine was captivated. The musician cradled the guitar in his arms like a beloved child. He soon lost his nervousness to the music. Carried on the warm breeze, the lilting rhythm drifted out over the barren landscape.

A steady flow of people made their way from the gallery to the pool area filling the seating in the pod-like rooms. Katherine noticed that the room beside them was the one with the tree and the hole in the roof. She admired the creativity of the man who created the space and the works of art that filled what in itself was a magnificent work of art.

Katherine's reverie was broken by Bruno bouncing down the stairs like a bomb about to detonate. She retreated to her seat and the security of Corinne's company. As he passed it, Bruno mimed diving into the pool.

"Another text from my granddaughter, asking if I'd phoned that model agency guy yet," Corinne said as Katherine sat down.

"You're going to have to phone him tomorrow. That reminds me my sister left me a message, I meant to ring her."

Katherine glanced at her own phone. She'd no missed calls or texts.

"There you are, well who's first on my dance card?" Bruno said hand outstretched.

"Oh we're fine right here Bruno," Corinne said.

"Nonsense, this sort of music is made for dancing." A trumpet solo heralded the liveliest number yet. Bruno began to shuffle on the spot.

Over his shoulder Katherine could see the dance floor was beginning to fill. Between the groups of women a very elegant older couple, the man wearing a panama hat and a blazer, moved together in a way that was only possible after decades of dancing in each other's arms.

The tune was an upbeat version of 'Guantanmera', a tune Katherine loved. What the hell she thought. There might be sunflowers on her dress, but she wasn't going to be a wallflower.

"If you're still asking Bruno, I'll join you."

"I knew you wouldn't let me down."

"Go girl," Corinne said.

When Bruno took her hand she had a flash of déjà vu, the oddest feeling. Katherine put it down to having knocked back her wine.

"What I lack in style and rhythm, I make up for in effort," Bruno said, swinging Katherine onto the dance floor. Other occupants had no option but to make space for them.

"That was what I feared," Katherine said, laughing to herself at the very idea of dancing with the big bear of a man.

At first she was extremely self-conscious, an apologetic smile fixed to her face. She could no longer see Ran. Bruno was not a natural dancer. He was liable to knock someone out with his flailing arms. But his enthusiasm and energy were contagious. Soon Katherine's awkwardness evaporated. She laughed as Bruno spun her around. Whatever tune he was moving to, it wasn't the one the band was playing. He twirled and spun her in a way that made her feel the centre of attention. Much to her surprise, Katherine was having fun.

When the music stopped a ripple of applause meant for the musicians was accepted by Bruno for his entertaining effort. Fanning herself, Katherine thanked Bruno and said she needed a drink.

"May I cut in?" Ran tapped her shoulder.

Katherine just nodded and stepped back onto the dance floor.

Chapter 11

Katherine couldn't sleep. She kicked off the sheet in an effort to cool down, knowing she was presenting herself on a platter to the mosquito she had played hide and seek with all night. The hands on her watch made a vertical line, six o'clock, half an hour of fitful twisting since she had last checked it. Grey light crept under the door.

Having dozed for an hour or so, Katherine had been awake since four. The freezer in the kitchen wheezed like a chain-smoking consumptive, but that wasn't what was keeping her awake, her mind simply didn't know it was allowed to switch off.

She had awoken abruptly realising that her room back at The Retreat was unlocked. There were six fifty-euro notes in the envelope she had wedged between underwear in the bottom drawer of the bedside locker. A regurgitation of her familiar financial worries followed and that of course brought Vincent to the forefront of her mind. And then she thought of Ran. It wasn't as if anything had even happened. But guilt only needed the merest hint of an opportunity to mount an ambush. Then it dawned on her. She sat bolt upright. Ran was simply the new Mark.

She wasn't going to be able to sleep now so she extracted herself from the ball of bedclothes. The t-shirt Corinne had given her was damp with sweat. She craved a shower but didn't dare wake Corinne. Dehydrated and with a headache looming, Katherine gulped down a glass of water.

The day's young light spilled into the atrium of the villa. From the living room she gazed out at the pale grey sea. Lights still flickered on the distant shores of Fuerteventura. Corinne's slow breath was audible from the master bedroom.

The living room was cooler, perhaps more conducive to sleep, so Katherine stretched out, propping a cushion behind her head. Her mind drifted back to the night before. She hoped she hadn't made a fool of herself.

***

Whilst she had been embarrassed at first to dance with Bruno she was nervous when Ran held her in an awkward waltz hold. They had jolted from side to side, never quite moving in unison. Ran had been full of chat, excited that an art dealer wanted to meet with him to discuss exhibiting his work in Madrid. His enthusiasm was infectious and Katherine listened, genuinely delighted for him. Part of her had wanted the music to speed up so they could separate and dance less self-consciously. The other part of her was far less chaste.

When the song ended they had sat on a low wall by the steps.

"What do you charge for your work Ran, if you don't mind me asking?" Katherine asked.

"It varies. That one upstairs is priced at five grand. Of course if it sells this place gets a hefty cut."

"That's a bit out of my range."

"You'd get a discount Katherine." Ran winked.

"How do you determine the price in the first place?"

"I suppose like most artists that's something I've struggled with for years. I think it really comes down to the value you place on what you do. If I don't think my work is of value, no one else will. The way I think of it is what would an accountant or a lawyer charge for a good six weeks' work?" Ran stretched his arms behind him which pulled his shirt tight across his chest.

"That's one way of looking at it."

"Will you finish that painting of yours in the workshop tomorrow do you think?" Ran asked, scratching his shoulder.

"That's the plan," Katherine said, dropping her gaze.

"I was serious in the car; promise me you'll stick with it."

"I'll be looking for some tips from you tomorrow."

"I'm sure I'll be saying this in the workshop, but always remember great art comes from in here." Ran put his hand on his heart. "Art comes from the inside out, not the outside in. If the purpose of art and I'm not just talking about painting, but all art, is to evoke emotion, then that emotion has to be on the canvas to start with. Remember when you're painting Katherine it's your imagination, your talent and your emotion that will make your work unique and authentic."

"I'm not sure I have the talent you think I have."

"I was saying to a student last week, the only thing worse than arrogance is selling yourself short. It goes back to believing in your work, owning your talent, being proud of it. Modesty is all well and good but if you want others to believe in you, you have to believe in yourself. "

It wasn't just what Ran was saying but how he was saying it that made Katherine forget the commotion of the party. She felt the world had narrowed to the spot on the ledge where they sat. She toyed with the hem of her dress. Here was a man passionate about his craft, his art. It was that passion, that energy that made him attractive, his physical attributes and there were many, were merely added bonuses. She followed his gesticulating hands, wondering what it would be like to be undressed by them.

"Oh look at him." Ran pointed to Bruno who had managed to drag Corinne on to the dance floor. "He'll do someone an injury."

"Do you mind me asking, what's the name of your aftershave?"

"You like it?"

Katherine nodded.

"Let me get this right, Aqua de Parma Intensa."

"I must remember the name." Katherine leant in. When

she would think of this night, she would think of that citrusy woody scent.

Ran just smiled. When she sat back her leg was still touching his. She didn't move. Neither did Ran. Katherine could feel her heart quicken.

She would have been more than happy to stay seated on the wall, but when Ran jumped up and suggested they join the others on the dance floor, Katherine accepted the offer of his hand to get to her feet.

As Corinne had said in the car on the way back, they had danced like no one was watching. The band was fantastic. Old familiar tunes mixed with modern songs and Latin beats that gave Katherine illusions of appearing on *Strictly Come Dancing*. She even joined Bruno in what Corinne said was a show stopping tango.

Later, Katherine watched in amazement as one of the women who had had their photo taken with Ran succeeded in separating him from their foursome, as skilfully as a lioness separating her prey from the flock.

She had wandered around the gallery space again with Corinne. Apart from a few stragglers and the waiters collecting discarded glasses and scrunched napkins, they had the exhibition area to themselves. Katherine enjoyed looking at the other works but her mind was elsewhere. She felt the artists were trying too hard to shock. Whether this was a theme for the exhibition or simply a trend in modern art she wasn't sure. The elderly couple who had been on the dance floor were also in the gallery. Corinne remarked that watching them, arms linked, dressed in their best, and loudly discussing the virtues of each piece, was the best thing about the exhibition.

As interested as she was in viewing the displays, and admiring the spirited couple, Katherine glanced out the window every opportunity she got. She had no exclusive rights to Ran. She didn't even know whether he had a wife, a girlfriend or even a boyfriend back in Israel. Maybe she was just confusing friendliness with flirtation. Of course he could dance with whoever he pleased, but that didn't stop her feeling like a schoolgirl, dumped by the guy who brought her to the prom.

Bruno was missing when it was time to go. He hadn't been seen in a while. Ran wasn't overly concerned, so it was just the three of them in the car heading back to Playa Blanca. Katherine sat in the back with Corinne. They felt like they were being chauffeured. It was still warm enough to keep the roof down. Katherine enjoyed the mild breeze and the velvet darkness. Shaded and shadowed by moonlight, the volcanic peaks loomed over them, their summits like charcoal lines on a black page.

***

The wind woke with the rising sun. Katherine could hear the pool cover flapping and the trees being shaken awake. She rubbed her eyes. Orange and pink flares now lit up the eastern sky.

There was no doubt Katherine had enjoyed the party. The music, the wine, the surroundings, the company and the novelty of finding herself at such an event made it a night to remember. But now in the morning light, with a sore head and tired eyes, she cringed at the thought that she had made a spectacle of herself. She had said yes and she had had fun, wasn't that what was important. Then again she had also said yes to getting back into the car with Mark, and last night, if he had asked, she would have said yes to spending the night with Ran. Could she justify the adulterous thought with the sound bite of living in the present? Could she justify it by knowing Vincent was cheating on her? Corinne had spoken about people repeating patterns. Katherine could clearly see her pattern now; an attraction to handsome dark-haired men, mental adultery, closely followed by feelings of remorse.

The light in the room meant any last hope of sleep had gone. When Katherine stood she felt lightheaded. She feared she wouldn't be able to keep her eyes open when they got back to The Retreat and it was Ran's masterclass that afternoon. The only thing for it was to get out into the morning light and hope some brightness and movement would help her get through the day.

Katherine splashed water on her face, wiped the sleep from her eyes and gave her teeth a rudimentary cleaning with her finger. Thankfully Corinne had left mouthwash in the bathroom. She stepped into her sunflower dress that she swore would not see the light of day again that week. A splash of perfume from a sample she discovered at the bottom of her bag would hopefully disguise the absence of a shower. She scribbled a note for Corinne, grabbed her bag and journal and let herself out of the villa as quietly as she could.

In the ten minutes it had taken her to wash and dress, the wind had completely disappeared. It was like someone had simply switched it off. The scent of jasmine hung heavy in the still air. Montana Roja glowed deep red. Katherine's shoulders were cool, but refreshingly so after the stickiness of the bedroom. Like miniature paper lanterns, clumps of bougainvillea flowers lined the narrow path that led to the seafront. The click of the gate seemed unnaturally loud.

Having grown up by the sea, the love of water had never left Katherine. She stood for a moment and drank in the view. The sea was a pale steel blue. A lone fisherman stood on the rocks below. Katherine loved the quality of the light, the long shadows and the sense of anticipation for the day ahead.

Whenever she needed to think Katherine would go for a walk. Whenever she really needed to clear her head she would drive to the coast and walk by the sea. Those walks calmed her. The sea always seemed to balance her.

A solitary jogger nodded as he passed. A seagull hovered

overhead. Katherine decided to head towards Playa Blanca, retracing their steps from the evening before. It wasn't yet seven, but already Katherine felt she'd made the right decision. The walk would do her good. She might even find a nice spot to just sit and write.

Katherine smiled when she saw several rotund and already deeply tanned tourists tuck towels around sunbeds in the prime locations as she passed the hotel pool. She was tempted to say '*guten morgen*'. She said '*buenos días*' to a young hotel worker walking towards her. A nicer stroll to work, a nicer commute she couldn't imagine. As expected, the supermarket in Playa Flamingo was closed, but it would be open at eight.

Walking past the harbour, a ferry to Fuerteventura was about to depart. A few fishermen were tending nets and refuse collectors were emptying bins. The day was starting.

The front in Playa Blanca was eerily quiet. The shop fronts were clear of concession stands and shuttered tight. Apart from the occasional jogger and cyclist, Katherine had the place to herself.

She wandered as far as the beach in the centre of the town. A little further on was the restaurant where they had eaten the day before. There was activity in the main street so Katherine climbed the steps to investigate. A group of men, including a few taxi drivers, recognisable in their maroon shirts that matched their maroon cabs, occupied a small dimly lit café. The locals must relish this time when they can reclaim their own town.

Across the street a van was unloading boxes of fruit. The sight of the crates of oranges, bananas and peaches reminded Katherine that she was hungry. Two boxes of nectarines, her favourite fruit were stacked by the door. They smelt ripe and were soft to the touch. Katherine gingerly stepped inside.

"Not open madam." The woman's voice came from the back of the store where she was sprinkling water over the displays.

"Could I just pick up a few nectarines?" Katherine asked, holding two in her hand.

The woman paused then shrugged her shoulders.

Katherine would have loved to smell and touch every colourful item on display but she didn't want to disturb the woman's morning routine.

"*Gracias*," Katherine said, hoping her pigeon Spanish would further placate her.

"Late night?" the woman asked.

"Yes."

The shopkeeper who was about Katherine's own age bent down behind the counter. "*Paraguayos*, you will like." She handed Katherine a flattened peach. Katherine instinctively smelt the dusty pink velvety skin. She had seen some in the supermarkets back home, but they were as hard as turnips, this one yielded to her touch.

"Taste, no charge." The woman took another one from the tray and bit into it herself, rolling her eyes.

Katherine sunk her teeth into the ripe fruit. The juicy sweetness was incredible.

"I'll take some." Katherine wanted another one for herself and a second for Corinne. Then in a moment of generosity she asked for a whole bag, she'd bring some back to The Retreat. Glancing over the enticing display, whilst the woman was getting her change, Katherine knew if she stayed any longer she could easily buy more than she could carry.

The colours and fragrant lushness of the shop brightened Katherine's spirits. There was already warmth in the sun when she parked herself on the bench overlooking the beach. She put her journal on her lap, stretched out her legs and bit into a second peach.

Opening the journal Katherine was surprised that she had already filled several pages. A lot had happened since she made her feeble attempt at her gratitude list during the first workshop.

She smiled at the extra one she had scribbled at the bottom of the page – '*I'm grateful for knowing Imelda,*' added when Imelda had shamed them all with her simple, honest and heartfelt list.

Her fingers were sticky now, but with her pen in her hand Katherine wrote in the margin of the page – '*I'm grateful for these peaches, this weather and this view*'. When she looked up she noticed the silhouette of a swimmer in the water. A man was swimming across the bay heading for the pontoon. What a way to start the day she thought. If she had a swimsuit she'd be tempted to swim herself. The water was so clear. As a teenager she used to jump off the harbour in Tramore, one of the few girls to attempt the fifteen foot drop. She smiled to herself at the memory and Tommy Plunkett jeering her – 'she'll never do it, she'll never do it'. Tommy didn't know it but back then there was no surer way to motivate her than to tell her she couldn't do something. That stubbornness, that iron willpower, had somehow been corroded over the years.

Katherine watched the swimmer churn through the water, nothing but head, arms and the occasional splash of feet. Dropping her eyes to her journal she laughed out loud at the memory of sitting on the loo in the restaurant where she had the boozy lunch with Declan and Suzy. Her writing was practically a scrawl – '*Don't get too serious, remember to laugh, especially at yourself*'. A nugget of wisdom from Morag and then Declan's throwaway comment '*We all just want to be loved, for who we are, not who we think we should be*'. It reminded Katherine of what Corinne had said at the restaurant yesterday, '*I want to be loved for who I am not who I pretend to be*'. Katherine added that in, just above where she had written '*I am Love*' followed by a string of question marks. She couldn't remember why she had written it. Maybe it was because she had just learnt Neide's partner's name.

The swimmer hauled himself onto the pontoon. Katherine shaded her eyes. Even from this distance she could see the man's hairy shoulders and back. He stared out over the ocean then lay down, his hands behind his head. The pontoon swayed beneath him.

On the next page were the sources of inspiration she had copied down from the flipchart. Reading them now they seemed quite obvious. She loved what Neide had said about motivation being motive plus action, and inspiration being in spirit. She crossed her feet on the wall. Katherine added *'getting up early'* and *'swimming'* to her list.

The next two pages were filled with everything she was forgiving herself for, everything she wrote when she had her meltdown after ringing Vincent, when Imelda had popped into her room. Taking the pen from her mouth she wrote what Corinne had said yesterday, *'a breakdown is just an opportunity to break out and rebuild'* and that *'she wasn't having a midlife crisis she was having a midlife awakening'*.

Katherine scratched the back of her arm. Two red bumps, the first mosquito bites of the week. She cursed the creature that had teased her all night. The swimmer on the pontoon was now stretching his legs and arms. He turned to face the shore. At first Katherine wasn't sure; she shielded her eyes and squinted. It couldn't be? She recognised the bald head. It was Bruno.

She didn't know whether to crouch down or stand and wave. He was a hundred feet or so away, but he was looking straight at her. It was definitely Bruno. Her brightly patterned dress was conspicuous. The next line in her journal was *'we resist what we need the most'*, something Ran had said at the creativity workshop. Katherine stood up, waved and called to Bruno. He motioned for her to stay where she was. Like a man half his age and size, Bruno ran to the edge of the platform and dived in.

He was a competent swimmer. Katherine had watched him traverse the bay with a steady, rhythmical pace, now he was sprinting towards the shore, hurtling through the water, propelled by fast-kicking feet. Gathering her belongings, Katherine removed her shoes and walked onto the cool sand.

Bruno was no Daniel Craig; he was more like a saturated teddy bear.

"Well hello again," he said, pulling off his goggles, catching his breath, still knee-deep in water. "You're out and about early."

"Very impressive swimming Bruno."

"And the physique, what do you think?" Bruno posed like a strong man flexing his biceps.

"Is it not cold?" Katherine stepped into the water. It only took a few seconds for her feet to adjust to the temperature.

"Invigorating. But remember what the cold does to a man too." Bruno laughed.

Katherine was reminded of the time she met Mark out jogging in the park. She wasn't sure where to look. Her eyes moved from the horizon to her submerged feet, to Bruno's stubbly face. She was aware of his hairy body and his black Speedos. There was a faded tattoo on one arm, probably going back to his navy days, a rite of passage rather than a fashion statement. His broad chest masked his ample stomach.

"Where did you leave your clothes?"

"By the rocks." Bruno nodded towards the far side of the beach. They began to saunter in that direction. Katherine kicked the water ahead of her.

"Where did you get to last night Bruno?"

"I got a taxi back. I'd reached my limit. I'm like a firework, I burn brightly but fizzle out quickly. How long did you stay?"

"Ran dropped us off about two. I haven't danced like that in ages. Every time I think of that tango! I'm a bit worse for wear though, I didn't really sleep."

"You need a good swim, best hangover cure there is."

"There's a lovely pool where Corinne is staying."

"Give me the sea any day."

"You don't need a wetsuit?" Katherine said.

"The cold never bothers me." Bruno wobbled his stomach. "Plenty of insulation. I've a friend who lives in Copenhagen and him and his two mates swim every morning at seven o'clock in the sea, summer and winter."

"That's hardcore."

"And they swim naked."

"No way."

"Imagine how great, how alive you'd feel after that. I'd go mad Katherine if I didn't swim. It clears my head, banishes stress, sets me up for the day. I've gotten my best ideas when I've been swimming; I've worked out many a plot splashing through the water."

"Really?"

"Absolutely. It's my meditation, my exercise, my brainstorming, all wrapped up in one. Plus it's my get out of jail card. I can eat and drink what I want, because I swim every day, that's what I tell myself anyway."

"As a child you couldn't keep me out of the water."

"What've you got there?" Bruno said, spying the bag of peaches. Katherine offered him one. "Oh my." Bruno devoured the peach in three or four bites, then flung the stone out to sea. "Could I be a pig and take another one?"

Katherine joined him, biting into her third peach of the morning. The law of diminishing returns didn't apply to the succulent fruit.

Whilst Bruno retrieved his belongings, Katherine parked herself on a flat rock. From the corner of her eye she could see Bruno wriggling from his trunks beneath his towel.

"Isn't this just a perfect moment?" Bruno said, positioning himself on a rock beside her, his towel wrapped high on his stomach.

The sun cleared the buildings on the far side of the town, igniting the beach. The cries of the seagulls seemed louder and from the town the clattering of shutters announced the start of the trading day.

"You must be staying close by?" Katherine asked.

"About ten minutes' walk." Bruno used the hem of his towel to rub the water from his ears.

"And you were saying you're staying with your daughter, Zoe isn't it?"

"Yeah, it worked out really well. Lisa, Zoe's mom and her husband have a place here, and I'm crashing with them for a few days. It's a bit cramped. Myself and Zoe are heading off on one of our adventures today, I can't wait. Then I'm at The Retreat tomorrow and I head home Friday."

"And where's home?"

"Good ol' London town, well Kentish Town to be exact. I'm not sure I'll be there much longer though. Zoe's heading to university in Edinburgh and I only stayed in London to be close to her. It's not a city I feel at home in."

"It's great that you still get on with Lisa."

"Matt's really cool too, but then we've all known each other for years."

"It's not many people who have such good relationships with their ex's."

"Most of the time that's because they don't have very good relationships with themselves."

A refuse collector was emptying the bins on the front. The prom was too narrow for the truck so he moved from bin to bin in a small van, its radio on full blast.

"Will you go back to the States, was it New York you said you were from?" Katherine drew circles in the sand with her toes.

"I doubt it. I don't have too many good memories from back then. And I hate what America has become. We won the cold war, but now America is the evil empire. Land of the free, it's such a joke. It's funny when I was out there swimming I was thinking and it must be my Italian blood, but I wouldn't mind spending more time in Italy."

"Italy is beautiful. And the food."

"Oh the food. I'd have to swim morning and evening. And the wine."

Bruno pulled on a pair of shorts festooned with red pineapples and a t-shirt that soon darkened where his body was still wet.

"You know what my ideal would be Katherine, I'd love to live someplace where I could swim every morning and when I'd look up from my desk I'd see water. Now I look out on a footpath, all I see is railings and ankles," he said, rolling his towel. "How about a coffee, I could kill for a caffeine fix."

"There was a place open just off the main street."

"Lead on McDuff. Here let me carry those." Bruno took the peaches. "What's the big notebook?"

"It's where I scribble down everything I'm learning at The Retreat."

"So it's empty then?"

"No, there's quite a bit in it actually and I'm sure there'll be a lot more after your session."

"Don't count on it." Bruno laughed, swinging the bag of peaches like a schoolboy with his gym kit.

Balancing herself against the railing, Katherine brushed the sand from her feet.

"Fuck. I didn't take my wallet with me," Bruno said, slapping his head.

"Fancy asking me for a cup of coffee and not being able to pay," Katherine joked. "It'll be my treat."

Heads turned when they walked into the dark café. Katherine was impressed when Bruno asked for two coffees in Spanish. No cappuccinos or lattes here. Two short black coffees were placed before them.

"I have to confess Bruno I've not read any of your books."

"You're in the majority then."

"Are they works of fiction?"

"You've heard of Paulo Coelho?"

"*The Alchemist?*"

"I write something similar, works of fiction, but I build them around universal truths or life lessons I've learnt, or more likely stuff I'm struggling with and trying to figure out. We teach what we most need to learn and all that."

"I must get some from you and you'll have to sign them."

"I tell you what; I'll put a few aside, fair exchange for the peaches, the coffee, the conversation and for risking your life during that tango."

They clinked cups.

"So what about you Katherine?"

"What do you mean?"

"You strike me as a seeker."

"A seeker?"

"On a quest for knowledge. You must be at The Retreat because you're looking for the big answers to the big questions, no?"

"When you put it like that, I suppose I am looking for new insights, new ideas, figuring out what I want."

"Here's what I've learnt, retreats, workshops, seminars, books, hell even my own books they're all variations on a theme. Now don't get me wrong they can be useful and good fun, but the answers you seek will never be outside you, they're always in there." Bruno tapped the top of Katherine's chest. He lowered his voice to almost a whisper. "We have the wisdom we need; all we have to do is be quiet and listen. Deep down we know what it is we want."

"I'm not too sure about that Bruno."

"Instinct, intuition, call it what you will."

"Let me ask you this, if there was one big life lesson you've learnt what would it be?" Katherine plonked her journal on the bar. "What should I write in here?"

"Apart from knowing you have all the answers to start with?"

"Apart from that, which is a bit too deep for me."

Bruno took the pen from her hand and twisted the journal around so Katherine couldn't see what he was doing.

"Right I'll give you two pieces of wisdom for the price of one, how's that."

"Bargain."

Bruno stood back and held up the journal. He had filled two pages with bold capitals. 'ENOUGH IS SUFFICIENT', and 'PUT HAPPINESS AHEAD OF APPROVAL!'

"Okay?" Katherine said, full of curiosity.

"People scramble to accumulate stuff, they want more of everything. Enough is never enough. What's the phrase, they strive but never arrive. You know until very recently I've lived most of my life being able to carry everything I own in the world on my back. So the first gem of wisdom is people don't realise that more stuff never brings more happiness, so enough is sufficient."

"That makes sense."

"The world is fuelled by a hunger for more things Katherine. But what people don't realise is that that hunger is really a hunger for meaning and that is something we can only figure out for ourselves. Of course I might be bonkers," Bruno said, laughing. "If I defined myself by what I own, I'm very poor, but if I think of the wonderful people I know, maybe the stuff I've created, my writing, the houses I've built when I was a builder, the small differences I've made, then my life is very rich."

"Ah that's a lovely way to put it."

"It's what we give that defines us, not the car we drive, the house we live in or our pension scheme. All that is bollocks."

"Eloquently put."

"I am a writer. It's funny I've met thousands of people all over the world, from all races, religions, ages and castes, and when you get to know people everyone everywhere wants to make a difference, deep down people are good people. It's the life we live that's the real legacy we leave."

"That's a powerful message Bruno and if that's what your writing is like, your books must be great reads."

"If only publishers felt the same."

"And the happiness and the approval bit?" Katherine said, running her hand over the page.

"Right, here's the deal, for you to truly listen to your own wisdom you have to make one promise to yourself. You have to promise that you will drop the constant craving for approval. You have to put your happiness ahead of the approval of others."

"I don't think I crave approval," Katherine said.

"Most people Katherine crave a constant stream of approval; in fact they will sacrifice their happiness just to be approved by others. I gave up that bullshit years ago, my happiness is too important. Take that bag of yours."

"What's wrong with it?" Katherine had the bag on the stool beside her, the Louis Vuitton logo emblazoned over it.

"There's nothing wrong with it. Why did you buy it?"

"It was a present if you must know."

"And I'm sure it was expensive and by carrying it you know that people will recognise it as expensive and they will view you in a certain way, either as part of the club or part of the club they aspire to. Really it's no different than that guy wearing that football shirt." Bruno gestured to the bearded man dozing in the corner.

"That's a bit harsh. I like this bag."

"Why?" Bruno shrugged his shoulders.

"It's practical, well-made, strong."

"And looks good?"

"Sure, what's wrong with that?"

"There's nothing wrong with having a nice bag, but if you have it to impress others, to make you feel good about yourself, then you're a bit deluded."

Katherine felt insulted. She'd bought him coffee, now he was making fun of her bag and calling her stupid.

"Corinne will be wondering where I am."

"Oh I've said too much, haven't I?" Bruno said, reaching to touch her arm, but Katherine stepped back.

"Anyway I'll see you tomorrow at The Retreat," Katherine said, picking up her bag and defiantly slinging it across her shoulder. She knew Bruno's eyes followed her from the café. She was annoyed. He might be full of life but he was also rude. She had a long walk back to the villa and her headache had returned. Vincent had bought her the bag for her birthday. She was annoyed then too because she had never been a fan of heavily logoed bags and she had remembered thinking that surely Vincent had known that.

***

Her dress was stuck to her back by the time Katherine turned the key in the door. It was only nine thirty but the sun was already hot and she had no lotion on her shoulders.

She deposited the tubs of yogurt she had bought in the supermarket into the door of the fridge and placed the loaf of fresh bread as well as the remaining peaches on the kitchen counter. She took her new swimsuit from the bag and just prayed it would fit. She might only wear it once, but if it meant a dip in the pool then the thirty-five euros it cost would have been worth it.

The door to the terrace was open. The pool cover was back and the sun danced off the surface. Katherine was about to call out when she spotted Corinne, sitting cross-legged on a sunlounger, staring out to sea. White earphones hung from her ears and her up-turned palms rested on her knees. Corinne was meditating. In shorts and a t-shirt the slender black woman was all knees and elbows. It was her expression that intrigued Katherine. She simply looked serene.

Katherine retrieved her journal and pen and sat at the table under the awning. It opened on the page where Bruno had written. Her first thought was that he had stretched the spine. She remembered what Corinne had said when they left the retreat after her disagreement with Pamela, how there was something inside her that was reacting to what she was hearing. Katherine knew that Bruno's comment about her bag wasn't really about her bag. But she didn't want to think about that now.

Keeping with the theme of the bold statements in her journal, she turned the page and in block capitals that matched Bruno's, she wrote – MEDITATE.

***

"I didn't want to disturb you, you looked so peaceful," Katherine said, when she noticed Corinne removing the earphones.

"You must have been up early."

"I've been to Playa Blanca and back," Katherine said, moving to the wall. "Got some gorgeous peaches and a few other bits for breakfast."

"Divine. You're so kind Katherine."

"And you'll never guess who I met? Swimming across the bay, I wouldn't have believed it unless I saw him. Bruno."

"No way, and where did he get to last night." Corinne flexed her feet, stretching like a dancer.

"Said he was burnt out, got a taxi back. You want to see him swim though Corinne, right across the bay and he climbed onto that pontoon, the one we could see from the restaurant. I don't know where he gets the energy. We had a quick coffee, then he starting slagging my bag."

"What was he saying?"

"He said I had the bag to be noticed or to be a member of a

club or something. We'd been having a good chat, but anyway."

"Oh." Corinne moved to the wall facing Katherine.

"He probably thinks I'm a moody cow."

"You'll see him again tomorrow. Which reminds me I must show you the photo I took of the two of you dancing."

"Oh Corinne, that'll be a delete." Katherine cringed at the thought.

"Nonsense you look so happy in it."

"You know the way you'd love to run your own workshops Corinne, well Bruno was saying that all the answers we ever need are on the inside that we won't find them in a book or at a workshop."

"Did he?" Corinne pondered the idea. She twisted her head from side to side, stretching her neck. "The way I see it is books and workshops are the vehicles, inner wisdom is the destination. We need tools, questions, exercises to help us access our wisdom. Of course the danger is some people just keep driving around, stuck in their vehicles."

"Addicted to courses."

"Exactly." Corinne stood up.

"You looked so blissed out meditating Corinne, do you do it every day?"

"I try to, even if it's just for five minutes."

"It's something I always wanted to do."

"What stops you then?"

"Time and I don't know if I'd be doing it properly."

"It's whatever works for you. I came across a lovely saying a few years ago. Prayer is where we ask God questions, meditation is where we hear the answers."

"Oh I like that, that's one for my journal." Katherine knelt to remove a few flowers and leaves that bobbed at the edge of the pool.

"Meditation got me through after Terry's death. Often I'd be sitting at home, my eyes stinging with tears, not knowing how I was going to cope. Thank God I had my faith. Every day I asked God just to help me through that day. About two weeks after Terry died I was sitting in my armchair, meditating or maybe I was just closing my eyes to the world I don't know, but I got this sense, this feeling on the inside and I heard the words 'you're being tested, but you are strong' in my head."

"Wow."

"Since then any time I feel overwhelmed or confused or challenged I just say a little prayer to myself, I ask God to help me – in my weakness I call on Your strength." Corinne looked to the heavens. "And it always seems to work."

***

Katherine was glad Corinne was in the kitchen when she dropped her towel and stood on the top step of the pool. The swimsuit was a little tight across her bust and she was glad she had shaved her legs the previous morning. Slight body consciousness was a small price to pay for a morning swim in such a pool.

From instinct Katherine held her breath and stepped into the water until it was up to her waist. She felt it cold on her thighs. She rubbed the water on her arms then bringing her hands together as if in prayer, she dived under. When she broke the water at the far end, all she could do was release a long slow sigh. Taking another breath she sank down and propelled herself from the wall.

Katherine floated on her back, her ears below the water; the only sounds the hum of the pool's filters and her heartbeat. She rolled over and put her face in the water. She turned, twisted and stretched, feeling the water on every part of her body. Swimming towards the sun she had to squint. Every stroke enlivened her. She did several lengths, but lengths weren't counted in a pool like this.

She sat on the steps and allowed the surface to get still. With minimal effort she pushed off, parting the sapphire blue water, causing ripples to sparkle and race to the edge. This was her meditation.

"How is it?" Corinne asked setting a tray down on the table.

"There are no words. I've decided Corinne; I'm staying here, to hell with The Retreat."

***

Katherine tidied up after breakfast allowing Corinne to stretch out in the shade. After washing the few dishes Katherine reopened her journal and under the last word she had written, '*meditate*', she added what Corinne had said – *prayer is when we ask the question, meditation is when we get the answer.*

Katherine couldn't wait to wash her hair. As she stepped into the shower she said a little prayer, not one of her usual ones, not the Our Father or Hail Mary that she said getting into bed at night, not even a begging one when worry and anxiousness swamped her. She simply asked for help. 'God I'm at a crossroads, guide me on the right path.'

She didn't expect an answer, so when a foreign thought popped into her head she was shocked. Rinsing her hair, watching the suds drain down the plughole, the words 'there is no path, you create the path', came to her. She stood motionless.

"I create my path by walking it,' Katherine said the words aloud.

Drying herself, Katherine was amazed that having asked a simple question, moments later an idea had popped into her head. Was that the answer? Was that God speaking to her? Was she connecting with her inner wisdom? She was intrigued.

Even though she was stepping into her sunflower dress again, Katherine felt renewed. She was excited to be heading back to The Retreat. And it was Ran's painting workshop that afternoon.

Chapter 12

It had worked out perfectly. Katherine spent the morning at the villa with Corinne; the rescheduling of the workshops meant she wasn't missing a thing back at The Retreat. She spent a blissful hour in the shade of the bougainvillea-covered awning lost in the cookery book she had borrowed from Carlos. She didn't understand the Spanish recipes, but the photographs inspired her. She sipped a mint tea and felt virtuous. The sleek yachts crossing the straits stirred dreams of sailing around the world. In her fantasy Ran was at the helm.

When Corinne woke from dozing on a sunlounger they made plans to drive into Playa Blanca before returning to The Retreat. Katherine wanted to get ingredients for the meal she had committed to cooking.

Whilst she did follow the occasional recipe, Katherine always described herself as an instinctive cook, not overly concerned with measuring cups or teaspoons. She didn't want the added pressure of trying something new when cooking for a large group, so she planned to keep it simple and stick with some tried and tested recipes, maybe with a Spanish twist. She had no hesitation in spending her money on supplies. If Neide refunded her great, but if not, the meal would be her gift to the group.

In the car, Katherine told Corinne about her experience in the shower. How she had said her little prayer and how moments later the words 'you create your own path' came to her.

"When you take steps, even baby steps towards your desired future Katherine, then that future is taking steps towards you," Corinne had said.

The concept consoled Katherine. The idea of creating

her own path, taking small actions in a new direction was practical and exciting. It was that sentiment that banished the concerns she once had about cooking an inedible meal. She was determined to enjoy the whole process from sourcing the ingredients, planning her menu, cooking the food and seeing the faces of those around the table smiling, their taste buds and appetites satisfied.

Playa Blanca was buzzing. It was as if hordes of noisy extras had descended on the deserted film set Katherine had strolled through at the crack of dawn. The two women made a beeline to the fruit and vegetable shop where the woman behind the counter recognised Katherine. Garlic, basil, thyme, lemons, olives and another bag of flat peaches went into Katherine's basket along with a tin of anchovies she discovered on a shelf of preserves. Corinne took the opportunity to get supplies for the villa. Katherine asked the storekeeper to recommend a good butcher's and to her surprise she suggested the supermarket across the street.

You can't go wrong with chicken was Katherine's thinking. In the supermarket she put four whole chickens into the trolley and added a ring of chorizo. She also got brown pasta, the basis of the vegetarian dish she planned. When Corinne mentioned dessert, Katherine said it would be nothing fancy, just ice cream, but she wanted to get it in the ice cream parlour she had spotted on the main street, where the sign over the door read 'Gelato'. When she finally managed to explain to the ice cream vendor what she wanted and having tasted what was on offer, they left with a pail of coffee-flavoured ice cream, to go along with the chickens, into the freezer box that Corinne had wisely put into the boot of the car. They also had two ice cream cones in their hands.

They struggled to keep up with the lines of dripping ice cream, the temporary nature of the treat just adding to their enjoyment of it. With the shopping in the car, they wandered to the front for a final stroll by the sea. The fresh, almost medicinal smell of a shop called 'Mystic' enticed them inside. By the entrance, a small boat was packed high with sponges. Large wooden sculptures, scented candles, local crafts, essential oils and handmade jewellery lined the shelves. Wind chimes and dreamcatchers dangled from the ceiling. They anointed themselves with samples of floral hand lotion and scent.

It was the sort of place Corinne said she could browse in all day. She restricted herself to a box of sandalwood incense. Katherine bought three handmade candles. She'd give one to Claire and Mags and keep one herself. She knew she had to get Rhona something more substantial, but she wasn't sure what would be appropriate for the woman whose accident meant Katherine was able to be here in the first place.

***

It seemed to Katherine that she had been away from The Retreat for more than twenty-four hours. She was happy to be back. With their arms full of bags and belongings Katherine and Corinne headed to the kitchen, skirting the questions from the others who were having lunch in the courtyard.

"Ah Katherine, I thought you'd run away," Carlos said, arms outstretched.

"Look what we have," Katherine said, depositing the bags on the big table. "Now quick Carlos, we have to get this into the freezer." Katherine extracted the container of ice cream.

"Even I say, Italy ice cream the best," Carlos said, licking his lips.

"And these are for the fridge." Katherine handed over the chickens.

"Ah you cook chicken and chorizo, like I say."

"I'm going to try and here's your book back, I had a good look through it this morning."

"I leave it here for you." Carlos made a point of placing the book on the counter.

"And be sure to take some of these." Katherine opened the bag of peaches.

"*Paraguayos. Muchas gracias.*" Carlos continued to unpack, showing Katherine where he was storing everything.

"I hope I haven't bitten off more than I can chew," Katherine said, rolling up the empty plastic bags.

"Nonsense, look at you, you're in your element," Corinne said.

***

Katherine wanted to get back to her room and change as quickly as she could, but Suzy and Imelda wouldn't let her pass the table without telling them about her adventures. There was much oohing and aahing when Katherine described the villa and how they ended up at the party. She talked them through what she had bought for the following night's dinner and with all the offers of help, Katherine felt she could easily end up just supervising.

Katherine was surprised to see Tonya sitting with the group, something the surly barrister hadn't done all week. Still dressed in black she was chatting away with Serendipity and Sophie, the three seemingly bonded since the workshop with Pamela.

***

"Listen up folks," Neide said stepping into the courtyard. "There's going to be a delay. Ran was just on the phone, he's running about an hour late. He's really sorry, but he's happy to extend the class to finish at six."

"I'm beginning to get a little fed up with all these rearrangements Neide." Bruce got up from the table. "This was supposed to be a week of workshops and I haven't been to one since yesterday morning."

"It's unfortunate but sometimes this happens."

"Is there anything we could do, so we're not just sitting around?" Marie asked.

"That's a good idea." Morag added.

"Is there anything on relationships Neide?" Declan twisted around. "I don't know about Bruce, but I felt I missed out yesterday."

Katherine could see Neide was uncomfortable with the mini revolt.

"Let me think. If you like we could do an exercise from the Relating Well workshop which was dropped this week to make space for Ran and Bruno in the schedule. It takes about an hour and is all about gaining new insights into relationships."

"It would be better than just sitting around. What does everyone else think?" Bruce asked.

"That makes sense." Marie was standing now. Katherine couldn't help thinking that she and Bruce were battling for the title of group leader.

"I was going to suggest you could run a little session," Katherine whispered to Corinne.

"I would have killed you if you did."

"Let's meet in the Big Room at two. So twenty minutes folks," Neide said. "I'll need to get the worksheets. Oh and by the way, there's rain forecast for later, maybe a thunderstorm, so we might have to have the evening meal indoors and just in case make sure the windows in your rooms are closed."

Better rain tonight than tomorrow night, Katherine thought. Her vision for her meal was a lantern festooned table, laden with steaming platters of food served under a starry sky.

***

With her well-worn sunflower dress scrunched in a ball and shoved into the back of her suitcase, Katherine put on her white blouse with the pinched in waist that always attracted compliments and paired it with her grey linen trousers. A lengthy and vigorous brushing of her hair and a light application of make-up and she was almost ready to go. Not bad she thought examining her reflection in the small bathroom mirror. Finally an industrial amount of deodorant was applied, her armour against the heat and humidity.

Katherine took a vacant seat in the middle of the semi-circle between Suzy and Morag. She was excited to be back in the learning environment. Her journal sat expectantly on her lap. Bruce was last to arrive taking his regular spot on the far left.

"Who would like to share what they took from the workshop yesterday with Pamela?" Neide asked switching on the fan in the corner.

"How to bag a rich man," Suzy whispered to Katherine, continuing where she left off the day before.

"For me it was simple, I'd never thought about setting myself goals in the context of relationships," Marie said.

"We can set goals in every area of our lives and that's something you'll all get a chance to do tomorrow." Neide said, remembering to light the sage.

"I thought what Pamela said about no matter what state your relationship is in, we do fifty per cent of the relating," Katherine said, in an effort to cease the gossip with Suzy.

"That's useful to remember, isn't it?"

"We loved writing down everything we want in our ideal man, we had fun with that," Sophie said. It was one of the first times Katherine heard the young Belgian girl speak in front of the group.

"We're still working on our lists," Tonya added. It was the first positive contribution Tonya had made. Could that actually be a smile on her face, Katherine heard herself think. The page now open on her lap was where she had written what Corinne had said about judging others.

"I must write out my list of what I'm looking for in my ideal man," Declan whispered.

"You'd only have two words on the page." Suzy laughed. "Jude Law."

"No, he'll play me in the movie of my life."

"He'll have to put on a few kilos then."

"Bitch."

"Now this exercise is all about enhancing an existing relationship," Neide said, picking up the stack of pages from the table. "I'm sure we can all think of someone that we don't get on with as well as we would like."

"I could be here until Saturday," Morag said.

"For this exercise just pick one person. You're going to do this exercise in pairs, taking turns asking the questions on this sheet."

"So it doesn't have to be your partner?" Marie asked.

"It can be a work colleague, a family member, a neighbour, the same principles apply." Neide moved to the flipchart. "This exercise is based on the golden rule of relationships, let me write it down for you – *you cannot change other people, you can only change how you relate to them.*"

Like everyone else, Katherine copied the rule into a new page in her journal.

"It's like what you were saying Katherine, we each do fifty per cent of the relating in our relationships, so if we are seeking to change or enhance a relationship, we have to change how we are doing our relating. Now what usually works best is that I will work through the questions with one person at the top of the room, so everyone can see what's involved and then you can split into pairs. So who would like to volunteer?"

Eyes looked at the floor and the hum of the fan got louder.

"This is a real opportunity to start the work of transforming a relationship," Neide said her eyes scanning the row of chairs.

Katherine could see Corinne gesture for her to volunteer.

After a moment's hesitation Katherine raised her hand. "I'll do it."

"Great, a round of applause for Katherine. Bring your chair with you," Neide said.

Katherine faced Neide at the top of the room. Katherine was apprehensive, but if this exercise helped her, then temporary embarrassment was a small price to pay.

"Now Katherine you've a person in mind, a relationship you would like to improve?" Katherine nodded. "We can use their real name, or if you prefer a fictitious name, whatever you'd be most comfortable with."

"Well it's my husband," Katherine said, looking at Corinne and Imelda's supportive faces. "So I might as well use his real name, Vincent."

"Okay, so first question Katherine, why do you want to improve your relationship with Vincent?"

"As I said, he's my husband. We haven't been getting on too well recently. I might as well say it; I think he's cheating on me."

There was an audible intake of breath from the group who leant closer.

"So why do you want to improve it?"

"Well I want to know where I stand; I want to know if my future is with him."

"All we can do with this exercise Katherine is look at the dynamics of the relationship and how you are relating to him. Do you feel you could improve how you are relating to him?"

"I'm sure I could handle it better." Katherine was aware of her arms folded tightly across her chest.

Neide turned to the audience. "It's important when you're doing this exercise that the person you're working with believes that it is possible for them to enhance the relationship, if they don't, the exercise will be of no benefit. And it's about taking personal responsibility too. If we are honest, sometimes we are just waiting for our partner to do or say something so we can apportion blame rather than owning our part in the relationship. So next question Katherine. What's the specific challenge you're facing?"

"How do you mean?"

"Is there an aspect of Vincent's behaviour that annoys you? Can you narrow it down?"

"As I said, things haven't been good, we didn't speak for a few days before I came away. He denied he was having an affair when I confronted him. Getting specific, it's trust, I simply don't trust him anymore." Katherine could see Imelda leaning forward, her hands joined.

"I'm just jotting down a few of the key things you're saying Katherine, so when we're finished I'll give you this sheet so you'll have a record of the exercise. Now this is a critical part. We get so used to seeing a relationship, seeing the other person from our own viewpoint, and that's especially true when the relationship isn't going well. We get rigid in our thinking and judgements until the other person becomes almost one dimensional. So now Katherine, I invite you to close your eyes, this will help you focus. I want you to put yourself in Vincent's shoes, imagine you are going inside his head. I want you, just for a few moments to look at the world as Vincent sees it. You've known him for years so you can probably do this more easily than you think. So for these next few questions I'm going to be speaking to Vincent through you."

The acrid scent of burning sage tickled Katherine's nose. She uncrossed her arms. She could feel all eyes in the room focused on her. The image of Vincent in the kitchen that night they had had the row came into her mind.

"So I'm asking Vincent now, what's your experience Vincent of relating and interacting with Katherine?" Neide said.

Katherine struggled to keep her eyes shut. It wasn't easy to view herself from Vincent's perspective.

"I don't know," Katherine said.

"Just breathe and imagine looking back at yourself, looking at Katherine through Vincent's eyes. That's it."

Katherine sensed the others perched on the edge of their chairs.

"What's Katherine like?" Neide asked in a gentle tone, almost a whisper.

"She can be moody and I don't know where I stand with her. She's up one minute and down the next. I can't seem to reach her anymore." Katherine was surprised at the words that came from her mouth, Vincent's words. Tears welled in her eyes.

"And what else?"

"I don't know what to do or say to her anymore. It really frustrates me. She's just going through the motions." Katherine continued to speak on Vincent's behalf. She sank into the chair. The first tear escaped.

"And Vincent what is it you need from Katherine?"

"I need her not to fly off the handle; I need her to acknowledge that we can't go on as we are." Katherine struggled to express the thought that now came to her. "I need her to realise that it's not been easy for me either." She wiped the tears with the back of her hand.

"Okay Katherine, you're doing really well. Open your eyes, that's the tough part over." Neide retrieved a box of tissues from the cupboard.

"I don't know where all that came from," Katherine said, embarrassed that she had cried in front of the group.

"You're just letting go Katherine. Tears in this room are always evidence of a breakthrough."

"I never thought about putting myself in Vincent's shoes like that."

"It has to help doesn't it? It opens up our thinking. And we're not even halfway through this exercise. Okay to keep going? So

Katherine, up to now why have you interacted and responded to Vincent the way you have?"

"Frustration, anger because I don't think he appreciates where I'm coming from. Maybe fear as well, and I suppose I'm reluctant to face some difficult truths."

"So how could you relate to him and respond to him more usefully?"

"Oh, that's a trickier one. Maybe I could be a bit more patient, be willing to listen and keep calmer when I am talking with him."

"What could be great about your relationship with Vincent?"

"If it could be like it was when we first met that would be great. We'd just chat about different things, the stuff we're interested in, there'd be more enthusiasm, we'd be spontaneous. It wouldn't be just the same old humdrum stuff. And you know sometimes I find myself censoring what I'm saying, second guessing myself because I'm afraid to do or say the wrong thing."

"So, what are you willing to do Katherine to make the relationship the way you would like it?"

"Have a proper conversation with him when I get back. I had sort of planned to do that anyway, but now I think I might be calmer, more patient, but stronger if that's the right word."

"What are you no longer willing to do Katherine?"

"I'm not going to run away. I'm not going to let him gloss over things that we really need to discuss."

"And the last question Katherine, what have you learnt from this exercise, these questions?"

"Maybe to be a little more compassionate, to see things from his side too and it's reinforced the need to have the open and frank conversation with him." Katherine paused. She looked up at the ceiling. "You know I think I might phone Vincent later, I've been putting off contacting him."

Neide handed Katherine the sheet with the questions and the responses which she had noted, then gave her a hug. There was another round of applause. Most faces in the room were smiling and none were smiling wider than Imelda and Corinne.

Bringing her chair back into the group Katherine felt lighter. Morag squeezed her arm and Suzy whispered a well done. Imelda gave her a big thumbs up. Katherine was proud of herself. Proud that she had volunteered and proud that she had what could be described as a mini breakthrough. She realised now that Vincent must be in a difficult place too. She didn't condone his behaviour, but maybe now they would be able to have a conversation, rather than a shouting match. If she was learning anything this week Katherine was learning to have compassion for herself and maybe now that compassion could extend to include her husband.

"That exercise is all about changing the filters through which we see and assess our relationships. Having done it, maybe Katherine can see Vincent and the dynamic of their relationship differently now and that gives her new choices, new options. Does anyone have any questions?" Neide asked. The room was silent. People began forming into pairs. "So Katherine you can observe, maybe float between groups if you wish."

"I might step out for a moment," Katherine said. She was going to strike whilst the iron was hot. She was going to phone Vincent.

***

Katherine couldn't get a phone signal in her room. She wandered around, waving the phone above her head, but the signal bar stubbornly remained flat. She sensed she had a window of opportunity to speak with Vincent before the injection of confidence, compassion and clarity wore off.

A single bar of signal coverage appeared when she passed the cactus garden. She decided to try the deck outside the walls, where she and Louise had painted the day before. Carlos was too busy tidying up after lunch to notice her pass through the common room. Thankfully, as soon as she stepped onto the deck, the phone signal stabilised.

Even outside the walls of The Retreat, there was barely a hint of a breeze. The heavy heat combined with an unexpected nervousness at phoning Vincent meant Katherine's deodorant was being tested to the full. It was almost three, he would be at work. It had been two days since their polite conversation about the weather. She told herself to be strong. It was ridiculous that she felt nervous phoning her husband, but she didn't know what he might say. Equally she feared that her new found resolve would shatter at any moment.

Vincent's mobile started to ring. Katherine was determined to show him that she was a mature, in control woman who wasn't afraid of whatever the future held. She just had to ensure that the child inside her wasn't seen or heard.

Katherine knew that if the ringtone cut off, he was purposefully ignoring her call, but she counted ten rings before his familiar voice message clicked in.

"It's only me; I might try you at the office," Katherine said, her first attempt at reconciliation thwarted.

A heat haze hovered over the parched panorama. Katherine could feel the crown of her head burning. She stepped into the narrow shade of the gable end. Below her, on either side of the road, small plots of land, hardly worthy of the label 'fields', separated by their stone walls, reminded her of the west of Ireland. Connemara with all the green extracted. Within the plots there were more piles of stones, miniature walls built in arcs and semi-circles. She had read that these were used to protect the crops from the wind.

Katherine scrolled through her phone and sent a text to both Thom and Claire.

"Hope u r having a gr8 week. Weather fab here, looking 4ward to seeing u both soon. Luv Mam."

She rang Vincent's office number. He always insisted that the company phones be answered within three rings. Out of habit Katherine counted them. It was answered in two.

"Hello Hunter and Associates, can I help you?"

"Jessica it's Katherine, is Vincent in?"

"Katherine, how are you? He's been out all day, have you tried his mobile?"

"Voicemail."

"He said he wasn't sure if he'd be back today, do you want me to leave him a message?"

"No you're fine. I'll catch him later."

Katherine was about to hang up when another thought popped into her head.

"Oh, Jessica, is Nicola there by any chance?"

"Nicola? No she's out sick today, could anyone else help you with anything?"

"No you're fine. Thanks. Bye."

More circumstantial evidence as Corinne would say, her judgemental mind homing in on coincidences that supported Vincent's betrayal? Guilty until proven innocent.

Katherine was more determined than ever not to let the situation with Vincent spoil the rest of her day. She wasn't going to go to pieces this time. Maybe it was the forgiveness exercise, the conversations with Imelda and Corinne, the exercise with Neide, or simply becoming resigned to her situation, but Katherine felt stronger on the inside. Her spirit, her fight had been slowly leaking from her over the years, now at least she felt she had plugged the hole.

***

"Ah Katherine, you want a cup of coffee? I make one for you?" Carlos said as Katherine failed to pass the kitchen unseen.

"Just a quick one, I'll have to get back." Katherine could feel the lack of sleep catching up with her. An early night beckoned.

"So what you cook with chicken tomorrow?" Carlos asked, putting a small cup of black coffee in front of her.

"I'm thinking I'll roast the chickens with loads of lemon and basil, maybe some chorizo." Minus the chorizo it was one of Katherine's reliable recipes. "I'll roast some vegetables as well, keep the vegetarians happy."

"Mmmm." Carlos rubbed his round stomach.

"This for tonight?" Katherine asked stealing a pick at the casserole dish ready to go into the oven.

"Lentil burgers."

"They look good, plenty of garlic I see," Katherine said. Right now, if she had a choice she would prefer a Big Mac. "Have you tried one of the peaches yet?"

"I'm going to bring two home, my wife loves them."

"What's your wife's name?"

"Lucia, she's a..." Carlos made a scissors motion with his fingers beside his head.

"A hairdresser? And have you and Lucia been married long?"

"Twenty-two years."

"Nearly as long as me. Any children?"

"Rosa and Valentina, and now three grandchildren, three girls."

"Ah, blessed art thou amongst women, eh Carlos."

"And big family wedding tomorrow, my sister's daughter. So excited."

"Your niece, that's lovely. Where's it on?"

"Here in Teguise, in the church and then at my sister's place, 'Valentina's' the restaurant maybe you see it, maybe you go sometime? It's my family's, named after my grandmother."

"I must check it out."

"People always ask, Carlos, why you not work there, but I say too much stress, too long hours, too much work. I like the easy work here and the nice people."

193

Katherine listened to Carlos speak about his family and the restaurant his grandfather established, now managed by his sister. She was reminded of what Bruno had written in her journal. At the beginning of the week she would have assumed that a mature man like Carlos, working in a place like this, was either lazy, lacked ambition, or both. How could a professional chef be happy producing a restrictive menu week in week out? But that was unfair. As he spoke about an actor who comes to the retreat every year, Katherine realised that here was a man who was completely happy with his life. Carlos didn't have to strive, he had already arrived. It was obvious his wife and family were his priority and his decisions in life reflected that. Lucia, Valentina and Rosa were lucky to have such a man in their lives.

Katherine left Carlos's kitchen thinking here's a man who didn't seem to have any ambition other than to be happy. It appeared he had found what everyone else at The Retreat was seeking.

Ran stood by the courtyard gate, his phone to his ear. He was back in his artist's garb, a faded blue shirt, worn jeans and sandals. Katherine waited for him to notice her, but he was too engrossed in his conversation.

In the workshop, the group were just beginning to share their learning from the exercise. Suzy was speaking. "It seems obvious now, but I chose my sister, we've never really got on. The question, what does she want from me, it took me a while to answer it, but then the word respect kept popping into my mind." Suzy spoke with emotion in her voice. It looked to Katherine as if a few of them had been crying.

Katherine put a reminder into her journal to do this exercise again with Joan in mind. She put a cross on the back of her hand to remind her to phone her sister.

"And what might be different now Suzy?" Neide asked.

"I think I will be a little more tolerant of the choices she's made in her life. We're chalk and cheese, we'll probably never be close, but I can appreciate that she has a totally different outlook on life than I do and that's okay."

"Lovely," Neide said. "When we change, our relationships change, that's the way it works. And Bruce how was that exercise for you?"

"Challenging. When I was working with Corinne, I chose to work on my relationship with my son. Looking though his eyes, I could see where he could easily view me as domineering. And what does he want from me; I think he just wants me to listen to him."

"That's a lovely insight Bruce. Most conflicts arise because people don't feel listened to."

An impatient gust of wind rattled through the courtyard. All heads turned.

"Anyone else?" Neide asked. Sophie raised her hand.

"When I worked with Tonya we both focused on the relationship with our mothers which was a coincidence, but it was strange because our learning was totally different."

"For me it was not to lose my temper or be aggressive," Tonya said.

"Whereas I felt I needed to be more assertive, not to just sit back and be silent," Sophie added.

"How interesting? That was good learning for both of you. You often find we end up working with the people we're meant to be working with."

"If I may Neide?" Corinne raised her hand. "There are two phrases I've picked up that might be helpful to Sophie. I find them useful when I want to be assertive in an appropriate way. I use this one quite a bit – 'I'm not comfortable with that.'"

"I like that," Marie said writing it into her notebook, the yellow stilettos that matched her skirt now discarded like bookends under her chair.

"The second little phrase to have in your back pocket is –

'that won't work for me.'" Corinne continued. "I hope that helps."

"And the simplest way to be assertive is to just say no," Imelda said.

"We can all have difficulty saying no, isn't that right," Neide said nodding.

Katherine wrote the word 'no' in her journal and circled it.

"There's an exercise you can do on saying no. Let me share this with you very quickly, I don't want to delay Ran." Neide moved to the flipchart and wrote the words '*no more will I*.' "You list the behaviours, the attitudes, the habits you are cutting out."

As Katherine copied the phrase into her journal she continued to write, ' – *no more will I accept Vincent's excuses or lies. No more will I avoid situations. No more will I put approval ahead of happiness.*'

"And there's another exercise," Neide said writing the words '*not to do list*' on the flipchart. "So as well as your to do list for the day or the week, you write out your not to do list, everything you are not going to do."

"Oh I like that one Neide," Suzy said. "Mine would be a long list."

"Now I see Ran outside. Why don't we take a quick ten minute break?"

Katherine and Suzy stayed behind with Serendipity to help set up.

"Let me give you a hand with that." Ran glided into the room taking the easel Katherine was struggling to erect. His aftershave immediately transported her back to the dance floor the night before.

"How did your meeting go?" Katherine asked.

"Looks like I'll be heading to Madrid in a few weeks, he thinks he can get the Thyssen-Bornemisza interested in including my work in an exhibition next February."

"That's a prestigious venue."

"I wanted to jump up and down but I played it cool. How are you after last night?"

"More tired than anything."

"Oh I heard all about last night, we're jealous we didn't get an invite," Suzy said putting the boxes of paint on the table.

Katherine left them chatting and dashed to her room to retrieve the painting she had started the morning before. She returned two minutes later, perfumed and excited.

***

Serendipity handed out paint splattered smocks. Katherine's had a tear down the side. Her carefully chosen, figure-enhancing blouse was now hidden by a plastic poncho that had seen better days. She chose the easel closest to the door.

"First of all folks my apologies for the late start," Ran said. "It's been a crazy week and I know I've messed up your schedule." Who could ever hold anything against that smile and those eyes Katherine thought? "Anyway, are we all set for part two? My intention for this afternoon is to share some tips and insights that will allow you to connect with your inner artist, whether you're a raw beginner who has never held a brush or someone a little more experienced." Katherine was delighted to be singled out by his glance. "I want you all to enjoy yourselves."

"I haven't held a paintbrush in my life," Morag said.

"You painted your front room before Easter." Louise laughed.

"Remember what we spoke about yesterday morning, it's not about doing anything perfectly. It's about enjoying the process. If yesterday's session was creativity or creation if you will, then today's is all about recreation, play. You can paint anything you like. Louise I know you have some final touches to make to your landscape. Katherine you have yours to finish as well. And if you're seeking inspiration, here's an idea, paint what you feel this retreat, these workshops mean to you?"

"Now that's an interesting proposition," Bruce said, paintbrush already in hand and with his beard and glasses perched on his nose, he looked every inch an artist.

"Sort of painting from the unconscious then?" Corinne said.

"Exactly, just allow yourself to paint what you're thinking, feeling, what you want to express," Ran said.

"I might end up with a Jackson Pollock?" Bruce said.

"So get stuck in, have fun with it and call me if you need me."

Arms reached for the tubes of paints spread out on the table. Plastic beakers were filled at the water fountain. Rainbows of colours were squeezed onto makeshift palettes. Katherine held back and stared at the painting she had started at the creativity workshop. She had got used to the purple circles, inspired by the shadows of the volcanic peaks.

At first she was distracted by the gusts of wind blowing her page, so with everyone's consent she pulled over the sliding door. Then she was distracted by Corinne who was using her whole arm to sweep dark green arcs over her page. She twisted her easel around and squeezed a dab of black onto her palette. She drew three vertical lines in the centre of the swirls, she wasn't quite sure why. At all times she was aware of where Ran was and who he was speaking with. After leaving Suzy laughing he moved to her corner.

"I think I'm stuck. I don't know if it's finished?" Katherine asked.

"Step away from it for a few minutes. Maybe even start something new then come back to it. Or think of it this way Katherine, what's trying to come into form on your page and is it there yet?"

"I'm not sure."

"Leave it for now. When I feel stuck I just try to paint my way through it. So don't try to paint Katherine, just paint and have fun."

Katherine took a swig from her water bottle.

"Listen up folks. As I'm moving around the room I'm hearing a lot of self criticism," Ran said leaning against the table. "Remember perfectionism is the enemy. The part of the brain that makes art and the part that judges art are separate. This is not about being perfect, it's about having fun, expressing ourselves with paint. Let your inner artist shine." There was a rustle of paper as Sophie and Tonya tore off their pages and started afresh. "Too often we are our own worst enemies, when really we need to be our own advocates."

Katherine doodled and splashed paint on a new page. She closed her eyes to access the magnificent view from the villa. She used nearly every shade of blue available to her, but like many more accomplished artists before her; she struggled to recreate the intense blue of the sea. Everyone else was absorbed in their creations. Katherine was frustrated because she desperately wished to impress Ran.

"Making progress?" Ran asked, leaning on the chair beside her.

"It's just not flowing today and I was so looking forward to this class."

"You are putting too much pressure on yourself Katherine. Remember what I was saying about all great art coming from the inside out. Start again and just paint what you're feeling, there will be nothing more authentic."

"Even if I'm feeling aaargh."

"Exactly, paint that aaargh." Ran laughed.

***

Katherine examined the swirling colours, the red, green and purple spirals on her page. It wasn't anything in particular but she had enjoyed the feel of the paint being transferred from brush to page. The time hadn't flown like it had when she was painting on the deck, but it had been an enjoyable few hours with plenty of light-hearted banter bouncing around the room.

Corinne had painted a tree, a web of branches fanning across the page. She said it just came into form and she thought it really symbolised what she was learning at The Retreat, stretching for the light, branching in new directions, whilst staying firmly rooted to the ground.

Ran invited everyone to bring their easels into a circle. Katherine congratulated Louise on finishing her landscape, a decent representation of the walls of the retreat and the expansive view from the deck. Serendipity had painted a butterfly which Katherine felt was the most accomplished piece in the room. She was at Art College after all.

Imelda's painting was full of bright bold colours. There was something childlike about it, an innocent playfulness that reflected the personality of the woman who painted it.

"Just like life, God chose the frame but I coloured it in," Imelda said.

"I like that," Ran said. "Daily experiences colour the canvas of our lives, but I'm the one with the brush in my hand."

Bruce had made a very decent attempt at a lighthouse and apart from Corinne's tree, everyone else had painted something abstract, their representation of what The Retreat meant to them. Katherine was more than a little perplexed about what was going on inside some of their heads.

"Remember we never have to explain our work," Ran said. "It's up to the viewer to interpret what they see for themselves. Just like a novel starts in the writer's imagination and finishes in the reader's, a painting starts with the artist's eye and is completed through the eyes of the viewer."

After a round of applause to recognise each other's efforts and a second ovation to thank Ran, Serendipity led the way in tidying up. She gathered the paint stained palettes to wash in the big sink in the kitchen. Smocks, with an additional veneer of use, were folded and replaced in the cupboard.

Katherine stayed where she was. Clipping her first painting to the easel she knew now what was needed to complete it. She added a dark vertical line, a simple stroke at the bottom of the page. Now it was finished. The one small adjustment transformed the great blobs of colour into the petals of a flower. The black lines she had added earlier were the stamens at the heart of the bloom. Some viewers might even see them as people in silhouette, facing a violet sunset.

"I might stay for a little while," Katherine said to Corinne and Imelda.

"I'm going to try to get back before the rain," Corinne said, her painting in her arms. "If you think of anything else you need for tomorrow night just give me a call?"

"Thanks for everything." Katherine gave Corinne a hug. "You'd better get going; I can smell the rain on the air."

"The thirsty earth licking its lips," Imelda said, waving over her shoulder.

"I think this is finished now Ran?" Katherine said.

"Oh, it really pulls the eye in," he said, scratching his shoulder. "You should be proud of it. Well done."

"I'm going to stay here for a bit. Thanks again for everything Ran," Katherine said, consciously taking an inventory of him, so she could recreate him in her mind, handsome and dishevelled leaning against the glass door.

"I'll pop back in before I go. Oh no, here's the rain," Ran said, before bounding across the courtyard.

Dark clouds loomed overhead. Large drops began to fall. Gusts of wind attacked the palm tree in the cactus garden. Leaves and whole clumps of flowers were tossed around like boats ripped from their moorings. The terracotta pots in the courtyard darkened as if coloured by an unseen hand. And there was the first rumble of thunder. Katherine pulled the door tight. Bullet-like rain pounded the roof.

Katherine dragged her easel to the table. The entire spectrum of paints was within arm's reach. She had the place to herself. Now it was playtime.

Katherine took the biggest brush from the box. She ran her thumb over the soft bristles. Red, she wanted to use red, the darkest red. A series of wallops was the only way to describe the paint being applied. When done with the red, she threw two shades of blue onto the page. A flick of the wrist and a line of dark green rained across the canvas to be followed by a flourish of magenta.

If she had looked around Katherine would have seen large pools of water form in the courtyard and through the vertical rain see faces at the door of the dining room marvelling at the power of nature. But Katherine didn't turn around.

When the foundation she desired was in place, she took a smaller brush and slashed through the layers, pulling and dragging and swirling the paint, in one continuous frantic motion, her energy building all the time. She was attacking the canvas, her inhibitions and inner censor squashed.

But she needed more than paint. In ferocious abandon, Katherine ripped the bracelet from her arm, snapped the cord and watched the tiny plastic pearls fall into the palm of her hand. She pressed them into the spiralling funnel of colour. The brush became an extension of her arm and her arm an extension of she didn't know what. She wasn't painting, she was creating. All that existed was the brush, the paint, the canvas and an unseen energy.

Katherine didn't know how long she had been standing at the easel. When she looked around she was astounded that a lake had formed in the centre of the courtyard. Water gurgled down the drains. She flung open the door and inhaled the cleansed air.

"What a storm." Ran leaped over the pools of water and stepped inside. "Could you smell the lightning? Wow Katherine, have you just done that?"

Katherine couldn't find any words. With the brush still in her hand she walked over to him, and kissed him passionately.

CHAPTER 13

It was a kiss that represented an entirely different way of life, a life of passion, creativity and spontaneity. Katherine savoured the lingering pressure of Ran's lips. The pleasure was all consuming. There was no space for thinking, let alone misgivings. Katherine simply felt incredibly alive.

It was Ran who stepped back and turned away. Katherine stood motionless. Every nerve in her body tingled. The damp air from the courtyard mixed with the oily tang of paint; it was the smell of adultery. Words would not serve her now, so she remained silent. In that moment she was willing to pay whatever it cost to retain the exhilarating feeling.

Ran smiled and brushed her arm, then sat on the table, pushing the tubes of paint to one side. Katherine felt as if she had shed a skin, layers of disappointment and drudgery discarded in a heap around her ankles. She felt new and powerful, a woman reborn.

Voices drifted in from across the courtyard, encroaching on the world just the two of them inhabited. Through the glass doors, Katherine became aware of figures dashing left and right, splashing through puddles. She could hear her name being called. It felt like she had forgotten to breathe. If she inhaled now, she wasn't sure what emotions would consume her.

"That was some storm, did you hear the thunder? The roof hasn't leaked again, has it?" Serendipity bounded into the room. Barefoot, she left footprints in her wake as she inspected the mural on the far wall for water damage.

"Look at what Katherine has painted. What do you think?" Ran said.

"Fab colours. And what are these you've stuck into the

paint, little beads? I love it." Serendipity flung her arms around Katherine. "You'll have to show the others, Neide will be so impressed."

"There's real passion in it, isn't there?" Ran said looking at Katherine.

"Beginner's luck," Katherine said joining them in front of the easel. She struggled to take her eyes from Ran.

Whilst painting, she didn't really see what she was doing, she felt it, now she forced herself to scrutinise her work with a critical eye. Three cyclones of paint, giant drops of colour and motion, red, deep purple and green were suspended on the white canvas. Katherine didn't know whether it merited Ran and Serendipity's praise, but she did find it pleasing to the eye. Had Serendipity or any of the others seen her kiss Ran she wondered.

"It really reminds me of the work of James Nares. Have you heard of him?" Ran said, hand on chin.

"Katherine you'll have to get this framed. There's a gallery just up the town that will do it for you and they're very reasonable," Serendipity said, leaning in to examine the brushstrokes.

As Ran inspected her painting, Katherine inspected Ran for clues as to what he was thinking. He had participated in the kiss, hadn't he? He didn't push her away. She hoped for a hint of lust in his eyes, but he was giving nothing away, only pride in a student who had exhibited talent.

"I think all this painting has me worn out and last night is catching up with me too," Katherine said, starting to tidy up.

"I'll finish putting everything away Katherine," Serendipity said, returning to the far wall and running her hand over the mural. "I think we've got away with it this time."

"Room 12," Katherine whispered to Ran. She dashed to the sink with her brushes and beaker before he had time to react.

"Katherine I'll do that, don't worry about it," Serendipity said, arranging the chairs back into their familiar semi-circle.

The storm clouds had released a censured sun. Katherine tip-toed across the courtyard avoiding the deepest puddles and clumps of dislodged bougainvillea. She slipped on a pile of sodden leaves and prayed that Ran wasn't still looking her way.

She dumped her bag on the bed and went straight to the bathroom to brush her teeth and apply a fresh layer of scent. Was she out of her mind? The madness of how she felt in the workshop was subsiding fast, but she was still ravenous for Ran's affections. Her heart pounded in her chest. She opened another button of her blouse and sat on the bed.

The heady cocktail of nervousness and excitement reminded her of another time she sat on the edge of a bed. As unfashionable as it was, she had been a virgin on her wedding day. Back then, a chorus of voices, an amalgam of her mother's, her sister Joan's and her form teacher Sister Philomena's, a resilient trio who preached the sinful dangers of pre-marital sex had prevented her from sleeping with Vincent before they were married. Those voices echoed now.

How times have changed. Katherine knew Claire had slept with at least two previous boyfriends, though it was never discussed openly. The closest they got was the one time Katherine had asked her daughter if she was being careful. A blasé shrug of the shoulders put an end to the conversation. She never wanted to think about what Thom got up to. He didn't have a steady boyfriend and perhaps that was worse. At fifty-one, Vincent was the only man Katherine had ever slept with.

Truth be known, twenty-six years ago she couldn't wait for their wedding reception to end. A two year engagement was two years of foreplay. She was the one who had assembled the archway of shoeless women and tieless men so they could get upstairs to the bridal suite. Many people say that their first time was somewhere between a disaster and underwhelming disappointment, but not Katherine. For many years sex with Vincent was fantastic and frequent. Then children, chores and complacency transformed what was once passionate and unpredictable into something too courteous and routine. Now when Vincent was in the mood her first thought was that she would have to change the sheets.

Perched on the bed she couldn't be sure if Ran would knock on the door and she wasn't completely sure that she wanted him to. Katherine realised she was trembling. She refused to countenance the questioning, the responsible, the logical voice in her head that was desperate to be heard. She locked it away and hid the key in the details of the room.

She jumped when her phone began to ring. She rummaged for it in her bag. Vincent's name lit up the display.

Katherine stared at the vibrating phone. The familiar ringtone and Vincent's name was a thread back to the real world, the world where she was a responsible married woman and parent with worries and concerns. She couldn't answer it, not now. It seemed to ring forever. She left it on the bed and went to the window. Ran was walking across the courtyard.

Eventually the phone stopped. It pinged to let her know Vincent had left a voicemail at the same moment Ran tapped on the door. She resumed her spot on the bed and flung the phone back into her bag.

"It's open." Katherine was surprised she sounded as calm as she did. It felt like she was about to leap from a high precipice and there was no safety net.

"I couldn't just go without saying goodbye," Ran said, looking over his shoulder.

Katherine knew straightaway that nothing was going to happen between them. He remained standing at the door.

"Well done again on the painting, I think you've really connected with something."

"I have to thank you for that," Katherine said.

"Nonsense, I just gave you a bit of encouragement." Ran shifted his stance. "Speaking of encouragement. I hope I didn't..."

"You don't have to say anything Ran. I'm sorry I threw myself at you like that. I don't know what came over me."

"There's no need to apologise, you were caught up in the moment."

"I don't know what I was thinking." Katherine felt embarrassed but relieved. The hopeful tension, the weighty expectation of sex had vanished. She could breathe again.

"You're an attractive woman Katherine and I've really enjoyed getting to know you."

"There's a but coming isn't there?" Katherine looked at her bare feet then slipped them back into her sandals.

"I've taken up many invitations over the years Katherine and I've done many things I'm not proud of and whilst your kiss was lovely, it just wouldn't be right, not for me anyway, not anymore." Katherine could see he was almost as embarrassed as she was. "I've a girlfriend back in Israel, and this time I want to make a go of it."

"You never mentioned her before." Katherine regretted the words as soon as they spewed from her mouth. He had no reason to share details of his personal life and she had no right to ask.

"Norma." Ran reached for his phone and showed Katherine a picture of a young blonde with braided hair wearing cut-off jeans. She was exactly the sort of woman that would be Ran's girlfriend, tanned, attractive and with perfect teeth. Even twenty years ago Katherine could never have competed with her. Now Katherine just wanted Ran to leave.

"Your son?" Katherine nodded at the bare-chested boy of about ten sitting at the woman's feet.

"Norma's son, Jessie, but we all live together." Ran slid the phone back into the pocket of his jeans that hung low on his hips. "Friends?"

Katherine nodded. For a split second she was tempted to fling herself at him. It was the way he dropped his head then looked up. But she had a modicum of dignity left. She would satisfy herself by picturing him standing by her door, with that exact expression. It would be a difficult image to erase from her mind when her head was on the pillow.

"God knows I'm no expert on relationships Katherine, but if I've learnt anything it's that falling into bed with someone else only multiples your problems. And yes the other person may never find out, but you will know."

"I'm old enough to know better too," Katherine muttered. She felt old and stupid. He must see her as just another middle-aged woman starved of affection.

"Now promise me you'll keep painting. One day I want to be able to come to one of your exhibits and say I helped kick-start this artist's career."

Katherine laughed at the idea, but nodded along.

"Sorry again for pouncing on you like that."

"You did take me by surprise." Ran laughed.

"I really don't know what came over me."

"You were just on a high. It's a fantastic feeling isn't it when the paint just flows from the brush. You connected with a part of yourself you had forgotten, that creative, free spirit and once you've unlocked that door Katherine there's no going back. But you have to keep picking up that paintbrush."

Katherine forced a smile.

"Look, I have to go, but here's my card. Drop me an email and let me know how you're getting on from time to time. I mean it."

Ran bent and kissed her cheek then he was gone, closing the door behind him. Katherine stayed where she was his business card in her lap. His scent lingered in the air.

***

Katherine felt numb, but numb was better than mortified. She eventually reached for her bag and switched on her phone. There was a text from Thom saying he would pop over on Sunday. Claire would be back from France too and the thought of both her children under her roof, for at least a few hours, buoyed her spirits. She then dialled voicemail.

"Kay, sorry I missed you and I know you rang the office too. Back to back meetings all day, sure give me a call when you get this. Hope all's well."

Katherine listened to it a second time. Vincent sounded more animated than usual. She couldn't help thinking that she was listening to an actor playing her husband, repeating lines from a well-rehearsed script. If she phoned him back now she wouldn't know what to say.

The room grew darker. The sun retreated from the courtyard. Katherine felt she had to get out. The instinct to walk, to clear her head pushed her from the bed and out the door. She managed to slip unnoticed by Morag and Louise who were hovering by the dining table.

Two cats languished outside the gates in a pocket of fading sunshine. The ground was still wet and the patches of cobblestones were slippery. Long shadows stretched into the laneways of the old town. An elderly woman, dressed head to toe in black temporarily stopped mopping her front step as Katherine passed.

The sun was losing its grip on the day, in an hour it would be gone. It was a more pleasurable stroll than the last time Katherine meandered through the side streets. On that first morning the sun was fierce and the town was packed with tourists for the Sunday market.

Her artist's eye appreciated the evening light, the shadow of a tree, an illuminated door. She took a few photos with her phone and enjoyed the peace of the deserted town. Paying attention to her surroundings, she told herself she was living in the present, but really she was avoiding stoking the furnace of her own thoughts.

She crossed the square where the market had been held, its only occupants now two local men who stood examining a car, hands deep in their pockets they intermittently kicked its wheels in that universal male language. The world was going about its business and would continue to do so irrespective of whatever Katherine thought about the eventful day.

She found herself drawn to the church at the top of the square. The main door was shut, but a side door was ajar. It was as much architectural curiosity as it was religious compunction that made her step inside. Katherine was greeted by old cold air trapped by the thick stone walls. The faded scent of candles immediately stirred feelings of reverence and contemplation. She moved slowly towards a side altar reluctant to disturb the heavy silence.

Katherine had long since dropped the habit of Sunday Mass. Vincent had never been religious and though Katherine made the effort especially when the children were young, Christmas and occasionally Easter were the only times she adhered to a commandment of her youth. However she would often pop into a church if passing, just to light a candle and take a few minutes respite from the franticness of life.

The side altar was dedicated to the Virgin Mary. Katherine dropped a coin into a slot on the wall and lit a candle whilst saying a Hail Mary. She then slipped into the first pew and knelt. She recited the Our Father to herself but got stuck on the penultimate line 'and lead us not into temptation'.

Dominating the main altar was a painting of Jesus on the Cross, a traditional interpretation of the crucifixion that didn't dilute the gore. It was an image that must frighten young children. As a child if she had misbehaved her mother would stand her in front of the picture of the Sacred Heart over their fireplace and make her look at the image of Jesus and say she was sorry. If she had been particularly bold her mother would say that her behaviour hammered more nails into his hands and feet.

A mother and young boy came into the church. The boy crumpled his cap in his hands. In an instant Katherine felt the loss of her own mother. It was almost a year since the doctor said she only had a few months. She saw another Christmas, which on more than one occasion her mother knowingly declared would be her last, rang in the New Year, then during the night of the twelfth day of Christmas, January 6th she died in her sleep. When the phone rang at ten past seven that bleak January morning Katherine knew exactly the ordeal that lay ahead.

The woman left taking her son by the hand. Hanging her head in her hands Katherine prayed for guidance and peace. When she sat back, her body felt heavy on the pew. Tiredness from the long and eventful day couldn't be kept at bay. She said another prayer for a good night's sleep and for all her family, including Vincent.

Closing her eyes, Katherine allowed the stillness of the place to envelop her. She felt her centre of gravity shifting down into her hips. The wooden bench wasn't the most comfortable, but she was quite happy to stay where she was for a while. A warm feeling settled in her chest.

***

"Katherine." There was a gentle tap on her arm. Katherine jumped.

"Imelda." The elderly ex-nun had slipped silently into the pew behind her.

"Oh I'm sorry, I didn't mean to startle you," Imelda whispered.

"No, you're fine."

"Beautiful church, isn't it? I've popped in a few times during the week."

"Very peaceful. I like these old style churches."

"Are you sure I'm not disturbing you?"

"No I was just sitting here; I've said my few prayers."

"When I was in Asia last year I got talking to a young man, a Buddhist monk, well a trainee I think, outside one of the temples in Cambodia, oh he had such a lovely face and a real mischievous grin. Bless him, he wanted to practice his English. After talking about Manchester United football club, of which I knew little, somehow the topic of prayer came up. I'll never forget it, in all his innocence he said isn't prayer just wanting to be freed from fear."

"He might be right," Katherine said.

"That stayed with me. I can still see his face. Then the next moment he asked me if I had ever met David Beckham."

A rattling noise from the back of the church caught their attention.

"I think that man wants to lock up," Katherine said. Over Imelda's shoulder a tall man with dark hair and a black jacket, but not a priest's collar, was jangling a weighty set of keys.

"If we hurry there's something I want to show you I think you'll like."

Imelda stepped into the aisle and genuflected. Katherine followed suit. The man busied himself as they passed. As soon as they were outside the door closed with a thud behind them.

"Where are we heading?" Katherine asked, keeping up with Imelda's brisk pace.

"You'll see."

Darkness was creeping through the town. They crossed a small park with stone benches.

"This is my favourite spot; I discovered it a few days ago," Imelda said. They had reached an elevated spot at the edge of the town where the entire island seemed to be laid out before them. The sun was sinking fast between the volcanic peaks and the western sky was aflame with every shade of orange, red and pink.

"What a view," Katherine said, easing herself onto the wall. "There's The Retreat." Off to the right Katherine could see the white walls of The Retreat and the deck where she had painted with Louise.

"Spectacular, isn't it?" Imelda said.

They sat in silence breathing in the majestic view. The sky condensed to crimson, then lavender, then midnight blue. Imelda pointed out Venus, the first star in the sky. A sliver of a moon hung low over the amphitheatre of summits. It had been a long and eventful day. Katherine had seen the sun rise in Playa Blanca and now she was watching it set in Teguise.

"Funny, I've always loved to watch the sun go down on holidays, preferably with a gin and tonic, but I couldn't tell you the last time I watched a sunset at home," Katherine said.

"We're too busy, aren't we? Sunsets always remind me of my place in the world and how small we really are, and how small our problems are in the bigger scheme of things."

"True." Katherine rubbed her arms. The earlier storm had left a chill in the air.

"It's only when our mind is at peace that we can see the beauty in the world around us, marvel at the immensity of views like this, see God in action."

"Sorry?"

"Oh, it's just something I say, God in action. I think of God as a verb not just a noun, so when I see sights like this I always think there's God in action."

"I like that."

"And it's funny too that we don't complain that the sky is

not orange enough or that the sun would be better if it set just a little further to the left." Imelda chuckled. "Everything is always as it should be."

"And of course we trust that the sun will come up in a few hours' time," Katherine said, smiling to herself. It felt like her little prayer in the church had been answered, this time by Imelda's words. Trust because everything will work out, my problems are tiny in the bigger scheme of things and the sun will come up tomorrow.

"My arms are getting a little cold Imelda, will we head back? It's lentil burgers tonight I believe."

"Lentils always give me wind, too hard to digest. I'm looking forward to tomorrow night though, are you all set?" Imelda said, linking Katherine's arm.

"Ready as I'll ever be."

"Sure we'll have a ball and we're not going to starve."

The two women retraced their steps past the church and across the square which was eerily quiet.

"Are you glad you volunteered for that exercise with Neide earlier, you seemed to get a lot from it?" Imelda asked.

"I have to say it got me thinking of the whole situation with Vincent differently, maybe a little more compassionately."

"Did you manage to speak to him?"

"No, and then I missed him when he rang back. I'll try him again now when I get back."

"Marriage difficulties or countries at war, nothing is ever resolved unless we talk. Oh I heard Serendipity rave about your painting."

"I don't know what was going on Imelda, maybe it was the storm, but I just lost myself in it. It was so freeing. I felt like a new woman."

"Good for you"

They stopped to look in the window of a craft shop. A pendant caught Katherine's eye, a green stone in the shape of

215

a teardrop. She peered closer to see the price, handwritten on a tiny sticker. "I think it says forty-five euros. That is a euro sign? I hope it's not four hundred and fifty."

"No point in me looking I don't have my glasses."

"I might pop back when it's open."

"That's what I like about the little shops around here, they're full of handcrafts, it's not all stuffed camels."

"Something like that would be a lovely reminder of this week," Katherine said.

"It's hard to believe tomorrow is our last full day. Where has the time gone?" Imelda said now linking Katherine's arm again.

"Now all I have to do is apply all my learning."

"You're right, knowing is one thing, doing is quite another."

"I know I need to sort things out with Vincent but sometimes Imelda and I probably shouldn't say this, but sometimes I feel like just running away from it all, starting a new life, in a new place where no one knows me and I could just be myself."

"What stops you being yourself right now?"

"Now I am myself and I certainly had fun painting earlier, but back home, I don't know."

"What's that Shakespeare quote? There's nothing either good or bad, but thinking makes it so. Sometimes we make life more complicated than it really is."

"It must have been a very tough decision for you to leave the convent? You don't mind me asking do you?"

"I prayed on it for months, years even."

"And how did you know it was the right decision?"

"I didn't, but I suppose I just couldn't ignore the voice in my head and the feeling that I wanted something different. If something keeps niggling away, we have to pay attention to it. The way I see it now is why would we get the ideas, why is that whispering voice there in our head, unless it's a signpost to something bigger and better."

"Back to trusting ourselves I suppose."

"And trusting that life is unfolding for us just as it's meant to unfold, and that God has something even bigger and brighter in store for us."

"That's a nice way of thinking."

"When I finally made the decision to leave the order, I felt lighter, that's the only way I can describe it. It was literally like a weight had been lifted. Maybe that's the only way I knew I was making the right decision." They turned into the alleyway to The Retreat. "If there is one piece of advice Katherine that I can share with you." Imelda stopped at the gate.

"I'll take whatever I can get."

"If you are feeling stuck and yearning for something different, a way forward or a way out of a situation, I always think we have to find a way in. The answers you seek are on the inside Katherine, in here," Imelda said, touching her heart. "The answers are always on the inside."

***

Most of the group had assembled at the dining table in the courtyard. Imelda joined them immediately. Katherine had a phone call to make. Strangely, this time her phone had perfect signal. She rang their home number, but the answering machine clicked in. Eight thirty on a Wednesday, she thought Vincent would have been at home. She didn't countenance the witnesses for the prosecution lining up in her mind. He answered his mobile on the second ring.

"Ah there you are it's been voicemail tennis today. How's it going?" Katherine was pleasantly surprised by his upbeat tone. She stopped pacing the room and sat on the bed.

"Good, there was a massive thunderstorm earlier; it's cleared the air though. How are things with you? I tried phoning home."

"I'm still at the office."

"At this time?"

"Meetings all day and a few people are out sick. The week is going well?"

"You know Vincent I'm so glad I came here. I know it was a last minute thing, but I have to say I think it's really doing me good."

"I'm glad Kay, you deserve the break."

"And the people are really nice. I ended up at the opening of an art exhibition last night."

"Not all tree huggers then."

"I'll have a few stories to tell you."

"And here's me slaving away at the desk."

Katherine thought of telling Vincent about Neide's partner's name, but such conversations are better related in person. "Was Claire in touch? I sent her a text but didn't get a reply."

"I spoke to her yesterday."

"How is she?"

"You know Claire, it is hard to get anything from her, but she sounded fine. If she was on the phone for a minute that was it."

"Thom texted to say he'll be over Sunday."

"Good."

"You must be hungry, or have you had your dinner?"

"Oh I'll get a Chinese on the way. Have you cooked your meal there yet?"

"Tomorrow night. I have to say I'm looking forward to it, everyone is chipping in."

"Well as long as you're enjoying yourself."

"I am and I've been doing some painting as well."

"I've been saying for ages you should be painting, you've always enjoyed it."

Katherine didn't remember Vincent encouraging her to pick up her brushes, but it was nice of him to say.

"Well I better let you finish up. Is anyone else there with you?"

"Not at this hour."

"Well, I'll give you a call on Thursday; my flight isn't in until late."

"I'll pick you up."

"Are you sure?"

"Of course, you've done it for me often enough."

"Vincent?"

"What?"

"Oh nothing."

"By the way Joan left another message on the answer machine. Did you get back to her?"

"Damn I forgot, I'll phone her now. Did she say what she wanted?"

"You know Joan, always cryptic."

"She'll be giving out about something."

***

Katherine stretched out on the bed. Not two hours ago she'd been willing to sleep with another man, now she had had the most civil conversation with her husband in weeks.

It was as if there was a lever in her head. Pull it back and she was the reliable, responsible Katherine, the familiar version of herself that could give Vincent the benefit of the doubt, focus on the good times they have had, and remember like everyone else he's doing his best. Push the lever forward and she was the carefree, spontaneous and passionate woman who could paint with abandon and kiss whoever she wanted.

Somewhat reluctantly Katherine dialled Joan's home number, there was no point in ringing her mobile she rarely had it on. Conversations with Joan were seldom pleasurable; she was usually moaning about something. It was easier to acknowledge her feelings of frustration and annoyance when she thought of Joan than the sadness that lay beneath them. Katherine knew she wasn't her sister's keeper and that Joan was well capable of making her own decisions, but Joan was the one who was still at home when their father died and she had stayed so their mother wouldn't be alone.

"Joan, sorry I'm only getting back to you now. I'm in Lanzarote for the week."

"So I heard, alright for some." Joan's voice had no humour in it. There was no 'are you enjoying your holiday', no 'what's the weather like', no asking after the family, she didn't even ask who she was away with. Katherine knew that from Joan's perspective such enquiries would somehow signal her approval of Katherine's flamboyant lifestyle, something Joan commented on every time they spoke. "There's a few things to sort out with the solicitor, when can you come down?"

"I'll check with Vincent when I'm back, but maybe the middle of next week if it's urgent." Making plans beyond the end of the week seemed surreal; a reminder to Katherine that life continued outside The Retreat.

"Let me know and I'll make the appointment, there's stuff to sign. And I've been going through the last of Mammy's things."

"I thought we'd done all that."

"There's all those boxes in the attic. If you want I can sort them out, most of it is probably for dumping anyway. I'm looking into getting the attic converted."

"You should make the house your own." Katherine never had any issue with Joan being left the house, after all she had lived in it her whole life, but somehow Joan thought that she did.

"I'm sure I won't be able to afford it." Sooner or later the conversation with Joan always came around to money. She had lost her carer's allowance and their mother's pension, but she was back full time at the tax office now and she had inherited the house, but Joan's gripe was that their mother didn't leave her any cash. When the funeral expenses were paid, the few grand their mother had in the bank would come to Katherine.

"Was there anything of interest in the attic?" Katherine asked in an effort to steer the conversation.

"Some books worth keeping. There's a few boxes of stuff that must have been Kay's which I haven't touched yet."

"Kay's?"

"It must have been put up there when the old house was sold. I've been getting young Pat from next door to help me, there's no one else I can ask, I can't be dragging and lugging everything myself."

"What sort of stuff?"

"Old newspapers, photographs, copies, some of our old school books. I don't think Mam ever threw anything away. But sure we can't live in the past," Joan said. Katherine knew it wasn't easy dismantling the cherished memories and possessions of someone's life. It had been painful helping Joan sort through their mother's wardrobe and cabinets.

Katherine listened to Joan speak, interjecting with the appropriate 'okay' or 'poor you' or 'that's awful', when she spoke about someone in the town dying. Vincent often joked that Joan was a professional funeral goer.

"I'm not going to be charged for this call, am I?" Joan said abruptly.

"No, I phoned you."

"Anyway I'd better go, so you'll be down this day week."

Katherine sensed that if she didn't do something to improve their relationship, after her mother's will was sorted out, they would probably lose contact completely and Katherine didn't want that. Joan was her only link to the past, to her life before Vincent and the children. Katherine resolved to make a conscious effort to get to Tramore the following week and perhaps on the plane home she would do the relationship enhancing exercise she did with Neide, this time focusing on Joan.

As she freshened up before joining the others, it wasn't Joan that occupied Katherine's thoughts, it was her aunt Kay and the boxes in Joan's attic.

Chapter 14

It was not a gentle awakening, a gradual return to consciousness, the morning light soothing and stroking her awake. It was the equivalent of being slapped. Katherine bolted upright, her t-shirt plastered to her back. She rubbed the sleep and congealed mascara from her eyes. Her mouth was dry and her top lip cracked. She gulped the last mouthful of water from the bottle by the bed. She was hungover.

Just one more night before she was back in her own bedroom with Vincent. That thought had played in a loop in her head between three and four a.m. A series of half dreams and wanderings followed. Far from refreshed, Katherine hauled herself to the window. The now familiar sight of Imelda, a woman twenty years her senior, stretching to greet the morning sun, made her feel even more inadequate.

She had dreamt that Vincent had been in the room with her, standing by the door just as Ran had done. In the dream Vincent was talking but she couldn't hear him. Then just before she woke she had been consumed by dread, convinced that someone was in the bed beside her. Even now it seemed so real, a heavy arm across her chest, pinning her down. Immobile, she had been afraid to even move her head.

Outside the brazen sun erased the remaining puddles from the previous evening's downpour. Katherine rubbed her temples; her head ached, she shouldn't have had the wine last night. The thought that in a few hours she had to prepare an evening meal for twelve struck her like a blow. She wanted to crawl back under the crumpled sheet. She felt exhausted and it was only eight fifteen.

The trickle of water from the shower did little to refresh her.

And this week was supposed to have been about clean living, detoxing the body and mind, feeling lithe and energised from the yoga at dawn, and serene from daily meditations. Katherine felt wretched. Drying herself, she rummaged in her bag for paracetamol. Cursing the empty water bottle she swallowed them dry. She didn't care whether it was macrobiotic or not, she needed a bucket of coffee and a mound of toast.

Getting dressed, she remembered she had dreamt again that she had been on the harbour in Tramore slipping and sliding on the green algae, feeling scared and powerless that she would fall into the sea. It must have been the conversation with Joan and the discovery of her aunt Kay's boxes in her sister's attic that stirred the unconscious. Like before, a fisherman in a boat had reached out to her. This time she could see the face as well as the strong arms. It was Bruno.

Scrutinising her refection Katherine decided she needed more than lipstick to face the day. Bruno's workshop started in an hour. She didn't like the way she had left him when he had passed comment on her handbag. He was a good man, if a little loud and direct. He didn't deserve her cold shoulder.

***

"Nothing like re-toxifying, is there?" Declan said from behind dark glasses. "Suzy's in a bad way, she's demanding breakfast in bed."

"You two were evil opening that wine," Katherine said. "I thought you were saving it for tonight."

"As if we held you down and prised open your mouth." Declan laughed. "We'll just have to get more."

"How can you even think of that now?"

"Take this." Balancing some fruit and bread on a plate Declan handed Katherine a multivitamin. "For the hectic lifestyle. Always works for me."

Katherine poured a cup of water and watched the orange tablet fizz and bubble. Its fruity zestiness was a welcome pick me up.

"Keep us both a pew won't you?" Declan said a plate in each hand as he headed back to his room.

Across the courtyard Bruno was setting up. Even if her head didn't throb she would need sunglasses to look at his shirt, a colour combination even more garish than she'd seen him in before. She remembered a phrase her mother used to utter, red and green should never be seen. He appeared to be alone, so Katherine seized the moment.

"Any of those peaches left?" Bruno said, stacking a pile of his books.

"Plenty but I'm keeping them for later." Katherine picked up a book with a bright yellow cover titled *Souled* the one Corinne said she had read. "I'll have to buy some of these later." The picture of Bruno on the back was a flattering one. "How did your trip go yesterday with your daughter?"

"We had a fantastic day. Did the grand tour, Timanfaya, the caves, had a great walk along the beach at Papagayo, even the thunderstorm was fun. We were soaked through, but we had such a laugh. A day for the memory banks for sure."

The way Bruno pronounced the words 'fantastic' and 'sure' betrayed his New York roots.

"I've never heard thunder like it," Katherine said, replacing the book. There were no prices on any of them.

"I believe some of you had a late one last night. It's party central with you Katherine, isn't it?"

"Oh don't talk. The anti-detox retreat. I mightn't be the most alert person this morning."

"I'll go easy on you then."

"I think I'll need a holiday when I get home. Anyway I'll leave my bag here and I'll be back in a few minutes," Katherine said.

"And a lovely bag it is too."

Katherine smiled as she walked back across the courtyard to finish her breakfast.

***

Twenty minutes later the semi-circle of chairs was fully occupied. It was the largest group of the week. Neide and Iam were sitting in on the creative writing and self discovery workshop, as it was labelled in the schedule, and Serendipity had joined them too.

Katherine's headache had eased. The caffeine, carbs and Declan's multivitamin certainly helped. She sat on the far right to take full advantage of the fan. She had kept her bag on the seat beside her for as long as she could saving the spot for Corinne, but she relinquished it for Sophie who wanted to sit beside Tonya and Serendipity. For the first time all week Tonya wasn't dressed head to toe in black, a lilac blouse made her look less dour. The little girl accessories in shades of pink remained. She was still a mystery to Katherine.

Corinne was the last to arrive taking the one remaining chair beside Bruce. From across the room Katherine heard her describe the storm as black rain and how driving was more akin to sloshing upriver. She was going to excel at this workshop Katherine thought.

Neide said a few words of welcome and listed all of Bruno's books and urged everyone to buy some as they were on special offer, ten euros each. Katherine wondered how many she could squeeze into her suitcase without being charged for excess baggage.

"Who here feels they have a book in them, or who feels they have what it takes to write a book?" Bruno said swinging his legs under the table and allowing his flip-flops to fall to the floor.

Eyes darted around the room. Iam's hand was the first up,

followed by Marie and Neide. Katherine thought Corinne should have raised hers.

"I'd love to write a coaching book," Marie said. "I've been gathering material for years." And no doubt an extra chapter or two from what she has picked up here Katherine thought.

"Have you started writing it?" Bruno jumped from the table and swung a chair under him.

"Not really, a few articles that's about it."

"Morag, you always said your life story would make a great book." Louise nudged her friend.

"A horror story." Morag laughed.

"Well, this morning is not about turning you all into authors; it's about helping you find your voice as a writer, to use the written word as a form of expression. I know you've done some creativity workshops with Ran and from speaking with Neide I think this session will build on what's gone before."

Katherine felt silly when she thought of how she had flung herself at Ran. She was relieved that he had shown more sense than she had and thankful that he hadn't mocked her. His pity would have been unbearable. She could easily beat herself up over a moment of madness, but she was resolved not to.

"I wouldn't know what to write." It was Louise who spoke, voicing what many people were thinking.

"Oh, we'll get to all that. I'll be taking you through everything step by step. I like to use the analogy of erecting a building. I'll give you the scaffolding, but you'll build your story, your building as it were, paragraph by paragraph, storey by storey – pardon the pun – even brick by brick, word by word."

"I like that," Iam said, scribbling away in his notebook.

"But going back to what this lady said." Bruno nodded towards Louise. "Every writer at times will not know what to write; the horror of the blank page. But remember today is not about writing perfect prose, or penning prize-winning poetry, it's about having some fun with words and your imagination.

All I want you to be right now is a little curious. Curious as to what you will create by the time we're finished. Deal?"

"Sounds good," Imelda said, as perky as ever.

"Now what's rule one of writing do you think? Any takers?"

"Having an idea?" Iam said.

"Maybe," Bruno said.

"Knowing your audience," Bruce said, from his seat on the far left.

"Perhaps. From my perspective it's this." Bruno jumped from his chair knocking it over. "Write. It's about showing up. Loads of people have ideas, but nothing gets written until you sit down and write. You put the pen in your hand or you sit at the computer. That's true for you and your coaching book," Bruno said, looking at Marie. "Or for your memoir." He winked at Morag. "Now that doesn't mean the words will flow, but they will never flow if you're not sitting waiting. You have to show up before the muse shows up. There are many times when I have to bribe, bully and beg the words into being, but they will never appear on the page unless I have the page in my hand."

"That makes sense," Iam said. "Do you mind me asking Bruno what inspires you to write?"

Katherine hoped Iam wasn't going to monopolise the session.

"I write because I'm a writer, just like a dancer has to dance, a singer sing or a painter paint. I wouldn't be me unless I wrote. Does that make sense?"

Most of the room were nodding. The note takers, Iam, Bruce, Marie and Tonya were busy jotting down the words of wisdom.

"If you're asking me what inspires me, well inspiration can hit anytime. That's why I carry a notebook with me." Bruno rooted in his jacket. "My little black book, full of ideas, snippets of conversations, descriptions of scenes and people that I might be able to use again."

Katherine wondered if Bruno had noted anything about her.

"So, rule one for writing is to actually write, to grind out some words. So it's time for you to start writing. Here's our first little exercise. It's very short but it gets you started. I'm going to give you the first sentence of a short story and I want you to write a few lines, whatever pops into your head. Ready?"

Bruno returned to the flipchart. Pens and papers were poised.

"The woman stood by the table. That's your opening line."

"How much do we need to write?" Declan asked.

"I'm timing the exercise at five minutes max. Don't worry about word count, sometimes the best stories are the shortest. Don't worry about grammar or spelling either, just write what pops into your mind. Maybe you'll describe the woman, tell us what she's doing, why she's standing there, where the table is. Just go for it."

Katherine turned her journal around, she would write in the back of it. She copied down the first line and tried to picture the woman.

"Write." Bruno hollered at the reticent group. Sophie jumped in the seat beside her. "It's not about writing perfectly formed sentences, just write." Katherine did as she was told.

***

The five minutes went by quickly. Bruno walked behind the group and asked for a volunteer to share their story. He tapped Morag on the shoulder just as Iam's hand shot into the air.

"You were writing away, are you up for it?" Bruno asked.

"It's not very good," Morag said.

"Pack the judgement; tell us about this woman."

"I don't have to stand up, do I?" Morag cleared her throat. "Fine as you are."

"The woman stood by the table. She had volunteered to speak, but now that it was her turn, she could feel her legs shake. It was the first time

she had spoken at Toastmasters, and the group were encouraging, but the words wouldn't come. She took another sip of water, but it went against her breath and she began to cough. It was a disaster. She wished she had stayed at home and watched Eastenders."

Louise was giggling away. The group followed Bruno's lead and gave Morag a round of applause.

"Great effort. So who's next?" Bruno asked. The moment Katherine looked up, Bruno winked at her. "Katherine?"

"I think mine's a little depressing."

"All this expectation management, just read woman."

Katherine raised her journal.

"The woman stood by the table. She struggled to remove the car key from the bunch in her hand. She laid them purposely on the table which she had wiped clean one last time. There was no point in leaving a note. If she chose to, she could have heard the echoes of family laughter. She wouldn't prepare any more meals or hear any more laughter around this table. It was time to go. There was no one left to hear her footsteps in the hall, or the click of the front door as she closed it behind her."

There was a pause when she stopped, then applause, but not from Bruno. He looked deep in thought.

"It's probably no good, but it's what came to mind," Katherine said.

"I love it," Bruno said, now standing with one foot on his chair. "I really do, bravo. So many questions. Where's she going? Who's she leaving? Is she going to kill herself by starting the car with the key in the garage? I can hear the sounds of her shoes on the floor. That's really good Katherine. When your words stir the reader's or the listener's imagination, when you evoke an emotion, happy or sad, then you're onto something. I really like it. Well done."

Katherine looked down at her page. Bruno's praise was a welcome gift. She could feel herself expand with pride.

Sophie had everyone laughing because the woman in her story was trying to assemble the table, but unable to follow the instructions she ended up having to prop it against a wall. Neide then read hers about a woman preparing a meal. It reminded Katherine of the task that lay ahead.

"To keep on track we won't do any more shares for now if that's okay, but four great stories, it just shows the power of the imagination. Now to some extent we're always writing about ourselves. Sometimes it's obvious, like when Morag wrote about a personal experience. Sometimes we're drawing from a deeper well, the depths of our unconscious. I don't need any of you to share and I normally wouldn't even ask the question, but as you are on this retreat, it's useful to ponder how what you've written relates to you and your current situation.

Katherine rubbed her eyes and turned the page.

***

"That was just to warm you up, now we're going to move up a gear. This exercise is called 'My Life.'" Bruno wrote the words on the flipchart.

There was a groan from the room, Suzy's being the loudest.

"I'll put that rumbling down to the late night I believe some of you had," Bruno said, turning around.

"Maybe some people don't feel their story is worth telling?" Neide said.

"All our stories are worth telling," Bruno said. "And I think deep down we all want others to understand our stories. So what you're going to do for the next twenty minutes or so is to write about your life up to now."

"I might need more than twenty minutes." Imelda laughed. "I'm probably the combined age of many people in the room. It will have to be the abridged version."

"I'm not going to impose any restrictions, just write what feels right to you. Ignore the grammar and the spelling, just keep the pen moving. And like before, I've the first sentence for you." Bruno moved to the flipchart. "This time I want you to start with '*Once upon a time there was a girl or boy named…*' and fill in your name."

"Just like a fairy tale," Imelda said.

Suzy and Declan were giggling like schoolkids. "Is there a happy ending?" Suzy laughed.

"Now there's an interesting idea. You're the author, so only you will know," Bruno said.

"Isn't there a school of thought that's all about dropping our stories?" Iam said, in a tone that Katherine felt was more statement than question.

"We have to know our stories first," Bruno said.

"Will we have to read them aloud?" Louise asked.

"We might do some shares, perhaps in pairs, but only if you want to."

"Are we writing in the third person?" Corinne asked.

"Yes, I find that gives us perspective and works well for this exercise, but if you want to switch to the first person you can," Bruno said.

"Do we have to stay in the room?" Declan asked.

"Wander off if you want to, but not too far, there's a few little prompts and nudges I'll want to share with you as you write."

Chairs were pushed back and hands reached for the spare pages on the table. Katherine decided to stay where she was. The breeze from the fan was refreshing.

"Remember, don't censor yourself, just write, keep the pen moving, have fun with it. It's about you expressing your story," Bruno said, raising his voice to those spilling out into the courtyard.

Katherine worried that if a few lines of a short story betrayed so much of what she was thinking and feeling, what would a few paragraphs, where she was the main character reveal.

"Now don't just be descriptive, write about what you loved doing as a child, significant events when you were growing up, your first love," Bruno said, before he too stepped into the courtyard.

Katherine twisted her pen. It was a tough exercise. She copied down the sentence from the flipchart.

Once upon a time there was a girl named Katherine.

She grew up in Tramore, a holiday town beside the sea. Her parents ran a bed and breakfast during the summer months. She had one sister called Joan. Every Saturday she baked with her aunt Kay. She loved making apple tarts. The smell of cinnamon still reminds her of those happy times. Kay died when Katherine was ten. Her parents hardly spoke of it.

After school, Katherine went to catering college in Dublin. Shortly after her twenty-first birthday she met Vincent, a musician and budding politician. He was Katherine's first serious love. They married in 1987 and had two children, Thomas and Claire. Thom as he likes to be known is gay. Vincent inherited a business from his uncle. He made a great success of it. Katherine has a good life. In recent times, with the children no longer at home, she feels lonely.

Katherine stopped writing. She was getting bored. She reviewed the words on the page, corrected the odd spelling and added an adjective or two in an attempt to make it more exciting. Was that it, her life to date in two paragraphs? If it was a script for a movie it would never be made. Change the names and it could be any woman's story.

She hoped the fact that she had already shared with the group, would mean she would escape reading aloud this time.

"I was thinking, rather than reading aloud, I want you to spend a few minutes reviewing what you've written," Bruno said once everyone had settled again. "Imagine it's a novel or a screenplay, who are the main characters? Are you even the main character in the story of your life? Is there someone who played an important role in your life that you haven't mentioned? What are some of the main themes of your story? What were some good and some not so good decisions the main character made, you in other words? What lessons has the main character learnt?"

"They're good questions," Neide said.

"And all great stories have conflict. What's the conflict in your story? Is the conflict resolved? In some stories conflict resolution can happen in surprising ways. Without conflict there is no character, true for stories and for life." Bruno added.

"That's deep," Corinne said. "It's a great exercise."

"Oh we could go deeper than that Corinne. What have you edited out? Who have you edited out? And on the subject of stories, we tell ourselves stories all the time. If you are worried about something back home, that doesn't exist here, other than in a story in your head, perhaps it's just time to tell ourselves different stories." Katherine couldn't help thinking Bruno was addressing her. "But back to this exercise, take ten minutes to glance over what you've written and pull out the themes, the conflict, the patterns."

The two mugs of coffee and several glasses of water meant Katherine needed to visit the toilet. She took the opportunity to step out. Crossing the courtyard, it was the word conflict that she pondered. Conflict with Vincent, conflict with Joan, conflict with herself.

***

"Now for my favourite part of this exercise – the sequel. Here's the first sentence." Bruno bounded to the flipchart ripping off the previous page. "'*I left the retreat in Teguise feeling...*'"

"Ah, interesting," Neide said.

"You two can adapt it," Bruno said to Neide and Iam.

"So we'll be writing this part in the first person?" Bruce asked.

"It makes it more personal," Bruno said. Picking up on a few confused looks Bruno explained the difference. "So use the word 'I', I wanted, I planned, I felt and so on."

"I see where this is going," Marie said.

"You're writing the script for what you want to happen next," Bruno said circling the group. "So it should be exciting."

"Another fairy tale," Suzy said.

"It's whatever you want it to be," Bruno said. "The last time I did this with a group, one very smart lady said that this exercise wasn't really about writing." Bruno returned to the flipchart. "But, r-i-g-h-t-i-n-g!"

"That's clever," Corinne said.

"Yes, righting the wrongs, resolving the conflicts, answering the questions."

"It's a goal-setting exercise too, isn't it?" Neide said.

"That can be part of it for sure."

"Which will tie in nicely with what's in store later," Neide said.

"Start with the mindset of what's possible for you."

It seemed to Katherine that the group was more enthusiastic about the exercise, but the blank page in her journal daunted her. To write anything now would mean answering the question, what do I want?

The group began to disperse. Serendipity, Sophie and Tonya installed themselves on the beanbags by the far wall under the mural. They started writing immediately. Katherine stayed rooted to her chair.

"You look a bit confused," Bruno said, dropping to one knee beside her.

"It's shouldn't be a tough exercise, but it's hard to know what to write."

"We know you can write, so it's not that," Bruno said.

"It's totally different writing about yourself, isn't it?"

"When I feel stuck, I get up and move. You know the

old phrase; we think on our feet. So I tell you what, I need a cigarette, walk with me for a bit and we'll see if we can't get you going."

With her pen and journal in hand Katherine followed Bruno across the courtyard. Marie, Bruce and the Scottish women were spread out at the four corners of the dining table. Imelda and Corinne were in the shade by the cactus garden.

Declan and Suzy stood conspiratorially in the alleyway outside the main gate, the sand-filled bucket for discarded cigarette butts between them.

"We need nicotine to get the brain in gear," Declan said. Suzy forced a smile as they passed by.

"We'll go around the block and you'll be gushing words and ideas by the time we're back," Bruno said pulling a packet of cigarettes from the pocket of his shirt. "I take it you don't smoke."

"I can't walk and write at the same time Bruno."

"We'll walk and talk first. So my dear, you will be leaving The Retreat tomorrow and you will be feeling what?"

"I don't know." Katherine looked at her journal as if it contained the answer. They turned towards the main street. Katherine spotted Corinne's car across the road.

"I'll take that for now." Bruno took the journal out of her hand.

"Just tell me, how will you be feeling tomorrow evening boarding the plane? Gut response, your honest answer."

"Scared."

"Scared, okay."

"Scared, but maybe just a little excited."

"So, your first sentence is – 'I left the retreat in Teguise feeling scared, but a little excited.' Good opening. What's the next sentence?"

"I had learnt a lot and I was eager to get clear, no, I was eager to put right many situations I had allowed to fester."

"There's a flow to that already. 'I had learnt a lot and I was eager to put right many situations I had allowed to fester.'" Bruno scrawled the words into her notebook. "Keep going."

"Top of my list was a long heart to heart with Vincent."

"That's a nice way of putting it. Great, see once you get started, once you give yourself permission to express what's on your mind you're away," Bruno said, closing the journal, the pen marking the page.

They turned right again up the hill towards the main square. Katherine didn't notice a shallow step and almost tripped. When Bruno caught her elbow she had an uneasy sense of déjà vu.

"I won't be able to remember all this Bruno."

"Yes you will. Let's keep going, you're on a roll. So after the conversation with Vincent, what's next?"

"So much depends on how that conversation goes?"

"How do you want it to go?"

"Now that's the million dollar question?"

"And what's your answer?"

"I want us to clear the air. I want everything in the open. I will share how I've struggled recently and I hope he opens up and we can talk everything through and rekindle what we once had." Katherine stopped in her tracks. "I've never admitted that even to myself this week. It has just struck me now. I want us to be the way we were, but I don't know if that's possible, if that's what he wants or not."

"But it's what you want?"

"Yes, it's what I want. Yes, it's what I want." Katherine said it again just to make sure the words felt right and they did.

"Good for you and that's also your first paragraph sorted."

"It's not really about the words on the page though Bruno, is it?"

"Words allow us to express meaning and feeling. We have twenty-six characters that we arrange on a page, but how they're arranged can change the world. That's the power of writing."

"The pen is mightier than the sword." Katherine reached for her journal, but Bruno twisted away from her and started walking at an even brisker pace.

"Not yet. Right, paragraph two, let me give you the first line. 'I was a little excited because.'"

"Because... because for the first time in years I felt a sense of possibility."

"Love it, keep going."

"I was painting again and I was reminded of my love of cooking and I was excited about bringing both hobbies back into my life."

"And how do you feel when you're painting and cooking? Is it the same feeling?"

"I lose myself when painting; I get totally absorbed in it. I think it's when I feel most alive. I only remembered that yesterday, at the end of Ran's class, funnily enough during the thunderstorm."

"And cooking?"

"With cooking it's the pleasure on people's faces when they're enjoying something I've prepared."

"Fantastic, always remember the emotions when you're writing."

"I'll never remember all this Bruno."

"You will because it's not fiction, it's real life, your life. Now one more sentence to get you into paragraph three and then I'll leave you to it." Bruno took a long drag on his cigarette.

"I really appreciate this Bruno."

"The power of a good first sentence and a little encouragement eh?"

"I see what you mean now. This exercise is about making things right, not just writing."

They reached the main square. There was no respite from the sun. Katherine could feel lines of sweat run down her back. A group of old men sat in the shade by the church putting the world to rights.

"So here's the sentence, I'll write it down for you." Katherine watched Bruno write on a new page.

"*If you had told me this was possible I wouldn't have believed you.*" She read the line aloud.

Bruno raised his eyebrows and lit another cigarette.

"What's possible for you Katherine?"

The question struck Katherine between the eyes. It stunned her. She continued walking towards the church.

"Do this last section yourself Katherine and I'll see you back at The Retreat," Bruno said.

Katherine nodded, the sentence on the page consumed her thoughts. She watched Bruno retrace his steps across the square. She decided to go to the spot beyond the church where she had watched the sunset with Imelda. She didn't notice Bruno look over his shoulder and smile.

Katherine sat on the same spot on the wall. The night before the expansive view was sharp, every shade and texture distinct, the shadows long. Now, a full strength sun scorched the colour from the land. She read the lines Bruno had written and added in what she had voiced during their walk.

'*If you had told me this was possible I wouldn't have believed you.*'

She read the sentence he had written at the top of a fresh page several times. She hesitated to put the pen on the paper, not because she was stuck, but because she was unsure of what might be unleashed. She counted the letters, fifty-two. One for each year she had been alive, one for each week of the year. Bruno had arranged them into a key, a key she needed to unlock a compelling future.

Katherine's pen began to move. Thoughts and ideas flowed from her in an avalanche of possibility that could no longer be contained. Soon her hand struggled to keep pace. She wrote for an hour without even looking up.

CHAPTER 15

Katherine filled eight pages of her notebook. Each page, dense with writing crackled as she turned it. It didn't matter that several paragraphs were barely legible; the words were clear and precise in her heart. She closed the journal and caressed the soft leather.

Bruno's exercise had resurrected something precious, a fragile dream, and Katherine tingled with excitement and possibility. The word 'yes' escaped from her lips. She was missing the second half of Bruno's workshop, but that was a small price to pay. Dreams and ambitions that she thought were dead, had in fact only been buried deep inside her. Over the years they had whispered to her, but she had ignored them, allowing daily urgencies and countless other habits and distractions to always take precedence. But no more.

Looking skyward, four paragliders caught her eye. They floated like feathers above the stark landscape. White clouds drifted in from the west, dripping over the volcanic peaks before being evaporated by the scorching midday sun.

It no longer mattered whether or not Vincent was having an affair, because she would get through it one way or another. It no longer matter that Thom was gay or that her mother had died. That was just life and she'd get through it. It no longer mattered that finances were uncertain, she'd survive. With the sense of possibility had come a resolute resourcefulness as deep as the pit where her dreams had been buried.

Everything that had happened over the last few months had led her to sit on the wall and to pour her heart's desires onto the page. It was a lighter Katherine who walked purposefully back to The Retreat. Irrespective of what happened over the next twenty-four hours, she could say now that her time at The Retreat had been successful. She had got what she needed, a renewed sense of vigour and purpose. If Bruno's exercise had been a key, it had opened a door to a vast treasure-filled room. She felt she had experienced the breakthrough that everyone spoke about.

***

"Ah Katherine you've made it back, we were beginning to worry," Bruno said, smiling. All heads turned. Neide looked as if she was about to say something.

"I'm sorry, completely lost track of time." Katherine sat down, noticing her bag was still under her chair and protruding from it, two of Bruno's books.

"Productive?" Bruno said, rubbing his bald head.

"Powerful."

"That seems to be the general consensus," Bruno said.

Katherine glanced at the other nodding heads. Imelda winked at her.

"You haven't missed too much Katherine. We did some shares and we spoke a little about how there are always two stories in every piece of writing, the unfolding story and the back story. This morning we just dealt with them separately; what has happened in our lives up to now and what we want our lives to be going forward."

"I see," Katherine said, savouring the cool breeze from the fan.

"And I've just thrown this question out to the group. As the hero or heroine in your own life story, what has to happen for you to live happily ever after?"

"I'm not sure if that's possible?" Suzy said. "I don't see life as being as simple as that."

"Happiness is not a destination, it's how we travel," Corinne said.

"Good one," Iam said, writing Corinne's words down.

"I think it goes back to our definition of success and what we want." Neide added.

"Of course we will all have our own definitions," Marie said. "I often ask my coaching clients that because how will you know you're on the right track unless you know your destination."

Katherine noticed a quote Bruno had written on the flipchart. She copied it into her journal.

'I am not what has happened to me. I am what I choose to become.' Carl Jung

"Does happiness equal success?" Bruno asked. "And is it a destination?"

"Success has to be a factor in happiness," Declan said.

"Are some people happy even though they may not be successful?" Bruno asked.

"Sure, but for me it's about reaching my potential and I don't think I'd be happy unless I was seen to be successful," Declan said.

"I agree with Corinne, I don't think success is a destination," Neide said. "We will never really arrive at success, but we will know if we are heading in the right direction."

"We may be going off on a tangent and I'm sure Neide this discussion is more your forte. I raised the point though because from a writing perspective it's always useful to know your characters' motivations. Everyone in life, or in a story, is making the best decisions they can, so they can be as happy as they believe they have a right to be. For me, success is part biography but the biggest part is belief, belief in yourself and belief in what's possible for you."

"It is not what happens to us but how we deal with it," Corinne said.

"Put it this way." Bruno continued. "We all know how each

of our stories will ultimately end."

"I think we'll have time to delve into this more in the afternoon during the goal-setting and motivation workshop," Neide said.

"If I may," Imelda said. "As someone who is perhaps older, I won't say wiser, but older, what I've figured out over the years is that the only true measure of success is the love that we have shared."

"Wow," Declan said.

Several people, including Katherine noted Imelda's words. Bruno just nodded, a broad smile lighting up his face.

"Now here's another idea for you all to ponder," Bruno said installing himself on the table. "What if we aren't telling our own stories but the story is telling us."

"Like something is being told through us?" Imelda said.

"I don't get it," Bruce said on behalf of most of the group including Katherine.

"What if our story is telling us?" Bruno repeated the question. Katherine could tell from his expression that the big American liked nothing better than to stir people's thinking, to drop a new concept like a grenade and see the reaction. "Imelda, what are your thoughts?"

"What struck me was that perhaps we are all characters in a bigger story, the story of life, life on this planet, with God, or the universe, the Divine Presence as the storyteller."

"That's deep," Bruce said, rubbing his beard.

Katherine felt as if her brain had already been stretched enough that morning.

"Our purpose in life is told through us." Imelda continued. "I'm probably not explaining it very well. That's just what came to mind when you said it Bruno, that how we live our lives is part of a bigger story, a bigger unfolding."

"It's an interesting concept," Iam said. There was silence

in the room. Sets of eyes searched the corners of the ceiling seeking hidden answers.

"You're really a philosopher Bruno aren't you?" Corinne said. "A modern day Aristotle."

"You should see me in a toga." Bruno laughed.

As the workshop began to wind down, Marie enquired about Bruno's writing process and Iam's request for tips for getting published led to a discussion about self-publishing. Katherine's attention wandered back to what she had written in her journal. 'If you told me this was possible I wouldn't have believed you.' Katherine loved that sentence. As Bruno brought the session to a close she scribbled down 'publish my own book of recipes'. Then she joined the others in giving Bruno a standing ovation.

***

"Joining us for lunch?" Corinne said. "I've news for you."

"I'll follow you across," Katherine said. She wanted to speak with Bruno.

"Bruno, these were in my bag?" Katherine exhibited the evidence when the others had left, most of them with newly signed Bruno Reye books in their hands.

"Shoplifting are you?"

"Seriously?"

"My gift to you. The peaches; putting up with my dancing at the party the other night."

"Oh please Bruno, let me pay for them and I'm the one who should be thanking you for your time earlier."

"You know I was delighted when you didn't come back."

"That's charming."

"You know what I mean."

"It was a powerful exercise."

"You were ready, that's all, I just gave you a little nudge."

"Thank you Bruno, I really mean that. This morning has

244

been life changing. If you are sure then about the books would you mind signing them for me?"

Bruno signed his name with a flourish. In one he added '*keep dancing*', and in the other '*what's possible?*' Very appropriate Katherine thought.

"I tell you what, you probably have plans but I've been roped into organising the dinner for tonight and you'd be more than welcome to join us."

"You're very kind; I'm catching up with Zoe later, so I'm not sure."

"Well the offer is there and you'd be more than welcome and your daughter too."

"I'll see what she says."

"Are you sure I can't give you something for the books," Katherine said, dropping them back into her bag.

"Go woman and have your lunch, you've earned it."

"See how practical this bag is, I can carry everything in it," Katherine said smiling.

"Almost as much as my Lidl bag," Bruno said placing his unsold books into a carrier bag.

***

With her plate stacked high with salad Katherine shuffled onto the bench beside Corinne.

"I phoned that model agent back," Corinne said, keeping her voice low so only Katherine could hear.

"And?"

"I'm meeting him next Tuesday. He thinks I could have a good chance of being in an ad for a range of soap. Can you believe it?"

"I can see you on billboards now."

"By the sounds of it they're looking for a united nations of women, you know all ages, shapes and colours. I'll be the old black woman."

"Oh please."

"He said he'll take a few Polaroids on Tuesday and see what the client thinks. Of course they may take one look at me and say no thanks."

"But sure you've nothing to lose," Katherine said, biting into a large forkful of spinach.

"He said it's a big campaign, magazines, maybe even TV ads."

"Will you get out of bed for less than ten thousand?" Katherine laughed.

"I'd get into his bed for ten thousand." Corinne shook with laughter. "I can only imagine what my Terry would be saying right now."

"He'd be saying you go girl."

"And I don't know what Nenah will say. I told you she's trying to break into modelling. What if the agency wants her old grandmother and doesn't want her."

"She'll be thrilled for you. You'll have to let me know how you get on Corinne; I'll be dying to hear."

"It could all fizzle out, but it's a bit of excitement isn't it? So what happened to you earlier?"

Katherine got so caught up in sharing what she'd written that Corinne had to remind her several times to keep eating her lunch.

"Well that sounds like a breakthrough to me Katherine," Corinne said, squeezing Katherine's arm.

"I don't know what happens next, but I certainly feel better, despite hardly any sleep last night."

"Savour that feeling of possibility, sometimes not knowing can be exciting, it means there's space for possibility or even a little miracle. And I like the idea that with vision comes provision. If you're seeking something that same thing is seeking you," Corinne said as they carried their plates into the kitchen where Serendipity was tidying up.

"Katherine let me know what you need me to do later," Serendipity said putting leftover salad into sealed containers. She was the latest in a line of people who had offered their services.

"What have I let myself in for?" Katherine said to Corinne.

"It'll be fun," Corinne said. "And a trailer for what's to come, judging by what you were just saying."

***

"Our last afternoon session," Neide said standing with her hands on her hips facing the group. A collective sigh filled the room. "Iam will be running the final workshop in the morning and I'll join you for the wrap up, but in the meantime wasn't Bruno's workshop fantastic? I took a lot from it myself."

Nods and positive words went up and down the line of chairs.

"As is so often the case, the timing has been perfect. I wasn't totally sure what Bruno was going to do, but getting us to think like the heroines or heroes in our lives and writing about what we would like to happen next, all ties in beautifully with what we are doing this afternoon. Now sometimes people ask me why we don't do this session on goal-setting earlier in the week, but I've found that we usually need to clear some stuff and recharge ourselves before we are in the right space to think about what we want to have, or do, or create in our lives."

"I agree," Marie said. "We have to be in the right frame of mind."

"Exactly, so hopefully having had the chance to relax and unwind here, connect with your sense of inspiration, have fun with some of the creative exercises, we can bring all that together and forge a little action plan so you can leave here feeling like the architects of your own lives."

"Sounds good," Bruce said.

"So let me tell you about the structure of the session. We will kick off with a series of questions I will use to encourage your thinking in terms of what's possible for you, as Bruno would say. That will be an individual written exercise. Now as you can see the magazines are back," Neide said picking up one from the pile on the table behind her. "Later you're going to have an opportunity to make your own vision board, a pictorial illustration of your goals."

"I've always found vision boards more exciting than words on a page," Marie said.

"Brings them to life," Neide said. "Then the last thing we will do is a little brainstorming exercise in small groups which will be a great way for you to generate momentum."

"Let's make sure we're in the same group," Corinne whispered to Katherine who nodded enthusiastically.

"I'm surprised there are any of those magazines left," Morag said.

"Which reminds me, if you've brought magazines with you, feel free to donate them before you leave tomorrow," Neide said.

"What time are we scheduled to finish this evening?" Katherine asked.

"Five at the very latest. I have to get ready for Carlos's niece's wedding and I know you will want to make a start in the kitchen. I hope everyone is helping out."

"She only needs to ask," Bruce said. He was the only person who hadn't approached Katherine with an offer of help. Even Tonya had come over during lunch.

"Are we ready to get started?" Neide said moving to the flipchart. "I want you to write the numbers one to twenty down the side of a page in your notebooks or on a blank sheet of paper." Neide wrote the numbers on the flipchart. "Then I want you to imagine you are like a child writing a letter to Father Christmas, listing everything you want. That's how we're going to start this exercise. Now in the past I used to ask everyone to answer the question, 'what do you want' twenty times, but recently I've found completing the sentence 'I would like to, or I would love to...' works better."

"So we write out everything we want to achieve?" Declan said.

"What you would like to achieve, to experience, to have in your life, to do, to give, to become."

"And what's the timescale?" Declan said.

"It's whatever you want, but I suggest five years plus. We will usually over estimate what we can do in a short time period, like a day, but we usually dramatically under-estimate what we can do over the space of a few years. Take this place, this retreat, this all started as a goal on a page. I hadn't a clue how it would happen, but the starting point was writing out my vision in an exercise just like this."

"Focus on the what first and the how will follow, isn't that the key to successful goal-setting?" Marie said, an orange stiletto dangling from her foot.

"It is because if we get too caught up in how something will happen, we are limiting our thinking," Neide said.

"But goals need to be realistic too. Isn't that the 'r' in smart goals?" Declan said.

"It depends on our definition of realistic?" Neide said. "And whether or not we believe something is possible for us."

"So it's a bit like the exercise with Bruno this morning," Morag said.

"You're building on it, translating what you wrote into specific goals."

"Can we leave the room?" Declan said.

"Not for this exercise because I've a few questions for you as we progress to encourage your thinking."

Katherine turned to a new page in her journal. She wrote the numbers one to ten down the side of one page and eleven to twenty on the facing page. She flicked through what she had written earlier, she wouldn't need to refer to it, those words were etched on her soul.

"Of course you don't need to limit yourself to twenty. Go for it. Two weeks ago there was a lady here who wrote down seventy-six well formed goals."

Katherine recrossed her legs and began to write.

I would like to rekindle my relationship with Vincent.

I would like to sit down and have an honest conversation with Vincent about finances and the future.

Whether these were goals or not Katherine wasn't sure, but they would be her immediate actions when she got home. Then she began to transcribe some of the sentences she had written that morning. This time she wrote them purposefully and in the neatest hand she could manage, inserting Neide's phrase before each of them.

I would love to run my own bistro serving delicious home-cooked food.

I would love to paint every day.

I would love my art to cover the walls of my bistro and my home.

I would love to have an exhibit of my work.

I would love to live and work by the sea.

I would love to attend an art class in Paris or Florence.

I would love to be the best mother I can to Thom and Claire.

I would love to have a better relationship with my sister Joan.

I would love to live in Italy or somewhere with a warm climate.

I would love not to have to worry about money.

"I can see most of you are writing away," Neide said. "A few tips for you. Keep your goals positively worded. So instead of saying 'I would love to give up cigarettes', write 'I would love to have a healthy lifestyle.'"

Katherine reviewed what she had written. She changed her last goal to '*I would love to feel financially secure.*'

I would love to fit easily into a size twelve dress.

I would love to see Thom and Claire settled in good jobs and happy relationships.

I would love to visit China.

"Also remember your goals should be your goals, not what you think someone else wants for you or what you want for someone else," Neide said circling the room.

Katherine crossed out what she had written about Thom and Claire.

"Here are a few more questions to stimulate your imaginations," Neide said. "What would you write down if you knew you couldn't fail? What would you write if you were not as self-conscious? What would you love to have or do just for the pure fun and excitement of it? What would make you a little scared if you wrote it down and it came true?"

"Oh I like that question," Suzy said.

Katherine allowed Neide's questions to stir and awaken more concealed dreams and desires.

I would love to spend a few days by myself wandering through the great museums and galleries of Paris and Rome.

I would love to write a cookbook.

I would love to complete a marathon and raise €5,000 for charity.

Katherine had something written beside the numbers one through to seventeen.

"Remember don't think about the 'how', remember the 'what' is all we are concerned about right now," Neide said, writing the word 'what' in bold capitals on the flipchart.

I would love to have a website that has information and menus about my bistro and examples of my painting, maybe even a blog like Thom.

I would love to cook a great meal tonight.

It was a short-term goal, but a valid one, Katherine thought. Only one blank slot remained on the page.

"Review what you've written and ask yourself, for everything you've noted what would that get for you or allow you to do or become?" Neide said.

Katherine sat back and scanned her list. And then it struck her.

I would love to be my true self every day

There it was, number twenty, the sum total of all the others.

***

"Now I want you to circle your top three or four goals. We'll call these your musts," Neide said. "Many goal lists are should lists or wish lists, let's turn the important ones into musts. For each of them, write down why you must do this, or have this, or complete this. If you cannot come up with reasons why you must achieve it, getting motivated will be a challenge."

Katherine found it the easiest exercise of the week. She started on a fresh page.

I must have a quality conversation with Vincent because he's my husband and I love him.

I must start painting again because I feel happy and free when I paint and it allows me to be creative.

I must have my own bistro or restaurant. It's what I always wanted but I never allowed myself to contemplate it. It's time for me to have my career.

I must be my true self every day because I'm exhausted and frustrated acting a role based on everyone else's expectations.

***

"Now before you attack the magazines, I've another little exercise for you, a visualisation. I think you'll enjoy this," Neide said. "You can drop your pens and paper for now. Just sit back and relax."

Katherine did as instructed. She stifled a yawn.

"I want you to hold up your hands and take a mental picture of them. Notice every detail about your hands, your nails, your rings, your knuckles, freckles."

"Liver spots," Morag said.

"Every detail, as if you're taking a picture of your hands."

Katherine's eyes rested on the three diamonds in her engagement ring and the gold wedding band behind it. On her right hand there was a blotch of sun burn across her knuckles and on her ring finger the yellow diamond solitaire Vincent had given her for her fiftieth birthday.

"Close your eyes and picture your hands, see them in your mind's eye. Now I want you to imagine what those very hands will be doing when you achieve one of your goals."

There was a snigger from Declan and Suzy, but Katherine stayed focused.

"Maybe your hands are holding something, a camera as you take a photograph in a place you always wanted to visit, a certificate, an award, a key to a door, or maybe they're touching something or someone. Just allow your unconscious mind to present an image."

Katherine could see her hands reaching up to hang a painting on an old stone wall above an open hearth. The painting was modern, full of colours and life. It was something she had painted herself. She could clearly see her hands gripping the frame. The fireplace was in her small restaurant. On the mantle rested bunches of dried herbs, some old books and a vase of wild meadow flowers. The image played like a movie in her mind. She could now see her hands straighten the cutlery on one of the wooden tables. From there she moved behind a large counter, and saw her fingers smooth the pages of the reservations book filled with names and numbers. It all seemed so real, so clear.

"Now, rather than hoping this will happen, expect it to happen," Neide said in a low voice.

Katherine was vaguely aware of movement beside her, but she stayed with the images in her mind. The colours became more vivid. Her hands were now on the sign on the door, turning it from closed to open. She could see her reflection in the glass. A lump formed in her throat.

"When you're ready you can open your eyes."

Katherine could feel her eyes welling up. The silence hanging in the room suggested others found the experience equally moving.

"Wow," Katherine whispered to Corinne.

"That's a great exercise," Marie said.

"Our imagination is a powerful tool," Neide said. "A preview of life's coming attractions according to Walt Disney."

"It's just wishful thinking though, isn't it?" Tonya said.

"Thought precedes action Tonya. Remember it's difficult to do something or achieve something unless we think about it positively and constructively beforehand," Neide said. "We have to believe that whatever we can imagine for ourselves is possible for us."

All eyes were on Tonya's expressionless face.

"Think of it this way Tonya," Neide said. "As a species why would we have an imagination unless it served a purpose? As I said earlier unless I could imagine having a place like this, it wasn't just going to happen."

Katherine wasn't sure whether Tonya was about to explode or whether Neide had defused her.

"Make sense?" Neide asked. Tonya nodded, as did most of the others.

"So, time to get creative. I've laid out some cardboard and glue and the markers are in the sideboard," Neide said, stepping away from the table.

Katherine was one of the first to spring from her chair. She wanted the *Food and Drink* magazine that was on top of the pile. Within seconds the magazines, many of them falling apart were scattered across the table. Grabbing one of the glue sticks, an old copy of *American Vogue* and one of the many copies of the *Lanzarote Gazette*, Katherine decided she would work on her vision board in her own room. She had bought two magazines at Dublin airport and planned to scan them for suitable images as well. No pictures could replicate what she had visualised, but perhaps they would serve as a reminder of everything she wanted to create in her life.

***

Her bedroom was stuffy. She left the door and windows open and switched on the fan to circulate the stale air. She straightened the bed before fanning out the magazines. Katherine wanted her goals, her insights and her writing from Bruno's class all in the one place, so she planned to paste the images into her journal.

The cover was hanging off the old edition of *Vogue* and many pages had already been ripped out. She quickly flicked through the designer advertisements that filled the first quarter of the magazine. A model in wellington boots standing in a field of cabbage caught her eye. The article was about green clothing. There was a picture of a walled garden. Growing her own herbs and maybe some fruit and vegetables was a worthy addition to the vision she had for her own restaurant. She wondered if Vincent had been keeping an eye on her vegetable patch behind the garage. Taking her nail scissors from her toiletry bag she cut out the image. She laughed to herself because it all seemed so obvious now. Her few rows of lettuce and rhubarb back home were just another clue as to her passion in life.

Katherine remembered she had read an article about The French Laundry, the famous restaurant in the Napa Valley. She found it in the *Travel* magazine and cut out an image of the kitchen and a beautifully laid table. She was not interested in Michelin stars, but the images were inspiring. She found another picture of an outdoor restaurant, with tables arranged around a fountain, photographed through a wisteria-covered arch. Maybe she could have a few outdoor tables for when the weather was warm enough.

Why not? Katherine said to herself. There was an advertisement for a dating agency at the back of one of the magazines. The image showed a couple in silhouette walking hand in hand by the ocean at sunset. It was a corny image, but she cut it out too. Maybe it could represent her and Vincent.

Shrieks of laughter filled the courtyard. Katherine glanced out and saw Declan standing beside the Scottish women who were working at the dining table. She could just imagine what was going on.

And then she found her stone fireplace. It was in an article about villas in Italy. The majestic villa with double height ceilings was nothing like her cosy bistro, but cropping the image, the old wall and large fireplace came pretty close to what she had pictured in her head.

Like pieces of a jigsaw Katherine arranged the images in her journal. She needed something that would represent her painting. The *Lanzarote Gazette* had an article on César Manrique. The picture of the white-washed walls, the brilliant blue pool and the pod-like rooms built in the rock didn't do the place justice. She smiled at the memory of dancing the tango with Bruno earlier in the week.

She cut out a picture of a Manrique painting. It would symbolise her art and how she had reconnected with her love of painting. She got to work with the stick of glue. As a girl she had kept a scrapbook. Forty years ago it was postcards from relatives on holidays, pictures of Abba and of Charlie's Angels and of course Parker Stevenson the dark-haired one from The Hardy Boys and Nancy Drew Mysteries.

Katherine filled four pages of her journal with images that represented her goals and dreams. She remembered that she had a spare passport photo in her purse. She glued it to the centre of the page then sat back on the bed and admired her work.

The heat and the lack of sleep were catching up with her. She could have curled up on the bed, but Katherine didn't want to miss another minute of a workshop. Gathering the magazines she left them with Morag and Louise at the dining table.

In the kitchen Katherine brewed a herbal tea. All calm before the storm, she thought. She opened the refrigerator; her four chickens were lined up on the shelf where she had left them. Memorable meals are a combination of great ingredients, imaginative flair and organisational skills. Tearing a page from the back of her journal she began to list what needed to be done.

***

"So for the last part of the session I want you to form groups of three. And we'll do this exercise standing up to keep it snappy," Neide said, quietening the room, as everyone was busy displaying their collages.

"I'm sticking with you on this one," Corinne said to Katherine. Morag made eye contact and their group was formed.

"So here's how it will work," Neide said. "In turn I want you to share the goals you have written, in particular your musts and why they're important. Speaking them out loud will bring them to life, make them more real. If we are seeking something different it usually means having different conversations, so see this as the start of a new conversation. Now if you've written something you would rather not share that's fine too, as ever this room is a space of non-judgement and confidentiality."

Top of Morag's list was to get her motorcycle fixed. She had been a biker all her life, but had given it up because she thought she was too old. This week made her realise she missed the thrill of the open road. She wanted to rejoin a local bikers' club, and go on a motorcycling holiday. She was reluctant to share one of her goals, but with just a little encouragement she said she always dreamt about riding her motorcycle along Route 66 from end to end, Chicago to LA. This was the goal that really made her face light up.

Corinne surprised Katherine in that she had only written down a few goals. She spoke about wanting to visit Jamaica, where her parents were born, connect with her roots as she said and meet some cousins she had never met. As she had mentioned to Katherine before, Corinne's dream was to run her own retreat, her own workshop centre. Corinne painted a wonderful image of a round room, with floor to ceiling glass, sea views and flooded with light.

Then it was Katherine's turn. Corinne had heard most of it over lunch, but Morag seemed impressed with the detail Katherine shared, especially when it came to her goal of running her own restaurant filled with her own paintings.

Energy levels in the room were high. Katherine found the snippets of conversation from the other groups fascinating. Declan was listing countries he wanted to visit, exotic places like Cambodia and Burma. Katherine smiled when she heard Serendipity say she would love to have her own art exhibition and to own a Louis Vuitton bag just like Katherine's. Looking at it under her chair Katherine realised that it had never been a goal of hers to own such a bag.

"How does it feel speaking your goals aloud?" Neide asked the room.

"Well I didn't sound as stupid as I thought I would," Morag said.

"Now staying in your groups, I want you to share your main goals again, your musts, and allow the others in the group to offer suggestions by way of actions or first steps you can take. So for the person whose goal it is, your job is to write down what the others are offering you. Don't debate the logic or reasonableness of their suggestions, or how you've tried them before; just accept the advice with gratitude. I guarantee that if you go into this exercise with an open mind you will gain new insights. Sometimes when our goals are reflected back to us we will discover something we overlooked before."

"Morag do you want to kick off again?" Katherine asked.

"Mine are very straightforward," Morag said. "Getting my bike fixed is simply getting the garage to look at it."

"And Route 66?" Corinne said.

"That's research on the web and I know someone, an old mate of mine Billy who did it a few years back, so I can ask him. It's not rocket science; I just need to get off my backside."

"What about my retreat girls, what do you think?" Corinne asked.

"Have a word with Neide, she's done it already," Morag said.

"I'd hate her to think I was trying to compete with her though."

"I don't think she'd see it that way," Katherine said. "You'd be so good at running workshops Corinne, wouldn't she Morag? I've learnt as much from you this week as I have from the people at the top of the room."

"You should do it," Morag agreed. "Start small, run a few workshops first, start building up your contacts, design your programmes, in some ways the location is secondary." Corinne started taking notes.

"What about renting a space, there must be plenty of halls and function rooms, even hotels." Katherine suggested.

"You know I never considered that. As long as the venue is suitable I don't need to own it, it just needs to be a great space with a great view," Corinne said. "Why did I never think of that?"

"And a hotel would make it a lot easier because you wouldn't have to worry about accommodation or food, you would just have to focus on your course."

"You know that's all I needed to hear. I was stuck on setting up a place like this, but why reinvent the wheel. Thank you.

And to think I've worked in hotels all my life," Corinne said. "So Katherine, let's see if we can help you out."

"Well having the conversation with Vincent that just needs to happen. The bistro, I don't know, I'll need all the help I can get."

"Do you know anyone running something similar? Could you learn from them?" Morag asked.

"My friend Mags has a café; I could certainly speak with her."

"And someone who paints and exhibits their work?" Corinne added.

"I've met many artists over the years. I could dig out some old business cards and brochures. There's one guy, I can't remember his name, but he had a fascinating story, left his job as an IT manager and now runs his own gallery in the west of Ireland. I've his contact details and I could certainly send him an email."

"Remember no suggestion is too silly, just keep the ideas flowing," Neide said.

"Maybe get some experience working in a restaurant first," Morag said. "Enter *MasterChef*. Would you need to go to catering college?"

"I did that thirty years ago," Katherine said, recognising another clue from her past. She wanted to be seen to be doing the exercise, so she noted the suggestions, but she had no intention of working for someone else or entering a cooking competition on TV.

"Like your suggestion to me is there a space you could rent, a premises or a studio. I remember you saying your husband was an estate agent, perhaps he has contacts," Corinne said.

"I never thought of that," Katherine said. She hadn't considered what Vincent would think of her ideas and plans, that was another conversation she would have to have with him.

"Of course tonight could be a test run," Morag said.

"What do you mean?" Katherine said.

"Yes, exactly," Corinne said. "Tonight this is your restaurant and we're your chefs and waitresses. If you enjoy it, if you feel like you're in your element, then that tells you something doesn't it."

"What would you call it?" Morag asked, "Your bistro, any name in mind?"

"You know I hadn't thought about that." But in a flash Katherine knew exactly what she would call it. "Kay's, I'd call it Kay's or Kay's Kitchen something like that."

"An abbreviation of your own name?" Corinne asked.

"Vincent calls me Kay, but I was thinking it's more after my aunt, she was a great cook and baker. I spent a lot of time with her as a child. That's when my love of cooking started."

With the exercise over Katherine resumed her seat. She pictured the front of her bistro and the name 'Kay's' over the door. She glanced at her watch, a quarter to five. Katherine sat on the edge of her seat waiting for Neide to wrap things up.

It had already been a momentous day. She now had to organise and cook the evening meal for the group. Katherine took a deep breath. She hadn't felt this excited in ages. The evening ahead would be a trial run, a way to test her dream. And there would be another test ahead as well, one Katherine never saw coming.

Chapter 16

Katherine lined up the four chickens by the large stone sink. The plump birds were cold to the touch. She rubbed coarse sea salt into their skins, she wanted them crispy. She reckoned they would take at least two hours in the oven. Each one would be cooked differently. The first with lemon, garlic and basil, was one of her regular dishes back home. The second, with tarragon, her favourite herb and the third, in honour of Carlos, would be served with chorizo and bulky croutons to soak up the juices. The final one would be a traditional roast with sage and onion stuffing.

Through the window Katherine noticed the others were slow to leave the workshop room. She had dashed across the courtyard as soon as Neide had brought the session to a close. Heat and responsibility meant sweat was forming on Katherine's brow. Only when the chickens were in the oven would she allow herself to relax a little.

"Now tell us what to do?" Imelda asked rolling up her sleeves. Corinne followed her into the kitchen.

"Onions first I think," Katherine said, grateful for the willing hands and encouraging smiles.

"Done," Corinne said, removing a knife from the block.

"If you wouldn't mind slicing one for under the chickens and I think because they're so big just one more finely chopped will do for the stuffing. You can use this pan," Katherine said, taking one from the rack over the table.

"Now there's no rush, let's enjoy the preparation as much as the eating," Imelda said, putting her cardigan on the back of a chair.

"I was going to roast some vegetables with the chicken, what do you think? Peppers, carrots whatever else we can find, some courgettes maybe."

"Leave that to me," Imelda said, taking the basket of peppers to the chopping board.

"And I was thinking of roasting a few potatoes as well, cutting them thick like chunky chips."

"Is there a peeler?" Imelda said, opening drawers. "Leave the old Irish woman to peel the spuds hah?"

"I need a wooden spoon," Corinne said, trying not to rub her eyes.

"That's never worked for me," Katherine said, laughing at the elegant black woman humming to herself, the handle of a wooden spoon protruding from her mouth.

Katherine lifted the pots of herbs from the window sill. The others still lingered in the courtyard.

"What's this one?" Imelda said, picking a thin leaf and chewing it. "Tastes aniseedy."

"Tarragon, I love it with chicken. A real liquorice taste don't you think?" Katherine said.

"Do you know what I love with chicken?" Imelda said. "Mustard, not English mustard, that's too hot, the French one."

"Dijon," Katherine said. "I saw some in that cupboard; make sure you take some to the table."

"I love loads of salt and pepper with my chicken and good crispy skin of course," Corinne said, temporarily removing the spoon from her mouth.

"Melted butter is about to go over these which usually does the trick," Katherine said, starting to grate breadcrumbs into a bowl.

"These courgettes will take hardly any cooking," Imelda said.

"What about keeping them for the salad instead?" Katherine said. "We'll use their flowers, too." Katherine broke the top off one of the courgettes. "I love these deep fried, but not tonight."

Serendipity bounded into the kitchen, followed by Sophie and a hesitant Tonya.

"Sorry Katherine, I had to tidy up the workshop room," Serendipity said. "Right, we're at your disposal."

"Could I put you in charge of the salad? Probably two big bowls and have a think about what we could do so it's different from what we've had during the week."

"I know a great dressing with wasabi and lime," Sophie said.

"I don't think there's any wasabi, but see what you can find in the cupboards. I saw almonds somewhere; they might be nice to mix in," Katherine said. "Oh I'll need some thyme."

"I'll get it," Tonya said.

"A good handful, you know where it is, in that pot across the courtyard. Now you two are the only vegetarians right?" Katherine asked Serendipity and Sophie. "I was thinking of sautéing some vegetables, a bit like a ragout and you can stir it through some pasta, what do you think?" The two girls nodded. "And there should be some chunky chips as well."

"Could you do with a few more hands?" Suzy said. Declan sauntered in behind her.

"Suzy would you mind setting the table in the courtyard, proper place settings would be nice for a change. And I was thinking about serving everything on big platters, what do you think? Perhaps you can find some candles or even a few flowers."

"Say no more, leave it to me." Suzy said.

"Now Declan, I'm looking for a strong man, up for the challenge?"

"You'll need to keep looking." Suzy laughed. Declan flexed his biceps.

"Fancy making some mayonnaise? It would go really well with the chicken. Have you made mayonnaise before?"

"I've opened a jar?"

"Get me two eggs, I'll separate the yolks and get you started."

"I could use this, what do you think?" Suzy said, pulling a pale blue tablecloth from a drawer. "I'm sure Neide wouldn't mind."

"Oh did you get more wine?" Katherine asked, instructing Declan to add the olive oil drop by drop.

"The white is in the fridge and the red is in our room, we got more of that Tempranillo, the one we tasted last night," Declan said.

"We did more than taste it," Katherine said.

"I think we should open a bottle now," Suzy said, at the refrigerator door. "We got a rosé as well, it should be nicely chilled – our aperitif, what do you think? Sophie, Corinne, fancy a glass?"

"We should have some music too, I'll get my iPad, this whisking would be far easier if I had a beat," Declan said.

"Be warned, it'll be camp classics all the way," Suzy said.

"My era then," Katherine said.

"Katherine, have a glass," Suzy said, pouring the rosé wine.

"You know I think I've a better use for this. I could poach the last of those peaches," Katherine said taking the bottle from her. "I saw a vanilla pod somewhere and I could use a sprig or two of lavender, there's loads out on the deck. Sophie would you mind getting me a few sprigs? We should have time; they'll only have to simmer."

"I'd better open a bottle of white then," Suzy said.

***

For over an hour an eclectic mix of dance music filled the kitchen. At Imelda's request Declan scoured his playlist for anything that resembled rock 'n' roll. When a re-mix of an Elvis tune was discovered, Imelda grabbed his hands and a jive ensued. Like the others Katherine enjoyed singing along, amazed she could remember the words to so many seventies floor fillers. Sophie, Serendipity and Tonya got their entertainment from the older women. They showed their youth by not recognising most of the Stock Aitken Waterman tunes that reminded Katherine of being a newlywed.

Bruce had hovered by the door, but a chorus of 'I will survive' scared him away. Organising the washing up hadn't crossed Katherine's mind until Morag said she would round up those who weren't involved in the preparation. Katherine had to laugh when Morag also said that she couldn't wait to hand the Marigold gloves to Marie, because they would match perfectly the yellow dress she had changed into.

"Tomatoes," Katherine shouted. She found the brown paper bag where Carlos stored a variety of tomatoes. "These are too good to cook, a tomato salad, what do you think?"

"I can do that," Tonya said.

"Maybe a few pinches of salt and some basil leaves, there should be a spare dish somewhere Tonya."

"Earthy sunshine," Imelda said bringing a ripe tomato to her nose. "The musty smell always reminds me of my father; he used to grow tomatoes you know."

"Tomato, melon, goat's cheese and mint is a salad I love. You have to have really good tomatoes though," Katherine said.

"Really?" Declan said.

"It works, tomatoes and melons are all the same family."

"We should probably leave the melon for tomorrow's breakfast," Serendipity said.

"How about adding some mint to the salad Serendipity, there's loads of it outside?"

"Carlos won't have to do anything next week, but heat up leftovers," Corinne said.

"When you walk back in the aromas are amazing," Suzy said, a bag of night lights in her hand.

"I just hope we're not forgetting anything," Katherine said.

"And so what if we are," Imelda said.

Opening the oven, Katherine inhaled a relay of aromas.

The tangy sweetness of whole garlic cloves steaming in their skins, the smoky paprika from the chorizo, the mellowing citrus of the lemon wedges. The chickens were already a burnished umber. Hot oil fizzled and spat when Katherine rotated them to ensure even cooking.

"Declan, these are too heavy for me, would you mind putting them back in," Katherine said, turning her attention to the peaches floating like icebergs in the pink winey liquid. "I'll reduce this down; it'll make a fabulous syrup. Folks, should I make some pesto?" A chorus of 'no' rang out.

"I'm getting hungry now," Declan said, grabbing a sliver of pepper.

"I should have thought about a starter," Katherine said.

"There's plenty already," Corinne said. "And I want to have room for dessert."

"Remind me to take the ice cream out of the freezer when we sit down to dinner, it'll need to soften. I must put a plate aside for Carlos too; I promised I'd keep him some," Katherine said, her mind working faster than her hands.

"This is the most fun I've had all week," Imelda said, finding space to wash a few dishes.

"Me too," Suzy said, lining up cutlery to take outside.

"What were some of your goals Suzy, if you don't mind me asking?" Katherine said.

"I want to own my own place, I've always rented. The ideal would be to have my design business on the ground floor and live above the shop as it were. Now if I won the lottery it would be somewhere in Chelsea or Fulham."

"You've always said that," Declan said.

"I loved that exercise when we closed our eyes and imagined our hands," Katherine said.

"You know what's funny and Declan don't laugh, I wrote down that I'd like to have a baby and I never thought I wanted to have children," Suzy said.

"Suze?" Declan roared. "You promised not to go to the dark side, all coupledom and babies."

"Well never say never," Suzy said, patting Declan on the arm. "It was that visualisation exercise; I could see my hands reaching into a cot."

"Well be careful what you wish for?" Declan said. "Will there be a man involved or are we talking turkey baster?"

Suzy threw a cloth at him.

"When I think of how I've bent over backwards for men in the past," Suzy said.

"Suzy we don't want to hear about your sex life," Declan said.

"You know what I mean, the time and energy I put into trying to make a relationship work. One of the big takeaways for me this week is that if I spend just a little more time working on my relationship with myself, I don't need to look to a man to make me happy."

"Are we talking about those toys you keep in your bedside locker?" Declan laughed. Suzy hit him again.

"You're right Suzy, if you're different, then your relationships are different too," Corinne said, starting to dry some dishes.

"My aha was similar," Tonya said. Katherine couldn't recall her sharing anything personal all week, so she stopped what she was doing. "I used to think respecting myself just meant stating my opinions, arguing my point, standing up for myself, I never knew there was another side to respect, self acceptance, self compassion even. It was Neide who said it to me a few days ago when I'd really worked myself up into a state, she said I was being too tough on myself."

"We can all be our own worst enemies," Suzy said.

"Anyway Neide suggested I drop any expectations I had about this week and just listen. Now I've struggled at times to hold my tongue, but I've probably learnt more than I thought I would."

"Good for you," Corinne said.

"I've surprised myself," Tonya said. All eyes looked in her direction. "When I interact with others from a place of self compassion then I don't need to attack or judge, because I can see now that in the past I was really only attacking and judging myself."

"Wise words," Corinne said. Imelda dried her hands and gave Tonya a hug. Katherine drew a long breath.

"In the spirit of sharing," Declan said, shifting his stance. "I have to say my biggest light bulb moment was earlier today, it was what you said in Bruno's workshop Imelda, how success is only really measured by the amount of love we have given or experienced. I can't remember your exact words, but I wrote them down and underlined them."

"That was powerful," Katherine said. "But sure Imelda is our very own guru."

"Our own Yoda," Declan said.

"I'm not that old and I can jive better than you." Imelda laughed. "Now Katherine if you can spare me, I'll be back in twenty minutes?"

Katherine suspected Imelda wanted to visit the church as was her habit in the evening. "I'd say by seven thirty we should be dishing up."

"Katherine come here, you have to see this." Imelda shouted from the courtyard.

"Right let me know what you think," Suzy said, grabbing Katherine's elbow as she stepped outside.

"Wow." Katherine couldn't believe the transformation. The dark blue cloth had been folded into a diamond shape in the centre of the table. The flowers from the common room had been split into several vases and old jugs and the entire table was dotted with candles in tumblers ready to be lit. "I hope you didn't carry those yourself?" Katherine said, nodding at the large flower pots that now fenced off the table from the rest of the courtyard.

"That's where Bruce came in handy. They really define the space don't they?"

"Listen to the designer talking," Declan said sticking his head out the door.

"It's stunning Suzy," Corinne said, photographing the scene with her phone. "Suzy, Katherine, let me take one of the two of you." Both women reluctantly posed.

"Where did you get them?" Katherine said gesturing at the large lanterns.

"Outside Neide's bedroom, I hope she doesn't kill me."

"Here's hoping the food lives up to the setting," Katherine said.

From the other side of the retreat they could hear Morag laugh.

"Someone's having fun," Suzy said.

"Morag's regaling the others with tall tales from her youth," Corinne said. "They're out on the terrace, watching the sunset. I'll let them know we're nearly ready."

"Declan I'll need your strong arms again, the chickens should be done and I want to let them rest for a while," Katherine said, returning to the kitchen.

There was no one in the courtyard to see the main gate open and Bruno step through.

***

"You made it," Katherine said, delighted but surprised to see Bruno. He had arrived at the worst possible time. She had just started to carve the chickens and the vat of pasta was waiting to be drained.

"So this is where the party's at? I just followed my nose," Bruno said, handing a bottle of wine to Corinne who greeted him with a kiss on each cheek.

"I'll set a place for you Bruno," Suzy said. "Unlucky for some we'll be thirteen around the table."

"Zoe not joining you?" Katherine asked, wiping her forehead and aware that Bruno's arrival had disturbed the symmetry of Suzy's table setting.

"No, but she said thanks for the invite. Can I carry anything out?"

A procession of platters filled the table where expectant appetites awaited. The cold dishes went out first. Serendipity and Sophie declared their salad to be Moroccan inspired, a tangle of lettuce, mint and parsley leaves, thin strips of cucumber and courgette, almonds and glistening like rubies, pomegranate seeds. Tonya announced her contribution by carrying out the tomato salad, now an infusion of succulent tomatoes, basil and olive oil just waiting to be piled onto the crusty bread that followed. The mayonnaise Declan had slaved over had been divided into two, crushed garlic and lemon juice had been added to one converting it into aioli.

Imelda returned and conscious that the elderly lady had done more than her fair share Katherine insisted she take her place at the table. Suzy got busy lighting the candles. Declan positioned his iPad in the window; light jazz would be the soundtrack for the meal.

Next out were the roasted vegetables, almost caramelised, they only needed a final grind of pepper. Sophie and Serendipity organised their own plates. The remainder of their 'ragout' was scraped into a bowl and dispatched to the table. Katherine hoped the food would stay hot. She tasted a potato wedge, chargrilled on the outside, fluffy and piping hot in the centre, just as she had hoped. She dropped two onto the plate she was assembling for Carlos, added chopped rosemary to the bowl of wedges then handed it to Corinne. Her attention turned to the pasta. Struggling to lift the large pot, Bruno stepped in. A good slug of olive oil and out it went.

Katherine could hear the chorus of appreciation that

welcomed each dish, but the meal's success would depend on how the chickens had cooked. They looked and smelt delicious. She sprinkled a little more salt across the crisp skins, roasted to a burnt umber. She then roughly carved each one, separating the breasts and legs, making them easier to serve. To each platter Katherine added more of the herbs that had been used in the cooking; she always liked the decoration to reflect the ingredients. The first round of applause erupted when Bruno placed two of the chickens on the table.

Jugs of iced water were filled; makeshift ice buckets located, wine corks popped. Katherine scanned the kitchen one last time; it wasn't a complete mess. She took a deep breath, straightened her top, picked up the tarragon chicken and remembering the Dijon mustard stepped outside to be greeted with a cheer. She slid the mustard in beside Imelda then took her place at the empty seat at the top of the table between Bruno and Corinne.

Heads leant forward to savour the enticing aromas. Camera phones flashed.

"What a feast," Imelda said pulling the steam to her face.

"Thank you Katherine," Bruce said. Glasses were raised and Katherine's efforts toasted.

"Tuck in before it goes cold," Katherine said.

"Now I want a little of everything," Bruno said, pulling a platter towards him. "Well a lot of everything."

"For what we are about to receive may we be truly thankful," Imelda said. A few amens followed, Corinne's being the loudest.

Hands reached, bowls were passed, chickens were lifted, sauces scooped, salads tossed and drinks poured.

"It tastes even better than it looks," Bruce said, from the far end of the table, raising his glass to Katherine. Imelda mouthed a thank you to Katherine having discovered the mustard at her elbow. One compliment after another flowed down the table.

Katherine reached for the tarragon chicken and began to relax.

***

"Just look at what you've created Katherine," Bruno said, topping up her wine glass.

"It was a team effort and Suzy arranged the table."

"Everyone is singing your praises," Bruno said. "And honestly, this food Katherine, you know the way to a man's heart."

"I'm glad you're enjoying it. We certainly had a great laugh in the kitchen, didn't we Corinne?" Katherine said, bringing her into the conversation.

"I hope you've roped some of the others into doing the washing up?" Bruno said.

"Morag has it all organised."

"She's quite a cook, isn't she Bruno?" Corinne said.

"That's what I've been saying and I used to think chicken was a boring dish," Bruno said, sinking his teeth into a chicken leg.

"Well, have you passed the test?" Corinne asked Katherine.

"What test?" Bruno said between mouthfuls.

"One of my goals Bruno is to run my own bistro, so tonight was a bit of a trial run."

"People would pay good money for a meal like this, I know I would," Bruno said.

"I don't know how you did it Katherine; you've managed by some extraordinary alchemy, to transform simple ingredients into the most sumptuous dishes. Carlos could be out of a job. And this mayonnaise, I'll be making some when I get home," Corinne said, adding another dollop to her plate.

"We've Declan's arm to thank for that."

"Could you see yourself doing this every night?" Corinne asked.

"You know I think I could. I should be exhausted, but I'm buzzing," Katherine said.

"A sure sign you're on the right track," Bruno said.

"And you can tell you've put your heart into it because it tastes so good," Corinne said. "I hope you realise you've discovered your calling Katherine. Oh didn't you say something about taking the ice cream out?"

"Damn I forgot," Katherine said, getting to her feet.

"Stay where you are, you've done enough," Corinne said, giving Katherine a hug then taking her empty plate with her to the kitchen.

"To your calling Katherine," Bruno said, clinking her glass.

Katherine took a moment to absorb the jovial scene. Conversations bounced up and down the table, glasses sparkled in the candlelight, remnants of dishes were being shared and crusts of bread used to soak up lingering juices. It was the delight on people's faces that Katherine would remember and cherish. This was easily the highlight of her week. She could now sit back and enjoy herself.

***

"I could keep eating, but I have to stop," Bruno said, pushing his plate away before reaching for a chicken wing. "Right, an experiment, you up for it, something I'm writing about at the moment. I want you to look around the table and tell me what you see."

"What do you mean?"

"It's a theory I have about how what we see reflects what's going on inside us, come on humour me."

"I see people eating, talking, laughing, drinking, is that what you mean?" Katherine said.

"Okay," Bruno pushed back his chair and indicated that Katherine do the same. "Take those two, Corinne and Imelda, what do they represent to you?"

"That's an odd question," Katherine said, but Bruno held her gaze. She took another sip of wine and looked at the two

274

women deep in conversation with Bruce. "They've been great friends to me this week; they're the two people I would love to stay in touch with. Two of the wisest women I've met and so generous with their time, I could chat to them all day."

"Okay, and Suzy and Declan, isn't it? I'm not sure of all the names."

"Now there's a double act, never a dull moment with those two. We had a gorgeous lunch last Sunday in a beautiful little tapas place just off the main square; you'll have to try it. They were the first people I got to know," Katherine said. She then lowered her voice and leant closer to Bruno. "But if I think about it sometimes they strike me as being a bit lonely, but who am I to judge. Good people though and great company."

"Keep going, the Scottish woman, Morag, the biker."

"Now there's a character. There's no messing with Morag, a wicked sense of humour, bit of a rebel. I suspect she's had a tough enough life, been hurt, but she just gets on with it."

"A face shaped by perseverance, I can tell," Bruno said. "And the woman from Northern Ireland, there across the table?"

"Marie, you know I haven't really connected with her, she pleasant but quite guarded."

"Usually a defence mechanism."

"And I dread to think of the size of her suitcase, I've not seen her in the same thing twice this week."

"And the girls?" Bruno said lowering his voice in case they overheard.

"Young women just trying to find their place in the world," Katherine said. She'd been wary of Tonya all week, but she saw her differently now.

"Would you want to be their age again Katherine?"

"I'm not sure, you?"

"I don't think so, growing older makes you appreciate life more, you don't take people for granted and you certainly don't take evenings like this for granted. And I'd hate to be all self-conscious again like I was in my twenties."

"I can't imagine you being self-conscious."

"I'd an operation to remove it." Bruno laughed.

"Of course I wouldn't mind having a figure like Sophie's."

"Oh please Katherine; you're a fine looking woman."

"That beats the usual not bad for your age." Katherine laughed, feeling herself blush.

"Don't tell me you've been brainwashed into thinking that you'd be happier if you conform to some unrealistic photoshopped image in a magazine, I thought you had more sense."

"I could certainly do with losing a stone and tonight hasn't helped."

"Get out of here woman. Look at this." Bruno lifted his shirt and grabbed his stomach with both of his hands. "This isn't fat; this is evidence of an abundant life. Here, see this fold, this represents the countless wonderful meals I've enjoyed, good times with friends, laughter, the odd glass, well crate of wine, even the waffles and maple syrup Zoe made for me this morning because she knows they're my favourite."

"It's different for men. Men develop stature, women just let themselves go. Wrinkles and grey hair and a man is distinguished, a woman is just old."

"Oh Katherine wrinkles are just life's way of saying you've earned your stripes and even if you live to be a wizened old woman, there'll never be a single wrinkle on your soul, or a line on your spirit. But I know better than to get into a discussion with a woman on this topic, so back to my experiment, tell me about the man with the beard."

"Bruce. Very intelligent, well read, a retired professor. I think he's struggled at times this week, felt a bit out of place. But what's this theory of yours."

"What we see in others is a reflection of aspects of ourselves.

276

So within you Katherine is the wise woman, the qualities you see in Corinne and Imelda, and if we go around the table, you're also the life and soul of the party, someone trying to find her way, someone who can feel a little out of place, someone who is defensive at times, and what else did you say, someone who was hurt in the past but who's getting on with it."

Katherine was about to say something but held back. She looked at Louise, the quiet, sometimes nervous woman, seemingly happy to stay in the background. She recalled her conversation with Louise when they had painted on the deck earlier in the week. Despite her two glasses of wine, Katherine felt there was some merit in Bruno's theory.

"We each see the world through our own eyes Katherine, our own filters," Bruno said. "Who we are determines what we see and what we see determines who we are."

"That was either very profound or complete nonsense," Katherine said squeezing his arm. Bruno's phone rang and he excused himself from the table. "What I see now is people waiting for their dessert."

Lively bantered bounced across the table. Everyone, even Tonya seemed to be having a good night. Morag was in full flow.

"If my mother, Lord rest her soul, knew of some of the whacky workshops I've been too," Morag said, rolling a cigarette. "Louise do you remember that outdoor place we went to with the tents in the field."

"Yurts," Louise said.

"Oh I've slept in one of those," Serendipity said, from the other end of the table.

"Not in a frozen field outside Dundee, I suspect. What were we thinking? All that native American Indian stuff, sweat lodges, what do you call it, Vision Quests."

"Oh I've heard of those," Declan said. The whole table was now tuned in to Morag's story.

"Oh Jesus, do you remember Louise what Rosemary said

about the vision quest thing she did. You had to wear a swimsuit in this big wigwam because you'd be sweating. Well, turns out swimsuits were optional. I can still see Rosemary's face when she was telling me." Morag could just keep the laughter in. "The man running the workshop, stark bollock naked, shovelling hot stones into this pit. Rosemary said she'd been married thirty years and had never seen a sight like it."

The table erupted in laughter.

"And he was a Native American Indian?" Declan asked.

"More cowboy than Indian if you ask me. The prices he charged. Poor Rosemary needed therapy afterwards."

"Oh Morag, that's too much," Katherine said, holding her side that was aching from the laughter.

"You must have done some far-out things Serendipity?" Suzy asked.

"Not really, I don't think so," Serendipity said self-consciously with all eyes now on her. "Well, don't say this to Neide, but at the beginning of the summer there was a guy here who ran a silent workshop. Oh I shouldn't say anything."

"You can't stop now."

"Neide will kill me, but anyway, after he gave a five minute talk about the benefits of sitting in silence, and I can see the point of that, he told us to sit or lie down and he'd come back in four hours."

"You mean he didn't even stay in the room with you," Morag said.

"No, he said it was easier for him to hold the energy for us if he was outside."

"Another cowboy."

"After about half an hour one of the men from the group got up to go to the loo, we weren't really supposed to leave the room and there was this guy, Greg something, cradling a cup of coffee and puffing away on a cigarette enjoying the view from the deck. All hell broke loose, everyone complained, people were asking for their money back. Neide never asked him back."

"There's plenty of charlatans about," Corinne said. "Playing on the vulnerable and naive."

"You know what freaks me out, and no offense to anyone here, but you know those Goddess dresses, tie-die and all that," Declan said.

"I knew you were going to say that," Suzy said.

"It was your fault. You dragged me to this Mind Body Spirit thing and what happens, this woman, with the biggest breasts I've ever seen dashes towards me, braless, dreamcatcher dangling from her neck and wearing you guessed it, a goddess dress."

"It was a good laugh though," Suzy said. "Do you remember the little woman; you called her a pixie, with the crystals."

"She said take this in your hand and all your troubles will go away and I said, love, it's not the first time I've heard that." Declan's punchline had the table in hysterics again.

"And remember the stall for clearing your aura," Suzy said.

"Yes, with an unfurled wire coat hanger."

"You don't see that on Blue Peter," Bruce said.

"And the three women in the rainbow coloured leotards." Declan continued. "I thought it was some sort of expressive dance, turns out it was chakra aerobics."

"That's new to me," Corinne said.

"Move over Jane Fonda," Declan said, refilling his glass. "What about you Katherine, ever been to any mad workshops."

"I've lived a sheltered life by the sounds of it."

"I've a story; I don't know if it's funny, it was actually a bit scary at the time," Sophie said.

"Go ahead dear," Imelda said.

"It was like the Mind Body Spirit thing you said Declan, but it was in a school. You could sign up for different classes. Me and my friend were wandering around and this tall man steps out of a room, saying his workshop was about to start, so we went in. Turns out we were the only ones in the room. He locked the door behind us saying he didn't want us to be disturbed."

"I'd be out of there," Morag said, tapping her cigarette.

"And what happened?" Suzy asked.

"We didn't have a clue what he was talking about, so my friend Sharon asked some questions which seemed to annoy him. The next minute he just closes his eyes and stops speaking. We just look at each other, thinking he's mediating or something. This goes on for thirty seconds or so and then he starts talking again. Ten minutes later he does the same thing. Sharon whispers to me that she thinks he's shutting down, you know blocking us out because we're annoying him."

"Weirdo," Morag said, waiting for the story to end so she can light up.

"Turns out he's a, what's the word, narcoleptic."

"Get out of here." Declan screams. There's a momentary intake of breath before the entire table explodes with laughter.

"Oh Sophie that's priceless," Suzy said wiping the tears from her face.

"Bless the poor man," Imelda said, her face red from laughter. "You can't beat a good laugh."

***

Serendipity and Morag followed Katherine's lead and gathered a few plates before returning to the kitchen. If she was at home Katherine would have used the chicken carcases to make stock. She was glad she had put a plate aside for Carlos because there was little left over. She laughed as Morag chased her from the kitchen brandishing the Marigold gloves that Katherine feared would be flung at someone sitting at the table.

Despite the lack of sleep and the long day, catching her reflection in her bathroom mirror, she looked and felt happier than she had done all week. The large suitcase in the corner, and the pile of unworn clothes mocked her. She contemplated changing her top but settled for a spray of deodorant and a touch of lipstick. She remembered Bruno's compliment and smiled to herself.

The chatter and laughter from the courtyard drifted into her bedroom. She stood for a moment at the door before closing it behind her. Her last night in Teguise. Katherine loved these evenings, good food, good company and the sensuous warmth of the night air. For the first time all week she wished Vincent was with her. He would have hated everything else this week, but he would have loved tonight. Katherine could easily picture him holding court at one end of the table.

Everyone had resumed their seats. Katherine assumed they were waiting for her to organise dessert. She hoped the poached peaches would hold their shape.

"Katherine, we've something for you," Imelda said standing and taking her hand.

"What's all this?" Katherine asked. All eyes were on her.

"We've had a little collection. Some of it went to cover the cost of the wine, but we all wanted to get you a little something, a small gesture to say thank you for cooking this magnificent meal," Imelda said.

Katherine was struck silent. She cupped her face to conceal her blushes. Imelda handed her a small velvet box.

"Oh there was no need." Katherine opened it slowly. The green pendant that she had admired the night before was inside. "Oh my. Thank you." Katherine felt a lump in her throat. "I'll treasure it. You really shouldn't have, you're all so generous," Katherine said, bending to give Imelda a hug.

"When we do what we love our true nature shines," Imelda whispered to her.

"To Katherine," Bruce said leading a toast.

Tears of a different kind were not far away. Katherine hung

the pendant around her neck. People came forward to admire it. The gift was totally unexpected and that made it all the more precious. That people she didn't know a week ago went to the trouble of recognising her efforts made her feel very humble.

Katherine couldn't keep the smile from her face as she and Corinne organised dessert. She cut the poached and de-stoned peaches in half, lined them up on a freshly washed platter, poured the reduced liquid, now a gooey syrup over them and added a few sprigs of lavender as decoration. A large bowl of yogurt through which Katherine stirred the seeds of a vanilla pod and a little honey, accompanied it. The second dessert, the one she had originally planned was a simple favourite, good quality coffee ice cream sandwiched between chocolate chip cookies. The coffee machine began to splutter and the kettle was set to boil. Corinne suggested people should serve themselves from the kitchen table.

The peaches were rationed so everyone got some. Bruno was the last in the line. He dipped his finger in the pink juice.

"Oh I've such a sweet tooth," he said, pulling over a chair. "Have you had yours yet?"

"I'll get some now," Katherine said taking her bowl to the table. They were the only two left in the kitchen.

"This is an orgasm on a plate," Bruno said, pulling the spoon from his mouth and rolling his eyes. "And the hint of lavender. You're an inspired cook, you know that."

"I do my best," Katherine said. She looked at Bruno and laughed. With his bald head, colourful shirt and peach juice dribbling down his chin he looked like a big baby.

"What?"

"Nothing."

"And we can't let this melt, can we?" Bruno said, pulling over the tub of ice cream.

"It can always go back into the freezer."

"Here, cook's treat." Bruno handed Katherine another

spoon. "Split it with you. You do know Katherine how you eat ice cream is a metaphor for how you have sex."

"Bruno."

"Do you politely lick around the edges or do you dive in." Bruno dug his spoon in.

"Enough of that talk. Here you need a napkin," Katherine said, handing him a paper towel.

"Right change of subject; you've had a good week?" Bruno asked, putting his hands behind his head.

"I can't believe how quickly the time has gone. I'd happily stay a few more days, but real life is waiting. I am looking forward to seeing my family though."

"You know, I can see the difference in you even since the other night."

"How do you mean?"

"You're more carefree or something. Do you know what it is, you've had an adventure this week Katherine. I always think people should have more adventures. Do you remember having adventures as a child? You'd go exploring, climbing, discovering."

"Oh yes, school holidays were the best. I'd head out with my friend Mary; we'd be gone all day."

"People today want too much certainty, they even try to schedule their fun. Did you ever hear such bollocks. Before this week when was the last time you headed off Katherine not knowing what you would do or where you would end up? I bet it was a long time ago. People have closed themselves to what life can offer them. They talk about lack of fulfilment, life passing them by; of course life is passing them by because they've shut up shop, they've stopped engaging with it. They want life to meet their expectations; they've put security ahead of joy, predictability ahead of fun. Life responds to how we show up, if you want certainty and predictability that's what you'll get. What's the phrase, their schedule is filled, but their life is far from fulfilled."

"We all have responsibilities though."

"Yes, including a responsibility to be happy. But the tricky part is we have to drop our expectations and get just a little more vulnerable, a little more uncomfortable, then life responds to us in ways we could never imagine. Think of the fun you've had this week Katherine, the party at the gallery, the workshops and even tonight, all because you went with the flow. Look at the gifts life gives you when you drop your own agenda."

"I hear what you're saying."

"Promise me Katherine you'll keep having adventures, what's the worst that could happen? Get the heart racing, take a few risks; dive into life, routine will kill you far quicker, believe me."

"Here you finish the ice cream," Katherine said, picking up her wine glass. She closed her eyes and inhaled the aroma. Red berries and a hint of chocolate, but that didn't really matter she was going to drink it anyway.

Then something unexpected happened, something she had never anticipated. Bruno placed his hand on hers.

"Bruno?" She had felt safe with him the entire week. The big American was like an older brother. His touch now changed all that. At the same time Katherine felt an uncanny sense of déjà vu. In her dream, when she was slipping from the harbour into the sea, a man with large hands reached for her. That same hand held hers now. "You've had too much to drink. Let's not spoil this evening."

"Your husband is a lucky man."

Katherine had been naive. All the clues were there, dancing with her at the party, the walk along the beach, helping her with the writing exercise, dropping the books into her bag, coming back to The Retreat for dinner, even sitting beside her all night.

"I won't apologise for liking you," Bruno said in a low, serious and very sober voice.

CHAPTER 17

All eyes watched Iam struggle with the projector and screen. Beads of sweat formed on his forehead. Katherine was glad she had managed to secure the seat on the right again so she had the full benefit of the fan.

"Please don't let this be death by PowerPoint," Suzy whispered to Katherine.

Iam Love, Katherine couldn't take him or his name seriously. He had been the butt of jokes all week, mostly instigated by Morag who had started calling him Gandalf. Once the grey accountant Colin Barton, he now dressed only in white and seemed to have an aversion to footwear. Rather than a mystical wizard Katherine thought his three-quarter length combats and baggy t-shirt made him look more like an overgrown toddler. The tufts of hair sprouting from his toes, calves, forearms and chest made Katherine think of caterpillars. He was a wiry man, some might even say scrawny. Suzy had labelled him and Neide 'little and large'.

"Can everyone see that okay?" Iam asked. The sunlight bleached the writing. Katherine could just make out the word 'agenda'. She sank a little lower in her chair.

"It's probably as good as you'll get it," Marie said. "You'll have to get blinds."

"Okay, we'll kick off. To start, I want to share my life journey with you."

Declan masked a groan with a cough.

"Then there's an exercise we'll do before Neide joins us for the final wrap up session and for those of you not dashing to the airport, lunch will be at the usual time, I know a few of you were asking earlier."

Katherine had been the last to arrive at The Retreat and she would be the last to leave, a fact she discovered over breakfast after the events of the night before had been regurgitated. Despite some sore heads it had been the most boisterous breakfast of the week. Photographs and videos were shared, greeted with shrieks of laughter and head-holding groans. Declan had recorded her and Bruno singing Ashford & Simpson's 'Solid as a Rock'. Katherine couldn't look at the video; the sound of her voice was cringeworthy enough.

Everyone viewed Katherine as the catalyst for their enjoyable evening, so a new wave of compliments revolved around her that morning. Neide had appeared to thank her again for arranging the dinner. She showed them photos of Carlos's niece's wedding. Katherine had been delighted to see The Retreat's chef looking very smart in a blue suit. Clean shaven he looked younger.

"Here I am aged seven," Iam said, a photograph of a young boy in short trousers standing beside a rose bush appeared on the screen. The orange hue and the child's clothes suggested the early seventies.

It was the first time all week that Katherine felt she was at a lecture. She knew that Iam had been an accountant, before as Morag put it; he had his overblown midlife crisis. His tone, stance and bullet points suggested much of the old Colin remained.

Some of his slides did have the occasional clever image; a man in chains, another man superimposed on a cliff edge, but the late night, the heat and Iam's monotone delivery made staying focused a challenge. Katherine played with her new pendant. Her thoughts drifted back to the night before, her conversation with Bruno in the kitchen and the question he had asked her after she removed her hand from under his.

***

"Are you married or are you really married Katherine?" Bruno's tone was philosophical. Withdrawing her hand and moving to the sink defused the tension between them, but Katherine knew she wasn't safe yet.

"What do you mean?" Katherine said, flicking him the briefest of glances.

"You know what I mean."

"I'm married and that's all there is to it." What if Ran had said something to Bruno? There's a pathetic woman in The Retreat desperate for a man. She pushed the dreadful thought from her mind.

"There's the habit of marriage, the occupation of marriage," Bruno said. "Then there's real marriage, two souls growing together, championing each other, where mutual love allows each to flourish."

Katherine busied herself rinsing plates; her heart felt like it was too big for her chest. She didn't know what to say, so she said nothing. If he got up from the chair, and turned her around she didn't know how she would respond. She wondered what it would be like to feel his hands on her body. Katherine knew that her rediscovered sense of self and feminine guile could save her, but at that moment she doubted her ability to muster either.

But Bruno stayed in his chair.

"The others will be wondering where we are," Katherine said hearing her name being called and the beginnings of a sing-song. She dried her hands and gave Bruno a conciliatory smile. She patted his shoulder as she passed. He touched her hand. In that one gesture she saw his vulnerability, his loneliness unmasked. She didn't want to leave him sitting there.

"Things haven't been great between me and Vincent for a while, but I want to work on it," she said, sitting back down. "Any more foolishness on my part would just add to my problems."

"You don't need to say anything else."

"In an exercise earlier this week I realised I'm responsible for how I show up in my marriage and in recent months I've hardly been there at all. You know Bruno at the start of this week I was convinced Vincent was having an affair and maybe he is, I don't know for sure, but I've cheated on him in my own head, so really what's the difference. This time tomorrow I'll be back home and I plan to have a new conversation with him, hopefully a conversation where we can start figuring out where we go from here. After twenty-five plus years of marriage I owe him that much. I owe myself that much."

"Come on you two," Suzy shouted from the door.

"We're on our way," Katherine said.

"Be warned, Declan has a karaoke app on his iPad," Suzy said, grabbing the last two bottles of red wine from the counter. "Don't be long."

"You deserve a man who worships you," Bruno said.

"I'm not sure I'd go that far." Katherine laughed. "Believe me, I'm far from perfect." She picked up a spoon and scraped out another mouthful of ice cream.

"It's not about being perfect, it's about being loved for being perfectly yourself."

"I'll buy that."

"Of course it has to work both ways. Loving someone else means seeing beyond their short-comings and mistakes, loving them as consistently as you love, say, your children."

Katherine knew she still loved Vincent; other stuff had just got in the way. "Coffee has to be my favourite ice cream," Katherine said, savouring the creamy bitterness and attempting to bring the conversation back onto safe ground.

"Don't listen to me Katherine, I'm hardly the expert. One failed marriage, two other failed long-term relationships. Well I shouldn't say that, I don't think you can use the word failure when it comes to relationships."

"What happened with you and Lisa?"

"Now that's a question."

"You don't mind me asking?"

"I wrote my first book in an effort to work out what happened between us and it wasn't a very good book believe me, but ignoring the self indulgent crap I wrote, the one bit of wisdom I gleaned from months of moping was that just as engagement precedes marriage, disengagement precedes divorce." Bruno shifted in his chair. "Do you know Katherine, I know the exact moment that marked the beginning of the end of each of my relationships? It was that split second when I chose not to tell Lisa or Misty or Rachel something, when I kept an idea, a thought and especially an emotion to myself. In that instant of repression the relationship started to die."

"Misty?"

"Don't ask."

"I hear what you're saying though."

"Repression leads to resentment, then point scoring. And if you're scoring points in a relationship both sides are losing."

"That's true."

"And then very soon you start speaking about your partner to others, revealing what should be sacred."

"Betraying the relationship."

"Exactly."

"But you and Lisa are good friends now?"

"Somehow we always remembered that we loved Zoe even when we disliked each other. She's been with Matt for what, it must be fifteen years now and they're perfect together and I'm genuinely happy for her. You know Katherine, if we are not trying to make people fit into our preconceived notions of how we want them to behave, relationships are not that difficult."

"Not everyone is as mature or as wise."

"It's just awareness. When you have the awareness to realise that when you are angry with someone, you're usually more angry with yourself. Me and Lisa made the decision that we weren't going to dig up the past, if you keep doing that there's no space for any sort of healing in the present and the future will be just more of the same."

"Wise words Bruno."

"Learnt the hard way, at the coalface of life."

"It's realising that it's not the other person's job to make you happy, isn't it?" Katherine said, putting down the spoon.

"Look at you getting all wise," Bruno said, nudging her shoulder.

"There you are. Come on, out," Morag shouted. "Katherine you have to see this." She grabbed both their arms hoisting them to their feet.

The dancing had started. Suzy, Declan and Serendipity were throwing some moves at one end of the table.

"Look," Morag said, pointing across the courtyard. There, by the cactus garden Louise was dancing all by herself. Arms raised, hips swaying, body twisting.

"Dancing to her own beat," Bruno said.

"And she doesn't drink," Morag said.

"I've seen this before, something just takes hold, a desire to express."

"Look at her, it's like she's shaking stuff off her," Katherine said.

"I suspect that's exactly what's she doing and she's not even aware of it," Bruno said.

"You go girl," Suzy said, having just spied Louise. All heads now turned, but Louise stayed in her own world.

"Jeez, I never knew she had it in her," Morag said.

"I wish I had those moves," Declan said.

"Beautiful," Imelda said mirroring some of Louise's moves whilst still seated.

"She's not dancing, she's being danced," Corinne said.

***

Iam droned on. Katherine looked down the line to Louise, perhaps the most alert person in the room. Katherine took Bruno's business card from her purse. As unconventional as the man himself, it was circular with serrated edges. So many ways to contact him; phone, email, website, Twitter, LinkedIn, Facebook, she wondered if she would use any of them. She would miss him. She liked how she looked through his eyes. Of everyone she had met that week, of everyone she had met in a long time, Katherine felt that he really knew who she was, he just got her. She could be perfectly herself in his company.

"Is everything making sense?" Iam asked. Katherine glanced at her watch; it had been a long twenty minutes. A few nodding heads did little to alleviate the uncomfortable silence that had made a home in the room. "Does anyone have any questions so far?" The hum of the projector was the only response. Katherine looked down the line. Morag's mouth was open; words queued on her tongue waiting to be spewed.

"It's not really working is it?" Iam said, his shoulders sagging.

Thankfully it was Corinne who spoke. "Could I make a suggestion? Just pull up a chair and talk with us. You've put a lot of effort into this, we can all see that and I think you've something valuable to say, but I don't think you need all the visuals, just talk to us, lead a conversation."

Iam considered her words. "Right, the stabilisers are coming off," he said, lifting the chair from behind the table.

"Maybe we could move into a circle?" Imelda said. Shuffling around, Katherine found herself beside Iam. He gripped a bundle of flashcards. His hands were shaking.

"Perhaps just focus on the key lessons you've learnt, what you want us to take away from this session," Corinne said.

"I'll give it a go. I just hope something half-sensible comes out," Iam said, tossing his notes onto the table. "Right, I know people think I'm mad, you probably think I've gone all hippy, the poster boy for a midlife crisis and all that. Why the hell does he call himself Iam Love? And I know what people say behind my back." Disarmed, many pairs of eyes searched their notebooks. "But all I can say is that the last two years have been the happiest of my life."

"Good for you," Corinne said, with an encouraging smile. "And what made the difference, because all any of us want is to be happy."

Iam's feet bounced on the floor. "I stopped struggling."

Now he had everyone's attention. Katherine put her notebook on the floor. The entire room seemed to be breathing again.

"I was brought up to believe that life is a struggle, that I had to grab life by the throat and go out and earn my living. Both my parents had tough childhoods, so they wanted me and my brother to have an easier life than they did. They were doing their best."

"Like most parents," Imelda said.

"I wanted to make them proud. But you know the scary thing, I worked for twenty years as an accountant and then as an actuary and at no stage do I ever remember purposely deciding to have that career. It just seemed to happen. I chose to study accountancy at school because I was always told I was good with numbers and if I studied accountancy it made sense to get a job as an accountant. Twenty-four years with London Underground, a good steady, pensionable job. I was settled as my parents would say. Now it wasn't all bad. I was earning good money, but the more you earn, the more you spend and the more you need to earn. Without knowing any alternative I had blindly bought into that big lie that seems to me now to be at the heart of so much misery. I believed that if I studied hard, worked hard, saved enough money, bought enough stuff, I would be happy."

"As millions do," Corinne said sitting back and crossing her legs.

"Unfulfilling consumerism, I think that's what it's called," Iam said. His hands were no longer shaking.

"So you changed your life completely after coming here?" Bruce asked from over his glasses.

"Was it the turning point? Not immediately, but the fact that I came here at all meant that I was searching for something. Phyllis, that was my wife, was going to be away golfing for a week and I'd come across a leaflet for this place on one of the girls' desks at work, so I decided what the hell. It was quite a last minute decision and I wasn't really sure what I was letting myself in for."

"A bit like me. I'm only here because a friend had to drop out," Katherine said, turning to face him.

"I remember Neide saying to me then that I'd been living in my head, divorced from my heart. At the time I didn't agree with her, we had a bit of a row. Of course I can see now she was absolutely right. But to answer your question Bruce, the final spur, what prompted me to make changes was actually an email.

"Did your friend Rosemary, who was here at The Retreat when I was here ever mention John the musician Morag?"

"Not that I remember."

"Well, John and I were each other's momentum buddies. We will be talking about momentum buddies later. Anyway John sent me an email a few weeks after I got back. It was one of those general how's it going emails. I was in the office, it was about four o'clock. I was typing a few lines in reply when I noticed the postscript he'd added. I'll never forget it. '*Remember Col you're always more than what you do.*' That had been my big learning from the week; I'd written it across the front of my journal. John was quoting it back to me. Despite all my good intentions I hadn't opened that journal since I'd come home, but those words..." Iam swallowed the emotion in his voice. An entirely different silence now inhabited the room.

"Those words leapt from the screen and hit me here." Iam

punched his chest. "I'd put it down to post holiday blues, but really I'd sunk back into the old familiar malaise, the quagmire of mediocrity as our friend Bruno calls it in one of his books. In that moment I knew I couldn't keep doing what I was doing. I looked at the files on my desk, the never-ending to do list and I just asked myself what was the bloody point." Iam stretched his arms and took a deep breath, as if breathing was a technique he was only learning. "You know folks the moments that shape our destiny are not heralded by fanfares; they're solitary decisions, made in isolation and silence when just for a moment our courage triumphs over our fear. Somehow courage found me that afternoon in that wood-panelled office with the view of the railway line. That evening I wrote my resignation letter."

"But wasn't that extreme, what did your boss say, your wife?" Declan was the one who voiced all the questions.

"Let me put it this way. A few years ago Phyllis and I visited Alcatraz. Something the guide said stayed with me. She said the greatest punishment for the prisoners was seeing the lights and hearing the sounds of San Francisco, the sounds of people free to live their lives. That's what it was like for me. For years I felt like I was observing life, never fully participating in it. The week here was a taste of freedom and when I went back home, well it was worse than before because I'd met people who were living, how can I put it, an uncontained life and there I was back in my cell again."

"But what about paying the bills, the mortgage, your responsibilities?" Declan said.

"And what about your wife and kids?" Morag asked.

"I'd been sensible my entire life. I studied hard to please my parents; I worked hard to give Phyllis and the boys a good life. But I'd had enough. You know I used to spend a chunk of each day dealing with pensions, deferred pensions and looking back I can see now I'd been living a deferred life."

"I think there's another type of life assurance called whole life?" Katherine said, drawing on her experience of working with Vincent. "That's what you are doing now, isn't it?"

"That's it, I must remember that," Iam said. "My sensibility meant from a security point of view we were okay financially. Fortune smiled on me too, or as Neide says it was just the Universe helping me out, showing me I was on the right path. At the time London Underground were offering voluntary redundancy packages, so I was able to leave with a lump sum which certainly helped."

"But what did Phyllis say?" Morag said.

"She thought I was mad. I embarrassed her. I think she was more worried about the gossip. Our marriage had been dying for years; it was a relief to put it out of its misery. I had pretended to be a husband and she had pretended to be a wife, two miscast actors in roles neither of us wanted to continue to play. And the boys have their own lives. Justin even said we should have separated years ago."

"It wasn't acrimonious then?" Katherine asked.

"Factual was how I described it to Neide."

"You must have been scared?" Suzy asked. "Surely you had doubts about leaving your work, your family, your home."

"Oh I did question my sanity as many others did too. I was scared, but you know at least I was feeling something; I'd spent too many years numbed to life. It was like when my brother thought it would be a good idea to teach me to swim. He threw me into the canal. When you have no choice, you do what you have to do."

"Like Columbus burning his ships," Bruce said.

"Exactly, there was no way back. They did offer me a sabbatical at work, and my director even suggested working part-time, but I had to make a clean break and when I heard myself say, that I needed to live full-time, I knew I was making the right decision. As an actuary I'd spent my time calculating probabilities, working with percentages and trying to make predictions with ever-increasing certainty. All that went and in its place was a life of uncertainty and one hell of a sense of possibility."

"Good for you," Marie said. "The phrase I use to describe my own situation is that it was only in jumping off the corporate ladder that I found my wings."

"I must remember that one too," Iam said. "Do you know the first thing I did, the day I left the office with my box of belongings; I sat in the park just across the road. I'd cut through it twice a day for years but I'd never stopped. I stretched out on the grass and looked at the sky. I craved open spaces. I'd spent my life living in boxes in every sense of the word, houses, cars, trains, offices."

"And when we die we're put in a box," Imelda said.

"I needed to be out in the open. I went on a spiritual retreat in Arizona, six weeks in the wilderness, slept under the stars, did vision quests, shamanic healing, it was incredible, a men-only group. We hunted, cooked what we caught, no phones, no technology, so liberating."

Suzy whispered to Declan, but he told her to be quiet. "Was that when you decided to change your name?" Declan asked.

"That was later, but the Indian chief we met gave us all Indian names, mine was Rushing Fox." There was a few titters in the group. "At the time it was apt. No the name change is quite recent, but I'd been thinking about it for a while. I did a lot of research. You know in many cultures people get the opportunity to choose their own names. In Japan, artists changed their name at that point in their careers when they felt they had become the artist they aspired to be. Many writers and film stars change their names, Cat Stevens, Cassius Clay. I didn't feel like Colin Barton anymore."

"But Iam Love, it's a bit much though," Morag said.

"It feels right to me. It's my commitment to what I believe is my calling for the second part of my life. I want to make my choices from a place of love not fear. I know now that I'm not and never was the roles I played. Like everyone else I'm always more than what I do. Who I am is far more important and who I am is love. That realisation was so huge in my life that I had to mark it; I had to do something significant, so I changed my name."

It was sincerity not pretension that Katherine heard in his voice.

"And I think this is a good point to link into the exercise I had planned for you this morning."

"But how did you end up back here?" Morag asked.

"I'd stayed in touch with Neide. When she heard I was at a loose end she asked if I could house-sit for a few weeks when she went back to Germany and I never left," Iam said. "We've been together now nine months and it's going great. With both complement each other. As Neide says herself, she's not the best with admin so I look after the business side of things for her. You know it's amazing how life works out when you step back, when you stop struggling. I never looked for accountancy work here, but just through casual conversations and word of mouth I've seven or eight bookkeeping clients. Only this week a pool cleaning company rang me."

"God works in mysterious ways," Imelda said laughing.

"Shall we take a ten minute break and when we're back, we'll give the exercise a go?" Iam said, getting to his feet.

"Can I just say thank you, thank you for being so honest," Corinne said. Her words were followed by applause. Iam blushed. "See you didn't need the slides."

There were no jokes about Iam or his name during the break. Brave, courageous, even ballsy were the words that peppered the courtyard conversations.

***

"Yesterday you did your goal-setting exercise with Neide, isn't that right?" Iam said standing at the top of the room. The projector, screen and laptop had been packed away. "For me, how you grow as a person as you pursue your goals, is as important as achieving the goal itself. So for the next little while rather than focusing on what it is you want to do, you're going to focus on the qualities you want to be, the characteristics or emotions you want to connect with. After all we're human beings, not human doings."

"I like the sound of this," Marie said, scribbling away.

"So review the goals you wrote yesterday and then ask yourself to achieve those goals what qualities do you need to display," Iam said. Katherine noticed how it was easier now for him to make eye contact with the group.

"Is this like the law of attraction?" Marie asked.

"Yes, you'll be harnessing the law of attraction because you'll be connecting with the qualities, with the emotions, not just thinking about them."

"What's the law of attraction?" Tonya asked.

"Think of it this way, physics tells us that everything is just energy including our thoughts. The law of attraction states that like attracts like. The universe responds to the energy you emit so negative thoughts will attract negative events, positive thoughts will attract positive events."

"So it's positive thinking?" Tonya said, toying with a pigtail.

"It's more than positive thinking, you have to connect with the feeling, you have to live the emotion in the present, otherwise it's just wishful thinking. The best way of connecting with the feeling is to form a little phrase or mantra that starts with the words 'I am.'"

"No pun intended," Bruce said.

"For example, I am happy, I am determined." Iam took the stereo from the cupboard and inserted a CD. "We're going to start with a short meditation to get us in the right place to do this exercise." A soft lilting instrumental filled the room. "So I want you to sit back, close your eyes and take some nice deep breaths."

Katherine noticed Corinne sit upright, her palms turned up. Katherine followed her example.

"In your own head, as you breathe in I want you to say the words 'I am' and as you breathe out say the word 'protected.'" Katherine could hear Iam breathe and repeat the words. A minute or so later he spoke again. "Now keep going, but change the word 'protected' to the word 'safe.'"

Katherine focused on her breath and the phrase 'I am safe'. She liked the floral scent of Suzy's perfume, freshly applied during the break.

"How did you find that?" Iam asked a few minutes later.

"Very calming," Corinne said.

"It's a powerful exercise because you're contradicting the feeling of being unsafe; of being unprotected which is really what fires feelings of worry and anxiousness. It's a great default mantra that one."

"I feel more at ease," Sophie said.

"That's the power of saying 'I am' and really connecting with it, not just saying it. What I want you to do now is grab your pen and paper, write 'I am' at the top of the page, then note what comes to mind, or rather what comes into your heart. Think of the qualities you want to connect with that will either help you in the pursuit of your goals, or simply those qualities or emotions you want to experience on a daily basis."

Katherine's journal creaked with the images she had pasted in the day before. She liked the 'I am safe' exercise so wrote those words in as a reminder.

"Oh, there's something else I meant to do with you first," Iam said, moving back to the flipchart. He wrote the words 'I am here'. "Think about all those times when you were physically in one place but mentally elsewhere. Even now your body is here in this room, but maybe your head is packing your bag or wondering about what's waiting for you at home. 'I am here' is a great phrase to say to get grounded in the present moment. Great for work life balance too, you know when your body is at home, but your head is still at work."

"I sure do," Declan said.

"But as I said, we have to feel the words, not just write them. So I want you to close your eyes again, repeat the words 'I am here' on the inside, allow your mind wander and just see what pops up." The music filled the room once more.

Katherine quickly relaxed into a pattern of deeper breathing. Her first thought was that her time at The Retreat was nearly over and that she would have two hours to kill in the afternoon before her taxi arrived. Make the most of the time that's left was the thought that followed. When Iam called time on the exercise a sense of gratitude had settled on Katherine, gratitude for everything she had experienced that week.

"As you said it's a good exercise for staying in the present moment," Marie said in response to Iam's request for shares.

"I had a different interpretation," Suzy said. "I am here, get on with living life."

"I felt something similar," Corinne said. "I am here, a spiritual being in physical form, celebrate the fact and get on with the business of living."

"I like that," Iam said. "No one is here by accident; everyone is born with a purpose. If someone else could fulfil your purpose then you wouldn't be here."

"I am here, so be grateful, that's what came to me," Katherine said. Nodding heads indicated others felt the same.

"Deal with reality, I am here, deal with the reality of that," Tonya said.

"Good one," Iam said.

"I had a different angle," Imelda said. "I am here, for me

that means God is here. I am the word; as the Bible says 'I am' is the name of God."

Not for the first time Imelda's quiet wisdom astonished Katherine.

"I was wondering if anyone would pick up on that," Iam said. "'I am that I am', the name of God. God, Divine energy, love, whatever label you use, is here in this room." Iam paused to allow people to ponder the concept.

Katherine wrote down what the others had shared.

"Now, back to the exercise, I want you to note what else you would like to attach to the words 'I am'. And remember feel it, don't just think it," Iam said, turning up the music again.

Katherine closed her eyes for a moment then allowed her pen to write whatever came to her.

I am happy.

I am content.

I am here and I am grateful.

I am ready for whatever happens next.

I am open to learning.

I am a good cook.

I am always doing my best.

She stared at the last sentence. It was easy for her to look back on events and wish she had made better choices. But even in those moments she now regretted, she had still been doing her best. She thought of her silliness with Ran and Mark and the arguments with Vincent. Yes, she had made mistakes, but she had always been doing her best.

I am gentle on myself.

I am compassionate.

Katherine turned back the pages and glanced down her list of goals.

I am determined.

I am focused.

I am optimistic.

She thought of the conversation she wanted to have with Vincent.

I am a good listener.

I am caring.

I am understanding.

"What you're doing with this exercise is determining how you want to show up in your life," Iam said. At the end of the exercise another sentiment rested on Katherine. She felt the emotion before she could form the words. With a lump in her throat she wrote – *I am loved.*

The group called out what they had written and Iam captured the phrases on the flipchart.

I am grateful.

I am brave.

I am resourceful.

I am resilient.

I am creative.

"I am loved," Katherine said, contributing what she felt was the most potent phrase she had noted. The words stirred a cocktail of emotions – vulnerability, openness, safety, warmth. If she dwelt on them Katherine felt she could easily cry.

"Good one," Iam said, adding it to the list. More words poured from the group.

I am full of potential.

I am attractive.

I am healthy.

"Now I want you to pick the one that means the most to you and reflect on it just like we did with 'I am protected', 'I am safe' and 'I am here'. So close your eyes once again and connect with the words, feel them, be fully with them for a few minutes," Iam said clicking the stereo on.

'I am loved.' Katherine allowed the feeling to swell within her. She knew she was loved by Vincent, Thom and Claire, each in their own way. But there was also a bigger love. Deep down she had always had a sense that she was protected. She thought of her parents and her aunt Kay, looking down on her, looking out for her, still loving her. Tears pricked her eyes. They weren't tears of sadness or even tears of happiness. They were tears of recognition, tears of realisation, the realisation that she was loved and that she would always be loved.

When the music ended, Katherine could see she wasn't the only one moved by the exercise. She passed Suzy a tissue. A gentle silence had entered the room.

"I can see that was a powerful exercise for many of you," Iam said, rejoining the circle of chairs.

Katherine remembered that after the lunch with Declan and Suzy earlier in the week she had written 'I am love' into her journal. She flicked back through the pages. She crossed out the question mark she had added back then, replacing it with the letter 'd'.

"Your name makes more sense to me now," Morag said, gripping a tissue.

"What was your phrase Morag, if you don't mind sharing?" Iam asked.

"I am a survivor," Morag said, wiping her eyes. "I am here and I am a survivor."

Hands reached to Morag in support. Katherine blinked away more tears.

"I started with 'I am loving,'" Suzy said. "It came to me when Katherine said I am loved. But during that exercise it changed." Suzy struggled to speak. Katherine rubbed her arm. "It changed to 'I am worthy of love.'" With the words out, Suzy could take a deep breath. "I realised that I've spent my life looking to others to validate the love I wasn't giving to myself."

"And you are so worthy of love. In essence that's what you are, that's what we all are – love," Iam Love said.

The words dropped into Katherine's soul. They settled easily, an old truth remembered.

CHAPTER 18

"It would make sense for us to be partners, don't you think?" Marie said, standing directly in front of Katherine. The sharp-featured life coach from Belfast had bolted from her seat as soon as Neide had asked the group to pick their momentum buddies. "I'm usually in Dublin once a month, we could meet up," she said, staring down at her.

A momentum buddy, someone to encourage and support you as you work towards your goals, someone who can hold you accountable if you so choose. Katherine cursed the fact that she hadn't pounced from her own chair and asked Imelda or Corinne. Now she was stuck with Marie.

"I suppose it makes sense," Katherine said, hauling herself to her feet. Approaching noon, the workshop room was stifling, even with the fan on full.

"I could even do some coaching with you," Marie said.

"Well, we'll see how it goes," Katherine said, writing her email into Marie's proffered notebook. She purposefully misspelt it, omitting the hyphen between her first name and surname. And she wasn't parting with her phone number, fearing a proliferation of texts advertising coaching courses in the Belfast area. Katherine had already given her number to Corinne and Imelda; she planned to stay in touch with them and possibly Suzy as well. She had no intention of initiating contact with Marie. The one time they had been left alone at the lunch table conversation had been awkward. After an uncomfortable few minutes they had both sought solace in their phones. Katherine felt that being at The Retreat was all she had in common with Marie and meeting her for coffee would be akin to meeting a teacher outside school having not done your homework.

"Now folks, we have two final exercises for you," Neide said, moving to the flipchart. "You know this is my favourite time of the week, when everything comes together."

"Should we stay in our pairs?" Marie asked.

"Yes, you're working with your momentum buddy on this one."

Chairs were dragged, seats swapped, cardigans and bags passed. Katherine stayed where she was within range of the fan. She marvelled at the colour of Marie's legs. Either she was spending every spare minute in a secret alcove sunbathing, or tinted lotions stocked her bathroom. She scrutinised Marie's knees and ankles for evidence that her tan had come from a bottle.

"The purpose of this exercise is for you to determine your top three actions, your three priorities for when you return home," Neide said. "But we're not going to call them actions; we're going to call them something far more powerful – promises." She wrote the words 'my promise list' on the board and beneath it 'I promise myself that'. "This is the phrase we'll use. You're going to write down the promises you're making to yourself. They might be the first steps towards some of the goals you noted yesterday, or maybe they'll relate to your learning from other workshops, whatever is most relevant to you."

"Why the word promise, not action or priority?" Marie asked.

"We tend to keep promises don't we? It's much easier to drop a commitment, or not follow through on an action, but we rarely break promises," Neide said.

Katherine didn't have to flick back through her notes as some of the others were now doing, she knew her priorities, she knew her promises, she had already made them to herself.

"Write out at least three, then share them with your buddy

so you can follow up with each other in a few weeks' time."

"What if we would prefer not to share?" Louise asked. All heads turned because it was rare that Louise asked a question. Even Sophie, the youngest and probably the shyest of the group, asked more questions than Louise. Morag looked particularly surprised because she was Louise's momentum buddy.

"Whatever is shared should be treated confidentially," Neide said. "But if you would prefer to keep your own counsel Louise, that's your choice."

One of the images Katherine had pasted into her journal had come loose. She loved the vision board she had created, the pictures that represented her goals and dreams. She had been gazing at it when she should have been proactively selecting her momentum buddy.

"I love that," Marie said pointing to the picture of the herb garden Katherine was smoothing out. Katherine quickly turned to a new page and copied down what Neide had written on the board.

"So remember to start off with the phrase – 'I promise myself that' and if possible put a timeframe on it, by the end of the week, by the end of the month, whatever you feel is realistic for you," Neide said, circling the room.

Katherine began to write.

I promise myself that I will have an open and honest conversation with Vincent, tonight if possible, even though I won't be home till late.

I promise myself that I will know how we stand financially by the end of next week.

I promise myself that I will source painting supplies by the end of next week.

"I presume we can have more than three?" Katherine asked.

"As many as you wish."

I promise myself that I will research what it takes to run a bistro. I

*will search the web, have a conversation with Mags and make general
enquiries. I aim to make substantial progress by the end of the month.*

Buoyed by his successful workshop that morning, Iam
rejoined the group. As was his habit he left his sandals by
the door as if he was entering a sacred place. Confounding
expectations, his workshop had been one of the most inspiring
of the week. Katherine told him so during the break and he
was genuinely moved by the feedback. With Declan and Suzy
listening in, Iam had spoken further about leaving the rat race,
although he put his newfound happiness down to the personal
development work he had done, without it, he said, he would
have quit the rat race, but would still have been a rat. Looking
at him now, laughing and chatting with Neide, Katherine was
prompted to add another promise to her list.

*I promise myself that I will try, as best I can, to make my choices and
decisions from a place of love not fear.*

This would be the hardest promise to keep. Suppose Vincent
was having an affair, all her learning from this week would be
annihilated by a tornado of emotions – disappointment, anger,
sadness, but it would be fear that would fuel the storm. Fear
would also be the ultimate enemy when they discussed finances.
Practically, she wasn't sure how she could make choices from
a place of love, but it was a noble and worthwhile aspiration.

"So when you're ready, share what you've written with your
buddy. Note each other's promises. Accountability starts here,"
Neide said.

Katherine listed hers first whilst Marie transcribed them
into her notebook. It was odd to see what was so personal, so
huge in her world, recorded by someone else as mere words
on a page. Katherine's happiness and well-being depended on
those promises, but Marie was writing them down as if they
were items on a shopping list. Our promises are really only
important in our own little worlds Katherine thought. Maybe
we all feel the world should be aligned to our every need and

want, whereas in reality, Katherine realised, life would go on whether she kept her promises or not.

"Right I'll tell you mine," Marie said, sitting up straight. "I promise that I will do what I have to do to promote my business and get to the point where I'm earning ten thousand euros per month by the end of the year. I promise that I will arrange a holiday in Thailand for myself and John by the end of the month. I would love for us to get away for Christmas and New Year."

"And your third one?" Katherine asked whilst scribbling down what Marie had said.

"This one is more personal. I promise that I will contact my sister by the end of next week. We haven't spoken in a few years. I'll be honest Katherine; she's popped into my mind quite a lot this week. I think it's time I extended the olive branch. I can't expect her to make the first move, she hasn't done the personal development work I've done, she's not as aware as I am."

"There was something Iam said earlier, I noted it in my journal, you probably did too, let's see," Katherine said, thumbing back through the pages. "We're always doing our best," she quoted from her notes. "I'm sure your sister is always doing her best."

"I don't remember that," Marie said recrossing her legs.

Katherine thought of her own sister. She had said to Joan on the phone that she would pop down to see her the following week. Now that would be a test of her newfound wisdom and tolerance. Whatever Joan said or did, she would have to remember that she was doing her best.

"Let me just check Marie if I wrote my email down right, I often forget to put in the hyphen, I've changed it recently." Katherine reached for her notebook.

"Folks, we need to keep an eye on the time and we've one final exercise for you," Iam said, handing out sheets of paper with The Bliss Retreat logo at the top. Serendipity passed envelopes down the line. "You're going to write a letter to yourself."

"Oh very good," Corinne said.

"Imagine what message you would love to receive in a few months' time," Neide said.

"Words of encouragement, a reminder of some of what you've learnt this week," Iam added.

"Exactly, some of your key insights," Neide said. "Or even a reminder of everything you should be grateful for. Remember that exercise way back at the beginning of the week."

"I remember Imelda's gratitude list," Katherine said, prompting the others to compliment Imelda again.

"We will post your letters to you in six months' time, or maybe just before Christmas, it would make a nice Christmas present wouldn't it?" Iam said.

"A participant a few weeks back described this exercise as writing a love letter to themselves," Neide said.

"Oh I remember those," Corinne said. "I suppose people don't write love letters anymore."

"A text or tweet if you're lucky," Suzy said.

"So shall we give it a go?" Neide said. Katherine didn't know what she would write, but she loved the concept. She could imagine opening it Christmas morning and being transported back to The Retreat, or to the wall in the park by the church, her learning rekindled, her drive to achieve her goals refuelled.

"What you write is for your eyes only so when you're finished, seal the envelope and address it to yourself. And here's a tip, don't reread it and don't bother editing it either, let it flow, write from your heart," Neide said.

"I'm not sure where to start," Louise said.

"Like any letter, start with 'Dear Louise,'" Neide said. "Think of it this way, if your best friend in the whole world was writing a loving, inspiring, encouraging, maybe even a little challenging letter to you, what would they write?"

"Some music might help," Iam said, switching on the stereo.

Katherine closed her eyes allowing the instrumental to harmonise her mood. When she felt stillness settle, she picked up her pen and wrote *'Dearest Katherine'* at the top of the page. For the second time that week her hand struggled to keep up with the flow of words. She didn't censor, she didn't edit, she didn't reread. She filled the page front and back. The very essence of what the week had meant to her was poured on to the page. She folded it in three and sealed the envelope, preserving it for a time in the future when it would be needed.

***

The usual chatter didn't fill the room when the last letter was collected. The exercise had prompted deep reflection. After soaring for five days in a world of inspiration, possibility and empowerment Katherine felt she was beginning to decompress. She would have to fight the feeling of deflation and the temptation to mourn the friendships made.

"So," Neide said, resting against the table. Along the semi-circle, the smiles were just a little forced. "We've just under an hour before we go our separate ways; let's spend that time sharing some of what we're taking with us."

"I could talk the entire time," Suzy said.

"I suspect we all could," Corinne added.

"I tell you what, perhaps if we just share one key learning," Neide said. "And let's do it standing up."

"Privy council style, keeps thing punchy," Bruce said, first to his feet.

"Why don't we form a circle?" Iam said. Feet shuffled round and Katherine found herself between Marie and Declan.

"Who wants to start?" Neide asked.

"I might as well." It was Declan who spoke. For someone whose sharp repartee had entertained them all week his expression was serious. "What do I say? Okay, I only came here because Suzy talked me into it and if I'm honest I didn't expect to learn a great deal, but in spite of myself I've enjoyed the week. So what am I taking away? I've always prided myself on the fact that I work hard and play hard, but this week has made me question that. It also struck me this morning that I've used that work hard, play hard mentality as a way of getting attention or pity or both. And the discussion we had in Bruno's workshop about definitions of success that really got me thinking too. How do I define success for myself? I think that's changing, or has to change, because the price of my old definition is too high. So what I'm taking away is really a question – how do I define success? I don't have the answer yet, but it's a good place to start." A round of applause set the precedent for those who followed.

"New answers and new solutions start with new questions, don't they?" Neide said.

"And I've learnt how to be conservative with toilet paper," Declan said. Knowing laughter filled the room. "Oh and I meant to say I've set up the Facebook page some of us were chatting about last night. The Bliss Retreat Tribe, that's what we decided to call it, wasn't it?"

"Other groups have done something similar," Neide said. "We must look at developing something on our own site, what do you think Iam?"

"A community section or blog maybe?" Iam said.

"Anyway who's next?" Neide asked, looking around the circle of faces.

Katherine contemplated volunteering even though she hadn't decided what she was going to say, but Imelda was quick to raise her hand.

"I've had fun," Imelda declared. "Specific learning, there was so much, but when I look back on the week that's my first thought, I've had fun. And you can't have much fun by yourself so I'm so grateful to everyone here for their friendship and for making this old woman feel young again."

"Oh Imelda, you'll outlive us all. I don't know where you get the energy," Suzy said.

"And I want to thank you Imelda for being so generous with your own wisdom, I've learnt a lot from you personally," Neide said, reaching across the circle and catching Imelda's hand.

"Hear! Hear!" Bruce said.

"You'll all have me blushing," Imelda said. "I don't know how you'd feel about this Neide, but there's a beautiful song I learnt recently that I'd love to share, it's all about going home."

"Wonderful," Corinne said.

"How about we keep going with the shares and then the floor will be yours Imelda," Neide said.

Sophie was the next person to respond to Neide's invitation.

"My mother arranged for me to come here this week," the young Belgian girl said. "She thought it would help build my confidence, help me get clear as to what I want to do with my life. I was scared, but everyone has been so nice. The goal-setting exercise was great. My goal is to move out of home." Laughter erupted. "Yes, my mother will be surprised. Now I still don't know exactly what I want to do with my life, but I've learnt that it's not about what other people want for me, it's what I want for myself."

"That's it girl, only you can live your own life," Morag said.

"So you're leaving here ripe with curiosity and full of possibility?" Neide said. Nodding vigorously, Sophie nudged Tonya to shift the spotlight to the next in line.

"When I project my problems onto others, it means I don't have to deal with them myself," Tonya said hands clasped at her chest. "That's what I've discovered this week and I've also realised, much to my relief, that no one is perfect. We all have our own challenges and struggles. Perhaps my issues are the most visible, there's no avoiding the size I am, but as I said to some of you in the kitchen last night I've spent a long time fighting the world, when really I've been fighting myself. So the first promise I've made is to be kinder to me."

"We can all relate to that one," Iam said.

"As I said to you earlier in the week Tonya, as a bigger person too, others will judge us; oh she must be lazy, irresponsible, stupid, but let other people do what they do, let's not judge ourselves harshly as well." Neide said. Katherine's eyes looked down to the floor as many other sets of eyes did too.

"My big takeaway was from this morning's session with Iam," Suzy said. "I've been waiting for Mr Right my whole life, but as I said earlier, until now I didn't really believe that I was worthy of love, worthy of being in a great relationship. In my letter I wrote that I'm the one I've been waiting for. It's not Mr Right riding into my life on a white horse; I'm the one on the white horse."

"Lady Godiva," Declan whispered to Katherine, but she ignored him.

"I took a lot from the relationship workshop with Pamela as well." Suzy continued. "She helped me realise that I'd been carrying the poison of every failed relationship with me and had injected it into my new relationships. No wonder they never went anywhere. So, I'm leaving a lot of baggage behind me this week as well Neide."

"That's what the baggage room is for," Iam laughed.

Hearing Suzy praise Pamela Lorne's workshop, Katherine wondered if she had missed out. Then again if she had stayed, she wouldn't have had the adventure in Playa Blanca with Corinne and that was an experience she wouldn't trade.

A sequence had now been established; the baton of sharing was moving around the circle. Katherine would be last to speak.

Bruce said that what he took from the week was the courage to try new things. Top of his promise list was his intention to join his local amateur dramatics club. Louise received a spontaneous round of applause when she said how she intends to trust herself and her instincts, rather than just relying on what others suggest.

"I'm still a little raw from the workshop earlier," Morag said being next in line. "It's not often a man makes me cry," she said to Iam. "Anyway here's what I'm taking away." Morag spoke fast, as if she had just one opportunity to get it all out. "I've done a lot. I'm a resourceful person, a survivor like I said earlier. I raised three boys by myself after my Eddie died. I got three meals on the table every day. They all have good jobs and are settled and I was able to do that for them. I was their father and their mother. That's what I'm taking away." She kept her head low. Eye contact would break the seal. Hands rubbed Morag's shoulders as applause rang out again.

"There's a quote of Mother Teresa's Morag that I love," Corinne said. "I can't remember it exactly, but something like – 'we, the willing, led by the unknowing, are doing the impossible for the ungrateful. We have done so much, for so long, with so little, we are now qualified to do anything with nothing.'"

"Beautiful," Imelda said.

"Except I'm no Mother Teresa." Morag laughed.

It was then Corinne's turn.

"If I may, I'm going to draw what this week has meant to me." Corinne turned to the flipchart and grabbed a marker. "Now this is my attempt at a tree. I've been sketching trees all week; I even painted one in Ran's class. So, each branch represents a different aspect of my life, my family, my friendships, my health, my finances, my work. This week I've got really clear as to what's important in each of these areas, especially work. At sixty-three, I now know what I want to do with my life, well the rest of my life. I got some wonderful insights yesterday mainly thanks to Morag and Katherine who pointed out some obvious facts that were staring me in the face. But this is my key learning. The trunk of the tree, this is the core of who I am, how I show up in each area of my life. This is the inner strength that feeds each branch and it's this inner strength that is even stronger as a result of being here this week."

Katherine marvelled at Corinne's perception and creativity.

"The roots, this is how I'm fuelled, how I nourish myself, when I connect with my creativity, when I turn inwards and this is what makes me stronger. I'm probably rambling on like an old woman. I could keep the analogy going, coping with the changing seasons, the challenges in life, bending in the breeze, being flexible, but I'll shut up now."

Marie was busy capturing what Corinne had drawn even though it was her turn to speak. Katherine felt she had been like a magpie all week more interested in collecting the tools and techniques than actually partaking in them.

"I've been amazed at everyone's learning and that's great testament to you Neide for the workshops you've put together. I'm leaving with a notebook full of wisdom."

"And if there's a specific learning Marie?" Neide asked when there didn't seem to be anything else forthcoming.

"That I'm quite a sorted person and I'm blessed to do the work I'm doing. Like Morag said, it's important to acknowledge everything we've done and achieved in our lives, I'm very lucky." The applause was half-hearted, more habit than spontaneous acknowledgement.

Perhaps Marie was a sorted person, but Katherine didn't quite believe her. Behind the veneer of perfect make-up and summer separates was a woman who hadn't allowed herself to be vulnerable for the entire week. She had retained her composure and coolness, but had missed the real rewards on offer. Katherine remembered what Corinne had said to her at the restaurant in Playa Blanca, without some sort of breakdown, there can be no breakthrough.

All eyes now turned to Katherine, the last to share. She had found what the others had said profound. There was no way she could match Corinne's analogy or Morag's vulnerability. Everyone had spoken openly and honestly, all she could do was follow suit.

"When I came here I kept hearing the word breakthrough," Katherine said. "I didn't know what it meant. Well I do now because I've had multiple breakthroughs."

"We should have multiple everything," Suzy laughed.

"These few days have been a real tonic and one I badly needed. What you said Corinne rings so true with me. I'm leaving here a stronger woman if that makes sense. I haven't a clue what I'll face when I get home, or what life will throw at me, but I'm not as scared by life, I'm not scared of change anymore. And there was something Bruno said to me last night that has stuck as well – greater happiness requires greater risk. I'm leaving here with the courage to take more risks."

"Fantastic," Neide said over the applause. "And from what I hear we should all be expecting invitations to the opening of your restaurant Katherine."

"Build it and we will come," Declan said.

"I love hearing how people have found their time here worthwhile. It's why I do what I do," Neide said. Iam took her hand, a gesture Katherine thought was sweet. "It's always fascinating because the same themes come up time and time again; being gentle with ourselves, having the courage to take more risks, appreciating everything we have to be grateful for," Neide said, acknowledging the different contributions. "I'm sure you have read those sentiments on the postcards and thank you notes on the noticeboard in the common room, but it's not the words that are expressed, it's what they mean to us. Suppose Suzy I told you a week ago that you were the one you were waiting for. It wouldn't mean anything to you. But having experienced the workshops, having participated this week, been open to whatever came up for you, you have connected with a beautiful gift of wisdom."

"So true," Suzy said.

"We are almost finished, but first I want you all to raise your right hands and give the person on your right a pat on the back, a big well done," Neide said. Much laughter ensued and many of the pats transformed into hugs. As had been decided at breakfast Bruce expressed some well chosen words of thanks on behalf of the group. A prolonged round of applause followed.

"Lastly, I want you all to point to yourselves," Neide said. The group did as instructed. "Now look where you're pointing."

"To our hearts," Corinne said.

"Exactly, not your knees, not your stomachs, not even your heads. Your heart, your first point of reference. Some of you have spoken about courage, leaving here willing to take more risks, having the courage to follow your own goals and dreams, or as we sometimes say, our heart's desire, well the word courage comes from the latin *cor* meaning heart."

"*Coeur* in French,' Sophie said.

"And *corazón* in Spanish," Neide said. "Most people come to a retreat like this because they're seeking some sort of change in their lives, but by the end of the week they realise that that means having the courage to change themselves and to listen to the wisdom of their hearts."

"Amen," Imelda said.

"So, Imelda, if your offer still stands, I can't imagine a better way to bring the week to a close."

Imelda cleared her throat and closed her eyes. Her gentle voice filled the expectant silence. Katherine read the unease on a few faces, but she was comfortable with the sincere emotion fenced within the circle they formed.

Imelda sang a slow lilting ballad. It was easy to imagine her, in her old life as a nun, raising her voice in prayer. What she sang now wasn't a hymn and Katherine didn't recognise the tune but the sentiment, a hopeful lament on the theme of going home was beautifully familiar.

'Let my light guide the way as I journey home', was a recurring line of the chorus. It didn't take long before several more voices, including Katherine's, joined in where they could. The song drifted across the courtyard and beyond the walls of The Retreat.

CHAPTER 19

It had been sad saying goodbye to the gang. They had all shared a unique experience, but after a week of introspection and insight their time together was over. Some friendships would not survive outside the walls of The Retreat, but Katherine resolved to make every effort to stay in touch with Corinne and Imelda. Corinne had promised her faithfully that she would email her the following week.

Suzy and Declan were staying in a hotel by the coast for a few days and everyone else had flights to catch. Katherine's flight wasn't until seven thirty. Along with Serendipity she had waved the shared taxis off, but as Serendipity and a local woman, whose look questioned why Katherine was still hanging around, busied themselves with mops and large buckets of soapy water, Katherine began to feel she was in the way. She occupied herself for twenty minutes browsing the noticeboard in the common room and the layers of postcards and thank you notes from people, mainly women, who had passed through the doors of The Retreat before her. This week has changed my life was a common theme. Katherine could appreciate the sentiment.

She perused the book shelves which she had meant to do several times during the week. 'Property of The Bliss Retreat' had been typed out and stuck on each shelf. There was no order to the books as far as Katherine could tell. *Conversing with Angels* propped against *Spiritual Childbirth*. A surprisingly thick book titled *The Beauty of Silence*, beside *Manifesting your Man*, with a creepy picture of a moustached man with a glint in his eye on the cover. Several titles by Paulo Coelho huddled together including four copies of *The Alchemist*. Rhona had suggested it once for their book club, but they had chosen something else.

Katherine picked up a book by the wonderfully named Oriah Mountain Dreamer. Deepak Chopra she had heard of too and Wayne Dyer's name rang a bell. There was a DVD of *The Secret* in German. Claire had bought her the book a few Christmases back, but she couldn't remember ever opening it. She made a mental note to dig it out when she got home.

"Oh, I've just the book for you Katherine," Serendipity said, plonking her bucket down splashing suds onto the stone floor. "Have you heard of *The Artist's Way* by Julia Cameron? My all time favourite, you'll love it. Here it is."

"A spiritual path to higher creativity." Katherine read the subtitle turning the red and gold book in her hands. She liked the image of the mountain and the flock of birds on the cover. The phrase *'an invaluable guide to living the artist's life'* from the blurb appealed to her. "You know I might borrow this. My taxi isn't due till four."

"You'll love it. Artist's dates are my favourite," Serendipity said, pushing the furniture back. "We'll do your room last Katherine, we're not kicking you out."

With two hours to kill, Katherine had a better idea, a final stroll around the old town.

***

Katherine settled herself on the wall of the small park adjacent to the church. She now considered this her spot. It was where she had sat when her pen caught fire contemplating Bruno's exercise, that powerful question – what was possible? Twenty-four hours later she still felt that sense of excitement and potential, the cumulative effect of her entire stay at The Retreat.

She took a few photos with her phone, but no camera could capture the essence of the place, nor what it meant to her. Forged from the tremendous violence of volcanic eruptions, she scanned the landscape below her. She wanted to imprint every shade of brown and grey, every parcel of green onto her memory because she knew there would be days to come when she would wish she was back here – peaceful, inspired and observing the world from a higher perspective.

It was appropriate that she was going to read Imelda's note sitting on the wall. After all it was Imelda who had first discovered the little park. Katherine retrieved the folded page from her journal. She knew Imelda had written out the poem she recited every morning whilst doing her yoga in the courtyard. That yogic peacefulness had stood Imelda in good stead when she discovered she had mixed up the time of her flight home. In the panic that ensued around her, Imelda remained philosophically calm. Katherine's lasting memory of the elderly ex-nun with the rusty hinges, as she referred to the arthritis in her knees, was of her leaning out the window of Corinne's car, shouting 'toodle-oo', as she was whisked off to the airport.

Katherine envied Imelda's elegant handwriting, no doubt the product of strict schooling. Uniform, with just a hint of a slant, it was the quality of handwriting that the words of wisdom scrawled in her journal really deserved.

'*To my friend Katherine*' was inscribed on one side, transforming the page of foolscap into an informal card. Imelda had taken her time with this.

Look to this day for it is Life, the very Life of Life.
In its brief course lie all the verities and
Realities of your existence;
The Bliss of Growth;
The Glory of Action;
The Splendour of Beauty;
For yesterday is but a dream,
And tomorrow is only a vision;
But today well lived makes every

Finding Katherine

Yesterday a dream of happiness, and
Every tomorrow a Vision of Hope.
Look well, therefore, to This Day.

Accredited to the poet Kalidasa, translated from Sanskrit.
With love from your friend,
Imelda
Keep on shining!

A final, precious gift from a wise woman. Katherine read the poem a second time allowing the words to seep into her soul before refolding the page and placing it carefully between the pages of her journal. The leather bound notebook was the tangible reminder of everything she had done and learnt over the week, but the lightness she felt on the inside was the real proof of everything she had experienced.

The journal would always fall open on the pictures she had pasted into it, her vision board, the images representing what she wanted to create in her life. She planned to reread everything she had written on the plane, embedding the knowledge she had captured. She flipped forward to the final entry, something Iam had said as they began saying their goodbyes. *Take what you've learnt this week and bring it back out into the world.*

Shifting position on the wall, she pulled *The Artist's Way* from her bag and flicked through the well-thumbed pages. A previous owner had underlined passages and written some notes in green ink. '*A little courage solves most problems*', was just one insertion Katherine found fascinating. One sentence had been double underlined – '*Ask for answers in the evening; listen for answers in the morning. Be open to all help*'. Each page had a quote in the side margin, a novel idea Katherine thought. The quote on one dog-eared page had been circled. "*We learn to do something by doing it. There is no other way.*" The quote was accredited to John Holt, Educator. Like all good quotes it represented the simplicity on the far side of complexity, a reminder of something Katherine knew deep down. No book would teach her how to have the conversation she needed to have with Vincent, she just had to sit down and talk to him. No one could teach her how to progress towards her dream of having her own bistro; she just had to take action. The same with painting, she had to paint.

She closed the book on her lap and savoured the warmth of the sun on her face. Memories of the week drifted in and out. Buckets of tears had been shed, tears of every kind. Tears of sadness alone in her room. Tears of laughter at the long table in the courtyard when she thought her sides would burst. And the tears of emotional release, those burning tears washing away old tensions and stresses that she had carried for too long.

But it was the unexpected friendships she would miss the most. Imelda and Corinne, Bruno and even Carlos, perhaps the wisest of all because he was perfectly happy with his station in life, a true guru disguised as a part-time chef.

There was no way she could explain to Mags or Rhona, let alone Vincent, those exquisite moments of insight when someone said something seemingly inconsequential and suddenly clouds of confusion parted and clarity shone bright.

Katherine grimaced at the embarrassing episodes too. At the top of the class during the relationship exercise with Neide, though that had certainly been worth it. The illicit kiss with Ran when she threw herself at him, just as she had thrown paint on the canvas when the thunderstorm raged. Thankfully Ran's common sense, and even if she didn't recognise it at the time, his respect for her, prevailed. That had been a narrow escape.

Shading the screen with her hand, she found the photo on her phone that Corinne had taken of her dancing with Bruno at the party at César Manrique's. That was mortification, not embarrassment, but with that big bear of a man you had no option but to surrender. She would probably always cringe at the picture, but the expression of joyful abandon on Bruno's face was contagious, even through a lens.

When people asked how she got on and they were bound to ask, so much would be communicated in the single word – great.

***

The only down side of being perched on the wall was that it wasn't very comfortable. One leg was numb. Getting to her feet, she took a pebble from the wall as a memento and dropped it into her bag. It was time to start the journey home.

As much as she wished it wasn't there, Katherine couldn't ignore the gurgle of anxiousness forming in the pit of her stomach, that niggling nervousness that if left unchecked would crawl out of her bowels and invade her entire body. She was going home to an uncertain future. There would be many new conversations with Vincent, but she couldn't be sure how he would respond. In the relationship workshops she had learnt that she was responsible for the fifty per cent of the relating she did in her relationship. She was determined to take full control of her fifty per cent. A renewed relationship was what she wanted; she hoped Vincent wanted it too. As she crossed the square in front of the church Katherine realised that the anxiousness she felt was simply the price she had to pay upfront for the possibility of something new and compelling.

She strolled past the restaurant where she had had lunch with Suzy and Declan on Sunday morning, when the wine, sunshine and easy conversation helped her relax into the week. She would have loved to have gone back, especially one evening, but that never happened. As much as she had enjoyed the salads at The Retreat, the spread of greens and pulses at lunch time was one salad too far. She did need to eat something, but Palacio del Marques was a place to linger and laugh. A sandwich at the airport would suffice.

Katherine loved the narrow streets of the old town. She took more photos, trying as best she could to capture the dappled light and the regimented whitewashed buildings, their brightly painted doors and hanging baskets the only self expression allowed. But this was no open air museum, the majority were family homes; some more cared for than others. Many front rooms were transformed into pop-up shops, coming to life solely for a few hours on a Sunday morning, tempting the weekly influx of tourists in a reversal of typical trading hours. Not strictly pedestrianised, the odd driver, either lost or brave, ran the gauntlet of looming walls and right-angled turns. These streets existed before the idea of a petrol engine ever entered someone's head.

She passed the art gallery she had visited at the beginning of the week. It was closed, siesta time. Two doors down a craft shop was open. The smell of leather enticed her inside. A thin woman with blonde dreadlocks swirled around the crown of her head, sat in the corner working a piece of leather through a machine. Katherine felt like she was intruding but the woman greeted her warmly. The aroma of leather was one of Katherine's favourite smells. She inhaled deeply the smoky, rich, almost oily scent as she browsed.

Leather bracelets, bangles and necklaces in black, brown and tan were laid out on a table. Ten euros each or three for twenty-five read the sign. She'd seen both Thom and Claire wear something similar so she picked up one for each of them and a third one because it made economic sense. She could certainly say they were handmade. The machine in the corner hummed as the woman slowly pushed a piece of leather through a stitching tool. Bags of different sizes and colours lined the shelves. Some were gaudy with too many tassels and studs, but a dark green one, racing green, a colour Katherine loved, caught her eye. It had a silver clasp and a sturdy zip. One hundred euros. A larger one beside it, in cream leather, was twenty euros dearer.

"Did you make all of these?" Katherine asked.

"Right here on this machine." The woman answered getting to her feet. "And all my own designs."

"I really like them. Have you been doing it for long?"

"Oh, twenty years off and on. You must be staying at The Retreat?"

"You don't get many tourists during the week I suppose."

"Your notebook, see." The woman took one just like Katherine's from the shelf behind the door.

"Ah, Neide said someone local made them and the leather cover of course, now it makes sense." Katherine caressed the cover of her brown leather notebook.

"So this must be your last day?"

"Flying home tonight, I'm just scouting for a few last minute gifts and you're one of the few places open."

"Well let me know if I can help you with anything and there's always a discount for someone staying at The Retreat, especially as you are a customer already. I can easily adjust the fasteners on those wristbands, if you like; I tend to do them at a standard size."

"They're for my kids, they should be fine."

"What age?"

"Oh they're adults." It struck Katherine that it was the first time she recalled referring to Thom and Claire as adults. "You know I'm also after something for a good friend of mine and I was thinking of a bag." Katherine wanted to get something substantial for Rhona.

"It's quite a classic this one," the shop owner said, picking up the cream bag.

"I can tell you really love your work."

"Life's too short not to and I'd like to think some of that positive energy goes into everything I make."

Perhaps it was a standard line the woman gave to every tourist who entered her shop, but she sounded sincere.

Katherine could never thank Rhona enough for persuading her to take her place at The Retreat. She knew her well enough to know that she would never accept money from her, but a gift and perhaps a voucher for afternoon tea would be graciously accepted.

"I think she'd really like that and the colour would match most outfits," Katherine said.

"And what about for yourself?" The woman asked placing Katherine's purchases on the counter.

"Oh I think I'm taking enough back." Katherine touched the pendant at her neck. "If you have a card I'll take one, I know my friend would love to know the name of the woman who made her bag."

"I'm Daphne." The woman handed her a leaflet from behind the counter. '*For the love of craftsmanship*' was written across the top, with Spanish and German translations as well.

"It's a good photo of you," Katherine said, examining the leaflet.

"I need to get more printed."

"Oh these are beautiful I love the way they catch the light," Katherine said, noticing a vase filled with tall twigs, and hanging from them, like jewelled leaves, was an array of crystal jewellery. "Do you make these too?"

"No, a friend makes them; I just sell them for her. She has a great website too. Unusual aren't they?"

"I love how they are displayed."

Katherine examined a small crystal angel-like figure and a charm bracelet. The figure had fastenings to wear both as a broach and necklace. Mags would appreciate it she thought.

"Now that's it, otherwise I'll end up buying everything," Katherine said, adding the sparkling figure to her growing pile on the counter. She hadn't got anything for Vincent, but there was nothing in the shop that would appeal to him. She could get him something at the airport.

With precise fingers Daphne lined up the handwritten price tags placing each one on the edge of the counter, like Sellotape awaiting wrapping paper.

Katherine glanced round the little shop again, just like the art gallery it had once been someone's main living room. The green bag stood defiantly on the shelf where she had left it. Would she regret not buying it for herself? Katherine picked it up again. It matched her pendant. Bruno would approve of such a bag. It reminded her a little of Corinne's bag as well. She looked at the handbag on her arm, the Louis Vuitton Vincent had bought her for her birthday. It screamed look at me and look at the person carrying it. The green bag cost a fraction of what it did, but it seemed to say, I was born in this room, made from my mother's love of the craft, take me out into the world.

"You know I shouldn't, but there's something about this bag I really like," Katherine said, trying it out on her arm.

"It's a great colour isn't it and a beautiful piece of leather."

Turning it upside down, Katherine ran her fingers across the seams. Then she noticed something embroidered on the base. She held the bag close – *sólo un amor*.

"Ah you found its name. I always stitch a word or phrase on to my bags," Daphne said, smiling.

"Something love?"

"*Sólo un amor* – only one love."

Katherine was not leaving the shop without it.

"And what about that one?" Katherine nodded to the cream bag set aside for Rhona.

"*Generosidad*, generosity," Daphne said, pointing at the stitching.

"It's a great idea."

"I tend to wait for the customer to notice first. It might sound a little loopy but I like to think that when someone buys a bag I'm sending that quality out into the world."

"Have you decided on a name for this one yet?" Katherine

said, reaching forward and rubbing the smooth burgundy leather in the machine.

"It usually comes to me when I'm working on it. Funny, just as you were coming in the door I was thinking of *esperanza*. In English you would say hope."

Katherine had a few crisp fifty euro notes in her purse. Apart from supplies for the meal, she hadn't spent much all week.

"So you say there's a bit of a discount going?" Katherine felt a little guilty for asking. She could well be the woman's solitary customer for the entire day, but as Vincent always said, if you don't ask, you won't receive.

"Let's see the two bags, two hundred and twenty, the three bracelets, twenty-five. And the crystal angel, that's twenty and as I said I'm selling that for a friend. I tell you what two twenty for the bags, plus the twenty for the crystal and the leather bracelets are my gift to you."

***

Buyer's remorse kicked in as soon as Katherine took a few steps into the street and switched the large brown carrier bag from one hand to the other. The feel good factor of supporting a local artist, the sentiment stitched into the bags, even the visualised gratitude of the intended recipients, was replaced by thoughts of a lighter purse and future penury.

She stopped to take a photo of the tree in the middle of the street, one of her signposts on the route back to The Retreat. Three cats were stretched out in the shade. Their unapologetic slumber filled Katherine with envy. The exertions of the week, fractured sleep and the thoughts of the journey home, made her want to curl up beside them. She longed for the cool crispness of her own bed.

"Goodbye cat," Katherine said, kneeling down beside the black cat with the three white paws that had the habit of stalking along her window ledge at night. The cat stretched and turned its back to her, as if it knew she was going home and that it was better off saving its energy for her replacement in room 12 who would be arriving on Saturday.

"Ah Katherine." She recognised the voice immediately. Carlos, coming from the direction of The Retreat, carrying the plate of leftover supplies she had put to one side for him. He looked smarter out of his kitchen whites. She was as delighted to see him as he was her. "We get to say goodbye. I thought you gone. I go to The Retreat to say goodbye and everybody gone."

"I see you got what I left for you?"

"*Muchas gracias. Fantástico.*"

"And yesterday went well? Your niece's wedding? *Fantástico* too?"

"*Magnífico.* They was happy. I was happy. Ah young love, we remember Katherine, young love. My heart sing for them. And last night, your *cena?*"

"*Magnífico.*"

"Yes, yes, Serendipity tell me all about it. You're so good. How do you say – overs?"

"Leftovers."

Carlos kissed his fingers, then deposited himself and the platter on a nearby bench. He beckoned for Katherine to join him.

"Look I show you." The bench was under someone's window. Katherine didn't think it was for public use, but she dropped her bags and sat down beside him. He proceeded to show her the slideshow of his niece's wedding captured on his phone, explaining who was in each photo, who was related to who, where they lived and what they did. Katherine didn't say she had seen some Neide had taken, allowing Carlos the full pleasure of reliving his niece's special day.

"She's beautiful," Katherine said, seeing the bride on Carlos's arm.

"Just like my daughter. So proud."

"What an attractive couple," Katherine said, pulling Carlos's phone closer to see the newlyweds standing in the centre of the altar about to walk down the aisle.

"My heart so full for them Katherine. So much love. *Amor* Katherine, *que es lo que importa.*" Katherine glanced up at him. "Love, that's what's important."

"You should be delivering a talk at The Retreat."

"No no, Carlos the chef."

"Carlos is a wise man." Katherine gave him a kiss on the cheek before getting to her feet and gathering her bags. "Now I have to finish packing and I might see if I can grab a quick bite to eat."

"Your taxi at four, Serendipity tell me. So I show you a good place for lunch, very special, the best tapas, very close." Carlos took Katherine's bags from her before she had a chance to protest.

"I'm not sure I have the time and I might just get something to eat at the airport." Carlos stopped in his tracks. "No plastic airport sandwich, Carlos look after you."

"I have to finish packing," Katherine said, trying to keep up with Carlos who was now a man on a mission. She was conscious of the time, but more than a little intrigued. It was an adventure as Bruno would say. She had just under an hour before her taxi was due.

They zigzagged left and right, before stopping at a nondescript door in an alley too narrow for the sun to bother with it. Carlos pushed it open and gestured for her to step inside.

It was a tiny courtyard dominated by an old rusty staircase. Three small wrought iron tables and a scattering of mismatched chairs jostled for space between pots of geraniums. Carlos pulled out a chair and instructed Katherine to sit. He sprinted up the staircase, shouting in rapid fire Spanish.

An old door was propped against a large bin in one corner.

If it wasn't for the few tables, Katherine would have felt she was trespassing in someone's back yard. Two minutes later Carlos returned with a glass in one hand, cutlery in the other and a cushion under his arm which he soon positioned beneath Katherine.

"Carlos where are we?"

"Tony, he's my friend and cooks only for locals."

"It's his restaurant?"

"Just a bar, but the best tapas. I ordered for you. Here." Carlos handed her the glass of what Katherine assumed to be a white wine. He sat on the steps anxiously awaiting her verdict.

"Oh Carlos!" Katherine sipped the golden elixir. She was never a fan of sherry, but this was a concoction like nothing she had tasted before, cool sweet nectar.

"I knew you would like." Carlos picked up his plate. "Tony will look after you; I must go, my wife waiting."

"You're such a good man Carlos." Katherine got to her feet and gave him a hug. "It was a pleasure meeting you."

"Next year you come back." Carlos's eyes looked to his feet.

"Oh, who knows, maybe." She kissed him on the cheek.

She laughed at his unique rendition of 'Love is in the Air,' as he lumbered back into the alley. She could still hear him as she repositioned her table and chair to find the solitary pocket of sunlight that managed to breach the courtyard walls.

Unceremoniously an elderly man, presumably Tony, wearing a misshapen jumper, deposited three dishes in front of her. She thanked him. He just nodded. Somehow his lack of conversation made the experience even more authentic. Katherine inhaled deeply. Whole prawns and chorizo sizzled in an earthenware dish. A basket of bread was begging to be dipped into the garlic and chilli oil fizzing away. Green peppers sprinkled with sea salt and a chicory salad with radishes, parsley, shards of cheese, and slivers of orange, dusted with paprika were the other dishes. Katherine couldn't have chosen a better selection herself. The aromas and anticipating the flavours was as much part of the pleasure as sampling that first mouthful.

Perhaps it was the simple surroundings or the unexpected nature of the meal, Carlos's generosity or the second glass of sherry, but it was one of the best dining experiences Katherine ever had. She took out her journal and added into her vision board *'wrought iron tables and chairs for outdoor dining and mismatched cutlery'*. Leaning against the unsightly bin she took a photo of her table setting framed by the pots of geraniums on the old staircase. It would be all too easy to stay here and miss her flight home.

She reopened *The Artist's Way* holding it in her left hand whilst her fork dangled in her right. She liked the idea of writing morning pages, a brain dump, clearing your head of all the gunk that gets in the way of creativity. It reminded Katherine that she had kept a diary for a few months when she was young, following the example of her aunt Kay who kept regular diaries. She remembered how Kay had a copybook, to record her thoughts, her recipes, her appointments. It was always on the kitchen counter beside her ashtray and the slops bowl for the hens.

She could use her journal for her morning pages, though the recommended three foolscap pages per day would soon fill it. The idea of simply allowing your hand to write whatever came to mind, no censorship, no rereading, no right or wrong, appealed to Katherine. She laughed at the idea mentioned in the book of simply filling the page with 'I don't know what to write' or a series of swear words. It would be a good way of recording her thoughts and actions when she returned home.

Reading ahead Katherine could see why Serendipity loved 'the artist's date', a block of time put aside to nurture the inner artist. She was reminded of the wonderful image of a tree Corinne had drawn on the flipchart and how her time at The Retreat had nourished her, fuelled her to be stronger in each aspect of her life. The artist's date could be a way for Katherine to tap back into what she had found at The Retreat, a way to feed her creative soul. Immediately trips to art galleries, massages, walks in nature, browsing food markets, visiting museums popped into her head as potential future dates. Perhaps that was what this entire week had been, one long and mostly enjoyable, date with herself. She had got to know herself again. And if this was how the date was ending, exquisite tapas in a secluded courtyard, then a second date was certainly on the cards.

Katherine sat back, swirled the remainder of the sherry round the glass, before savouring the last mouthful. She closed her eyes and inhaled the lemony pepperiness of the geraniums. It had been a gift of an afternoon. She was so glad she hadn't stayed in The Retreat clock watching. But it was now time to go. Reluctantly, she climbed the steps and shouted her thanks into what appeared to be a storeroom. Tony saluted from the far door. She left a ten euro note under one of the plates as a tip.

Stepping back into the dark alleyway, she could feel the effects of the two glasses of fortified wine. She was getting to know these streets. The three cats hadn't stirred; they were still stretched out beneath the tree in the middle of the road. Her late lunch had quelled the anxiousness she felt about going home, at least temporarily. She quickened her step. She didn't have time for a shower, just a change of clothes.

The courtyard of The Retreat was wet. Buckets of water had been thrown and sloshed down drains. She tried as best she could to keep her sandals dry. Katherine went straight to her room and dropped her new purchases onto the bed. She had ten minutes before the taxi was due. The glasses of sherry had banished her buyer's remorse and examining the leather items she was genuinely delighted that she had bought the few gifts, including the bag for herself.

It may have been giddiness from the drink, but a thought entered Katherine's head that seemed like absolutely the right thing to do. Before she had time to change her mind, she tipped the contents from her Louis Vuitton handbag onto the bed. It was still in very good condition, practically new. Vincent was unlikely to notice, not right away anyway, and so what if he did, it was hers to do with as she pleased.

She began to transfer her belongings, sunglasses case, purse, lipstick, compact, comb, tissues, passport. She even found a home for the photos of her children and Vincent, her parents' memorial cards and the novena for travellers she always brought with her when flying.

When she was sure it was empty, she ripped a page from her journal and wrote: *'To Serendipity, my gift to you. Thanks for everything and for recommending The Artist's Way. Enjoy. Love Katherine.'* She could already hear how Serendipity would tell the story about how she manifested her Louis Vuitton bag, and maybe she did.

The last thing Katherine did before hauling her suitcase into the yard was take the first picture she painted in Ran's workshop, the painting that started out as a flower, but had transformed into people silhouetted by a setting sun and spread it out on the desk beside the framed picture that had fallen from the wall earlier in the week. On the back of the itinerary she wrote: *'Neide, perhaps you will find a frame for this and a wall to hang it on. Thanks for an incredible week, Katherine.'*

***

The wheels of her suitcase rattled across the cobblestones. She had managed to squeeze Rhona's bag into it but only by filling it with her own laundry first. She had no sooner replaced *The Artist's Way* on the bookshelf than Serendipity told her the taxi was at the top of the lane. Neide and Iam were nowhere to be found. Katherine would have liked to have thanked them in person. Her final hug with Serendipity was all the sweeter, knowing the surprise that awaited her.

Before stepping over the threshold Katherine took a final glance around the courtyard. The workshop room, the tree and cactus garden, the sprawling bougainvilleas, the deep purple one that tumbled over the archway into the bedroom block which could have been a postcard, and of course the long table outside the kitchen door. It would be nice to return one day, but Katherine knew her experiences this week could never be replicated.

Seeing her struggle up the lane, the driver, cigarette dangling on his lip, relieved her of her suitcase. As Katherine settled into the back seat she knew that the time for learning and reflection was over; the time for doing was almost upon her.

***

On the journey to the airport Katherine couldn't shake the niggling feeling that she had forgotten something, but she couldn't think what. Perhaps it was just her hasty packing; she certainly knew she had all her essentials. She patted the green leather bag on the seat beside her and imagined Serendipity's reaction.

Pale Celtic skin and an assortment of county jerseys confirmed that she was in the check-in queue for Dublin. Katherine felt tired, but she hoped she didn't look as wilted as some of the holidaymakers shuffling towards the check-in desk. The couple behind her obsessed about the weight of their bags.

In duty free she picked up a bottle of local red wine that she hoped Vincent would appreciate, perhaps they might even share it. The discounted whiskey was too good a deal to pass on. For a moment she thought she saw Bruno, but it wasn't him.

The flight was on time. She had a window seat and thankfully the seat beside her remained empty. An elderly man sat by the aisle. They exchanged some conversation, which helped pass the time. He looked years younger than his declared age of eighty-two. His accounts of his hill walking expeditions in Lanzarote made Katherine feel positively lazy. He would have got on famously with Imelda she thought.

When Katherine gave him the synopsis of her stay on the island, the man listened with a genuine air of curiosity. He had visited Teguise on a previous trip. Before returning to his book he offered Katherine his definition of a happy life – a head empty of worry and a stomach full of good food. Katherine nodded in agreement.

She had texted Vincent when she was boarding and he had replied saying he was meeting her as planned. What she feared most was Vincent's silence, that he would look at her and say nothing, that her being away changed nothing. But deep down she knew she had changed and if she had changed then the world around her, including her relationships, had changed.

Katherine enjoyed the four hour flight. No longer earthbound, soaring above the clouds she looked down on the world where everything seemed smaller, including her problems and worries. She was on the right side of the plane for the spectacular light show that was the setting sun at thirty thousand feet. She watched the horizon turn rose, then mauve, then orange until the fading light condensed into a narrow gash of red as the sky above it darkened until somewhere off the coast of Portugal she was staring into the blackness of the night sky. Her eyelids grew heavy. By the time the sun would rise again she would be in the comfort of her own bed.

It was only when the plane banked to the left over the familiar dark outline of Howth, with the golden lights of Dublin beyond, that the old pang of anxiety made a fist in her stomach. She found herself breathing quite purposefully.

***

Walking the sterile corridors of the airport Katherine could feel gooseflesh on her arms. It wasn't just the chill of the night air, but anticipation, the leap into the abyss of the unknown.

She wanted to say goodbye to the elderly man but there was no sign of him at the baggage reclaim. She sent Vincent a quick text to say she had landed. 'Waiting for you' was his immediate response. She had a voice mail from Serendipity, the poor girl sounded as if she was hyperventilating. At the bottom of her bag she found the stone from the wall by the church and dropped it into her jacket pocket. Standing by the carousel she scanned the photos on her phone. She was sorry she didn't take more. She was looking at the one of Bruno dancing when she spied her bag.

Suitcase in one hand and her new handbag proudly on her shoulder, her journal slotted inside, she headed towards the exit and the green, blue and red channels. She had plenty to declare. She fully expected to be stopped by the posse of custom guards, but she walked straight by them through the double doors. A sign read, '*no turning back beyond this point*'.

Her heart pounded in her chest. She scanned the faces but couldn't see him. Then movement at a pillar to her right. She had thought about Vincent for most of the flight and seeing him walk towards her was like seeing a photograph move. Katherine felt that all her living moments had culminated in this one.

She stopped in front of him. He kissed her cheek. Katherine dropped her bag and gave her husband a hug. He smelt familiar.

"You're looking well Kay. You must have had a great week."

"An incredible week, I've so much to tell you."

"We've a lot to talk about, don't we?" Vincent said. Katherine nodded. He took the handle of her suitcase. She noticed his wedding ring. She found the stone in her pocket and squeezed it tight.

As much as Katherine tried to ignore it, her bedroom still smelt of damp. It rankled that the surveyor's report never mentioned it and there had been so much done to the building before she moved in. The oil burner and scented candle on the dresser would have to do for now. What she really needed was a spell of dry weather.

The new gutters had been tested during the night. Rain had woken her at three and a head full of checklists had kept her awake. She had watched the flimsy orange curtains begin to glow from four, but must have dozed off in the warm light, because it was now half eight. Katherine couldn't remember the last time she had stayed in bed as long. Thankfully the few hours rest had eased the pain in her shoulder, which she had strained painting the ceiling in the restaurant. With only four days to go, she didn't have time to nurse any pulled muscles.

By some stroke of luck, or inconsistent local planning, she had a view of the harbour. Over the rusted galvanised roof of the vacant property across the street, she could see the arc of the bay and an advancing tide. Part of the charm of the place was the thick walls and deep window ledges. In time she planned to make a proper window seat, but that was on the 'nice' to do list, not the 'absolutely must, by the end of the week, critical' list.

Unpacking the remainder of the removal boxes was this morning's priority. She had stubbed her toe too many times on the ones squeezed between the bed and the old wardrobe. If the other boxes were anything to go by, a high percentage of shoes and bags would go to the charity shop. How many did she really need? As Mags said, packing was a state of mind. If she had been as ruthless packing in the first place she would have saved a fortune on removal charges.

"Mam are you up?" Claire called from downstairs.

"I'll be down in a sec," Katherine said, opening the bedroom door.

"Want anything from the shops?"

"Do we need milk?"

"There's half a litre."

"Pick up some anyway, there's change in the biscuit tin," Katherine said, straightening the bedclothes. It was ironic because in two days' time several gallons were due to be delivered.

It was amazing how quickly new habits formed. They had only been in Kenmare three weeks and tentative routines were emerging from the chaos of starting over, or Act Two as Katherine called it. Hearing the front door click shut, Katherine returned to the window. She watched Claire kneel by the buggy and tuck the blanket Rhona had knitted around Luke's little legs. When it wasn't raining Claire had got into the habit of doing a loop of the town as soon as she had fed him.

Katherine loved watching the two of them together, especially when Claire didn't realise she was being observed. From moody teenager, to college dropout to single mother, it wasn't the life she wanted for Claire, but it was the life she was living and in this moment her daughter looked perfectly happy. The nights when she cradled Claire's head, soothed her worries and wiped her tears were now few and far between. Watching her kiss Luke's forehead then stride off towards the main street, made Katherine's heart sing. Funny how it took Luke's unexpected arrival to establish the sort of relationship she always wanted with her daughter. She was there for Claire and now Claire was here for her.

***

At the time it had seemed like a blow upon a wound, Claire announcing she was pregnant the same week they discovered Joan's cancer had spread. That had been the worst week of Katherine's life. Joan's steely defiance won her first battle, but as she said that week in March, she didn't have another fight in her. She fought the cancer long enough to see Katherine's grandchild, the first of the new generation. Luke Jonas Hunter, if it wasn't for him, for his innocence and potential, his blissful unawareness, Katherine wasn't sure how she would have coped. A parent's passing was part of the natural order of things, a younger sibling dying, eroding away within nine months of diagnosis, was just wrong and so unfair.

As Katherine now knew, when you witness life leak from the eyes of someone you love, you are changed forever. Perhaps that was what Joan's passing and Luke's arrival, just over a year ago had taught her, apart from the gift of life everything else was small stuff and Katherine no longer sweated the small stuff. If she had needed another push to pursue her dream, Joan's passing had been it. Life was simply too short. And as it turned out, the contents of Joan's will had given her another gift too, the means to take action.

***

Across the narrow landing, the spare bedroom would in time become her office, now it was the dumping ground for everything that hadn't yet found a home. The laptop, perched on the table hauled up from the kitchenette, was her first stake in the ground. Clicking it on, it wheezed to life. She really only had today to get the room ready for Corinne. She knew her friend well enough to know she wouldn't mind a few boxes in the corner. She took a mental note to get some flowers to brighten the space, chrysanthemums if possible, Corinne's favourites.

The excuse of a desk was as chaotic as Katherine's head. She located a rubber band to contain the heap of leftover flyers. She regretted having the date of the opening printed on them; they would be redundant after Friday. She ripped open the manila envelope Vincent had sent down with Claire. The only item of post to merit her attention was the new Bliss Retreat Programme. Neide had used her testimonial again. She knew Bruno was concentrating on his writing this year and Ran had moved on too, exhibitions in Dubai and Abu Dhabi according to his Facebook page. Curiously there was no mention of Iam anywhere on this year's brochure.

She glanced at the stack of folders beside the desk, the mountain of bureaucracy she had accumulated. Correspondence with solicitors, estate agencies, insurance companies, the food safety authority, the health service, the enterprise board. At one point she had contemplated taping blood pressure tablets inside the cover of each of them. At the bottom of the pile was her folder from the 'start your own business' course. If 'business planning', 'managing your finances' and 'marketing', had been replaced with 'staying sane', 'developing a thick neck' and 'resisting the urge to strangle pen-pushers', she would consider extracting it from beneath the weighty evidence, the practical reality of actually starting your own business.

There was an email enquiry from the local newspaper about Friday night's opening. It was another reminder that what she was doing actually involved other people and other people's expectations. Yes there were moments when she questioned her sanity, opening a bistro in her mid-fifties, but as Corinne kept reminding her, she was breathing life into her dream. Katherine was investing everything she had, financially, emotionally and physically. Big dreams demand a big price, worry, sleepless nights, self doubt, but Katherine willingly paid that price because she knew, without a shadow of a doubt, that she was doing exactly the right thing. She had never felt more alive.

Katherine ran her hand over the pink post-it note stuck to

the wall. '*What if it is a roaring success and you are blissfully happy?*' It was her favourite mantra and the single best antidote for the occasional bouts of irrational thinking that, if left unchecked, had her homeless and destitute, abandoned and unloved.

Katherine was thrilled that Corinne planned to stay for at least a week. They hadn't seen each other since the New Year apart from the Skype calls, but they weren't the same. Her sympathetic ear, the gentle prodding, the encouragement and insights, the mutual support, all evidence of a true friendship that had only really blossomed outside the confines of The Retreat.

Of course, Katherine knew exactly what Corinne would say when she noticed the magazine picture Katherine had stuck over the spare bed. It was what Corinne said every time she was reminded of her starring role in the soap advert that had graced many glossy magazines and had even been on a billboard in Times Square. '*Who wants to see an old black woman with her bits hanging out?*' But like millions of other women, Katherine thought it was an inspiring image. A grandmother, approaching seventy, with shining skin and eyes, the history of her life in every laughter line and wrinkle, gazing defiantly, but lovingly at the camera.

Katherine knew too that Corinne couldn't wait to visit the old lighthouse. Recently renovated and reopened as a guest house, Katherine only discovered it when out walking with Claire and Luke. The minute the owners, a retired English couple, showed her the space at the top with the jaw-dropping sea views, Katherine knew that Corinne would run a workshop there. When they had spoken that evening Corinne was practically in tears, it was the space she had been visualising for years, a round room with a sea view. And knowing Corinne's work, hosting a workshop in a lighthouse, well, it was just right on so many levels.

Katherine quickly scanned the rest of her emails, a mixture

of administration, good wishes and spam, nothing that couldn't wait until after a mug of coffee, a slice of toast and her morning pages.

***

She had bought her own copy of *The Artist's Way* within a week of returning home from The Retreat. It was now a well-thumbed and much underlined resource. The ritual of writing her morning pages had been the one constant in her life over the last three years. With only a handful of exceptions she had sat with a pen and pad in her hand every morning and dumped onto the page the multitude of thoughts spiralling around her head.

There had been days when her pen was so heavy it almost tore the page. Days when her tears stained the ink. Days when she ranted and filled the pages with everything that terrified her. But there were also days when she knew what she had written was the answer to an unspoken prayer. On the days when no words came she listed everything she was grateful for. There were the days when she laughed at her own stupidity and days when she hardly wrote at all, but just drew what was on her mind. Sometimes those sketches found their way onto a canvas where they transformed into something intriguing, even beautiful. That had certainly been the case with the painting she called 'The Vortex' that now took pride of place over the fireplace in the restaurant.

***

Katherine scavenged through the boxes in the corner, optimistically labelled office supplies, for a fresh pad. She found a half used one in the box she had taken from Joan's attic, the one containing the remnants of her aunt Kay's life. Katherine had spent many hours sifting through the old notebooks, shopping lists, Christmas card lists, medical prescriptions and newspaper cuttings. She sought clues as to why one woman's life ended tragically at the age of thirty-three. Initially the snippets of Kay's inner life, her irregular and often illegible diary entries, recorded in cheap copybooks, fuelled her curiosity, but soon it became apparent that what she was reading was merely evidence of an ordinary woman's ordinary life. If Kay's fragmented and frequently undated journaling revealed anything, it was a hidden world of frustration, disappointment and mood swings that perhaps today would be diagnosed as bipolar disorder. Perhaps Claire hit the nail on the head when she said Kay was just a woman who struggled to find her place in the world.

Kay's old cookery books were fascinating especially the handwritten amendments and recipes they concealed. Katherine had resurrected Kay's bread pudding and apple tart recipes, both of which were now proudly on her menu, preceded by 'Aunt Kay's'. The best treasure she unearthed was a photograph hidden in the pages of the Elizabeth David book. It was an image rich with memory that had brought tears to Katherine's eyes. In it, Kay was smiling, looking directly at the camera, beside her, ten-year-old Katherine was deep in concentration. They wore matching aprons, their sleeves pushed high on their arms and their floury hands resting on the edge of earthenware bowls. The photo was now framed beside her bed. A large copy of it took pride of place behind the counter downstairs. A close up of their hands had been incorporated into the design of the menus.

And there it was, her old journal wedged in amongst Kay's stuff. She hadn't been looking for it, but since the move, she'd been aware that she wasn't sure where it was. The feel and smell of the leather cover brought her straight back to The Bliss Retreat. It was the doorway to other smells and memories; the scent of the sun lotion she rubbed into her shoulders every morning, the herbs in the courtyard and the aromas from whatever Carlos was cooking in the kitchen.

Katherine often wondered what her life would be like if she had never boarded that plane to Lanzarote, or if Rhona hadn't broken her leg. But as Corinne was so fond of saying, life has a way of ensuring we are in the right place at the right time. Despite her apprehension about what was ahead, on this Tuesday morning in June, on her knees in a bedroom of her new home, Katherine knew that she was exactly where she was meant to be.

***

The coffee machine hissed and gurgled into life. Propped against the Formica worktop, which she should have had replaced when the main kitchen was being renovated, Katherine opened her old journal. She smiled at the images in her vision board. There wasn't any exposed brickwork in her place, though stripping back the wallpaper in the dining room she had discovered a layer of faux red brick wallpaper, a throwback to the seventies. Scanning the early entries was like getting reacquainted with an old friend. Her very first gratitude list had been a meagre effort. They had certainly become easier over the years, even if life at times, wasn't particularly easy. What she had written then was still relevant now, but in a different, more profound way.

I'm grateful for my health.
I'm grateful for my children.
I'm grateful for the friends I have.
I'm grateful that I was able to come here.
I'm grateful for my lovely home.

She ran her finger over the last line. Of course she had added an appendix to her list after Imelda had shared her gratitude list with the group.

I'm grateful that I know Imelda.

The journal held two letters, both of which had arrived

Christmas week, six months after her time at The Retreat. She opened the one postmarked England, the one she hadn't written, the one she never expected to receive.

Dear Ms. Hunter,

I'm writing this on behalf of my mother Sheila Prescott, who came across your contact details in the address book of her neighbour and friend Imelda Ryan. I'm contacting you with the sad news that Imelda passed away on December 8th.

My mother found her sitting in her armchair by the window. As you may have known, Imelda had a heart condition, though from what my mother tells me, it never held her back. It certainly brought my mother comfort to hear the doctor say that she had passed away peacefully. My mother said the book she was reading was still open on her lap and her rosary was beside her. Knowing Imelda as she did, she was convinced that Imelda knew her time was up and that she was ready to depart this life.

There was a small service and burial organised by the convent. I don't know how well you knew Imelda, or for how long and I'm sorry if this letter comes as a shock, especially just before Christmas. I confess I didn't know her well myself, but I know my mother was very fond of her and will miss her.

Yours sincerely,
Josephine Radley

Katherine clasped her green pendant. She couldn't help smiling when she thought of Imelda. Watching her balancing precariously on one foot doing her unique morning yoga, her ever-handy restorative bottle of brandy, waving wildly from Corinne's car whilst being whisked to the airport. The only heart condition that woman ever had was that her heart was too big for this world. She could only too easily imagine Imelda's laughter at the fact that she had labelled the brandy on the drinks menu '*Imelda's pick-me-up*'.

Mug and toast in hand, Katherine crossed the hall to the main kitchen housed in the extension that was added in the early eighties when one side of the old house was converted into a restaurant. She took a photo of the pristine kitchen and tweeted '*the calm before the storm*' to her two hundred and thirty-two followers. It had been Thom who had persuaded her to join the world of social media. Just as well because it was mainly by reading his tweets and status updates that she knew what her eldest child was up to. Somehow he was making a living in New York, part street photographer, part fashion blogger. A portfolio career as he called it. She was just one of his sixteen thousand followers, but the only one who insisted on regular phone calls.

Her storeroom shelves and industrial freezer were filling fast. She was thankful she had taken Peter's advice about opening night. A tasting menu sounded opulent. Yes there were seven courses, and forty diners, a scary two hundred and eighty plates, but two courses were cold and could be assembled beforehand, another was soup and the rest would be relatively easy to prepare and dispatch in a uniform and timely manner.

After rejecting the first mentor the enterprise board had assigned to her, a man seemingly intent on treating each meeting as an audition for Dragon's Den, Katherine got to work with Peter Roche, a former pub and restaurant owner himself. He was a straight-talker who emphasised crawling before walking and knowing the margin on everything. He was the rock of common sense Katherine needed. If Corinne provided the moral encouragement, the confirmation that Katherine's life was evolving in accordance with the blueprint etched on her soul, Peter Roche provided the practical advice that ensured

Katherine retained a roof over her head and food on her own plate.

Squinting into the morning sun, she stepped into the backyard. Wherever she looked there was something that needed digging or dumping. It frustrated her because she could see the potential of the space, an outdoor dining area, something few restaurants in the town offered. There wasn't a view to speak of, but cleaned up and with a few shrubs and flowers, a border of lavender was what she was visualising, it could be beautiful. The grass was soaking wet and needed scything, not just mowing. She didn't have a lawnmower; it's not something you think of when tentatively dividing assets, but Ger next door said he was happy to cut it for her.

In time the raised bed against the far wall would become a herb garden and the two sheds at the back could be converted into her studio, or if she listened to Peter, a function room she could hire out. In his words, she needed as many revenue streams as she could get. Nature was slowly consuming the wrought iron table, the solitary piece of outdoor furniture. The thyme plant she had defiantly placed on it served as a reminder of what she planned to create.

It was warm enough to sit outside. Katherine returned with a coffee refill, another slice of toast and the last of the heather scented honey she had bought at the market. She took a chair from inside, deposited herself at the table and began to write her morning pages.

I'm grateful for the sun on my face. Hopefully there will be many more mornings when I can start my day out here, plan my specials menu and not be up to my knees in wet grass and weeds. Now there's another feeling of déjà vu! I never know what that means, but I'll take it as confirmation that I'm aligning with my true self as Corinne would say. This honey is really good; I wonder could I get a few jars at cost to sell? What's that nursery rhyme, 'the Queen was in the garden eating bread and honey?'

Just four days until I jump off the cliff. I have to remember that a thumping heart is a sign of life, not just nerves. Everyone keeps saying I'm doing the right thing. It's always nice to hear that.

Claire said that Vincent was saying at the weekend how proud he was of me. He'd never say it to my face. She says I should invite him down for Friday, but I'm not sure. I'll phone him later, I don't have time for second guessing him.

I must check what time Corinne's plane is in tomorrow and I should probably phone the lighthouse and see when it would suit for us to pop over. There's no point in saying we'll go at the weekend, there will be too much to do.

I do worry about Claire. I didn't dare mention anything about her going back to college in September. It would be a shame if she didn't finish her degree. How do I care about her and not worry about her? Maybe I should just sit with that question. I know she has her own path in *life and I have to keep remembering that it's not my job to walk her path for her.*

There's a little robin hopping along the wall. I should get a bird feeder. Sing a song of sixpence, that's the nursery rhyme.

Taking a gulp of coffee, Katherine turned the page. Her phone pinged. A text from Bruno.

"Any chance of getting fed next week? I was thinking of popping over? I'll be in London with Zoe."

Bruno's regular texts always made her smile. The heartfelt poem he sent her after Joan's death contained words of solace that had supported Katherine through her grief. She treasured all his writing and treasured their friendship too. Rhona of course could never credit the fact that Katherine was now good friends with her favourite author.

She thought for a moment before replying.

"As long as you don't scare away the diners!"

She pictured him by the lake in Italy, in the old boathouse he had bought with the advance for his next three books and was renovating one room at a time, at what he said himself was the glacial rate of a room per year. Several times he had invited her to visit, and she had eventually agreed to a long weekend in September, under the proviso that everything was running smoothly with the restaurant.

"That's if you have any diners."

Katherine laughed out loud. At The Retreat Bruno had spoken about the importance of adventures. The man himself, equal parts kind and outrageous, impulsive, yet so patient, represented the biggest adventure of all. It was a thought that excited but also scared her.

She couldn't think of a suitable retort, so ended their

exchange by asking him to let her know his plans. He signed off in his usual way, "*Ciao bella.*"

With her phone still in her hand, she opened Facebook. The Bliss Retreat Tribe page had never really taken off, but she did enjoy keeping abreast of what people were doing. Top of her newsfeed was another of Morag's entertaining posts from her trip across Australia. She really was a one woman show, her pithy humour and one-liners perfectly suited the brief status updates. The account of her trek across America on her motorbike had been worthy of a TV series, 'hairy bikers plus one' was what she had labelled her adventures. Last week, she had posted a picture with Louise who was in Melbourne with Martin. They were celebrating their first wedding anniversary, thirty years after they had celebrated it the first time.

Despite not living anywhere in the vicinity of Bali, Katherine kept getting invites to 'party nights', featuring some celebrated DJ she had never heard of, that Declan and his boyfriend were running. Over the years, he had kept his online friends entertained with his escapades. During his year-long sabbatical when he travelled around Asia, he met a New Zealander, referred to initially as Mr Big, whilst volunteering with an NGO in Thailand. Declan never returned to his advertising job. They opened a beach bar and club in Bali, with the inspired name 'Eat Play Lust'. Katherine couldn't be sure, but she suspected that the young boy appearing in many of their candid photos was his partner's son from a previous relationship. Katherine had learnt that the sense of belonging we all seek, even our definition of family, is often not what we expect it to be.

She never heard directly from Suzy, though she did see a picture of her in an article about interior design in a Sunday newspaper. Up to a few months ago, you could be certain that Suzy would be the first to comment on Declan's posts, their double act and double-entendres transferring to the written word, but there hadn't been a comment or even a like from her in ages.

A month ago, on their first night in Kenmare, Katherine saw another member of The Bliss Retreat Tribe. Having fish and chips on their laps, Katherine had screamed at the TV causing Claire to jump and frightening Luke. There was Bruce in an advert for life assurance, one of those where you get a pen even for enquiring. At The Retreat he had confessed his desire to get involved in amateur dramatics and Katherine was delighted that the retired professor was breathing life into his dream too.

***

A shouted hello grabbed her attention. With mug in hand she walked around the gable end. Johnny the painter was back to finish the signage out front. Not always as reliable as she would have liked, the ginger-haired man with sideburns to rival Elvis, did have good attention to detail which Katherine valued more than punctuality. He had been due on Saturday. Mixed in with the banter about the weather holding, she managed to persuade him to put a lick of paint on the back door for no extra charge.

With one phone call less to make, she returned to her morning pages.

> Johnny is back at last to finish the paint job; I just hope that pale green looks ok. I'm delighted with the new counter, the desserts and cakes will look great behind the glass. Peter says I should hold off, but if everything goes well I'd love to start the afternoon teas soon. It's a growing market and apart from the hotel no one else is doing them and the mark up is far better than lunches. I'd need to hire another waitress though.

Somehow and I don't know how but everything is falling into place. Maybe it's as I read the other week that when you're doing what you're meant to be doing, it shouldn't be difficult – help, luck, whatever you call it eases everything along.

I'd the radio on in the kitchen last night, all eighties music, it brought me back. I'd never really paid attention to that song 'Flashdance – what a feeling' by Irene Cara before. "Take your passion and make it happen, pictures come alive, you can dance right through your life." It made me think of my vision board. I found the journal in with Kay's stuff. It's beside me now, funny to be flicking through it again.

Of course the music reminded me of Vincent too.

Katherine's pen hovered over the page. Her old journal contained her very first attempt at morning pages, written the day after she had returned from the retreat.

***

On the journey from the airport, Vincent had spoken of every inconsequential thing which was comforting at first, but then infuriating. It was only when the kettle was boiling and she was perched at the kitchen counter that she had delivered her well-rehearsed opening lines. At the time it felt like an out of body experience, that someone else was speaking, the calm, measured tone was foreign to her.

"There's a few things I need to say Vincent and it's important for me to say them." She motioned for him to sit beside her. Vincent looked at his hands. She had waited for him to make eye contact before continuing. "I want to apologise. I've found the last few months incredibly difficult, whatever the cause, my mother's death, stage of life, I don't know, but I want to start by saying I'm sorry."

Katherine had feared she would cry, but she didn't, not then. She had remained composed when she told him of her foolishness with Ran and Mark. There was a lump in her throat when he placed his hand on hers, at once communicating that she was forgiven and to keep going. She had steeled herself for what her honesty might unleash in him. She had spent hours running through all possible scenarios and developing a recovery plan for each. By the time she took her first sip of tepid tea, she had said everything she wanted to say. Whatever would happen next, she was immensely proud of herself.

Following her example and a little tentative at first, Vincent spoke in an equally open and frank way that must have felt alien to him, but liberating too, at least that's what he said afterwards. Her tears only came when Vincent told her about not wanting to let her down. As she suspected, they were in financial trouble, he couldn't protect her from that stark fact anymore. He'd been too lax with the business accounts and the Revenue were starting to ask questions. He apologised too, blaming his snappy demeanour and secretive behaviour on trying to keep their heads above water. He admitted that there had been times when he could easily have taken advantage of situations with other women. Katherine bottled the urge to know names and places, knowing that would only be a detour away from the place of truth and openness she wanted them to reach.

But there was a possible escape route from their financial

woes. Zenon, the financial services firm were interested in acquiring the insurance side of Vincent's business and offering Vincent a directorship. Katherine absolutely meant it when she told him that she didn't care if they had to sell the investment properties, or if they needed to downsize. There were many things in their lives they could simplify. She told him she had already started by giving away her designer bag.

After writing those first morning pages, gushing about a fresh start, Katherine, bolstered with renewed confidence told Vincent of her dream to run her own bistro. She knew him well enough to know that his instinctive response to anything that wasn't his idea was scepticism. He didn't respond negatively, in fact he barely responded at all, consumed as he was with the Sunday papers. At the time Katherine brushed it off, he had a lot on his mind. However, deep inside, a barely audible alarm bell sounded. Subsequently, she described that moment as the time when the first of many new veils descended between them.

And then life sideswiped her with Joan's diagnosis and the frequent trips to Tramore that ensued. The decision was made to sell the business and that in turn was a catalyst for more change. Thom announced he was going to America and Claire wanted to drop out of college. Katherine's full-time occupation became worrier. They moved house, a smaller place closer to the city to reduce Vincent's new commute. Katherine mourned the loss of her large garden and vegetable plot, but did what she always did, tried to ensure everyone around her was happy and manage as best she could. On the road of compromise however, Katherine was learning that it was very difficult to turn back.

***

Katherine turned the page of her pad and continued to write.

I had that dream again last night, the

one where I'm in the rowing boat in the bay, my clothes floating in the water and I'm trying to fish them out with an oar. In it I'm feeling overwhelmed, that's hardly a surprise. Maybe it has something to do with Kay drowning, who knows.

Corinne is bound to ask what's the story with Vincent. The bland answers won't satisfy her. Wide awake at four o'clock I was thinking of that question she asked me when everything was coming to a head—what is life asking of me that I'm still withholding? Well now at last I think I can answer it — I've let go of trying to fix everything, I've stopped resisting life, I've stopped trying to keep everyone around me happy and I think my family are actually happier as a result. How weird is that?

Of course it would be easier to hate Vincent, but he's done nothing wrong. Sure he could have been supportive and enthusiastic about my dream, but it was my dream, not his. He wanted to stay in Dublin, I didn't. He wanted to extend his contract with work, I just had to give this place a go having reached the point where the pain of not doing it was greater than the pain of doing it.

Like everyone, he's doing his best, I have to keep reminding myself of that. Others can label our situation however they wish, trial separation, growing apart, not having anything in common anymore, but only we know the truth, at least our own versions of the truth. I'm sure like most men Vincent would prefer a neater, more finite state of affairs, not this muddle of uncertainty, but that's just the way it needs to be right now. I've spent too long putting bandages on a wound that wasn't healing, time to let some air at it.

You know maybe we have just evolved to a new stage in our relationship, just like we moved beyond the infatuation of first love to newlyweds, then the mutual dependence of being parents, now we simply need to be apart for a bit. It's a road without a map which is scary, but my emotions guide me and right now they're telling me I'm moving in the right direction.

Chatting to Mags yesterday, I said I've unyoked myself from Vincent, I was a moon now I'm a planet, or something like that. She asked about my wedding ring, but I told her, I won't stop wearing it, he'll always be in my life, we have the unbreakable bonds of children, but maybe the time is coming when I'll move the ring to my other hand. Bruno might *be here next week. I do like spending time with him. That has to mean something!*

There are times when I miss Vincent, I miss telling him things. For thirty years we were the witnesses to each other's lives. Just like with Joan and those waves of grief, when I allow myself to miss him, to sit with that emotion, and don't try to distract myself from it, it passes and a different emotion settles, usually courage or calmness. As Corinne says, to heal you need to feel. I don't wallow in it though, I've no time for that, I made the decision to leave, but I do give myself permission to feel what I'm feeling. I'm human, not superwoman.

Katherine twisted her wedding ring and checked her phone. She had filled her three pages and her coffee was now cold. She picked up her journal and removed the other letter concealed in its pages.

Dearest Katherine,

You are an incredible, loving, joyous woman who is always doing her best.

Always remember the week at The Retreat where you connected with what was truly important to you, your family and the importance of appreciating everything you have in your life. Pick up your journal frequently and revisit all your learning and insights. Some messages you cannot hear often enough –

I am loved

I am always doing my best.

Know the goals you wrote came from your heart, that they represent the path to your true happiness. No doubt there will be bumps in the road but keep going. As Imelda would say, life challenging us is just God testing us. You are up for the challenge.

If change comes, embrace it, because change is the dance of life.

Don't be your own worst enemy. Gone are the days of putting yourself down. Don't sell yourself short, don't say no to your own dreams, others may say no, but don't add to their chorus.

Sometimes it may be difficult to love Vincent, but love him anyway. He will always be the father of your children. If your paths diverge, know you can walk it alone because you will never really be alone. Listen to your inner wisdom and seek help wherever you can find it.

Laugh more and dance more, no more hiding, let your true self shine and know the world is a richer place because you are in it.

Love and blessings

Your best friend Katherine

There had been times when Katherine felt the letter had been penned by a stranger. She found it hard to believe she had written it three years ago, almost to the day. She really should have the precious page copied and laminated. She placed it securely back inside her journal, between the pages containing the 'I am' exercise. That had been one of her favourite exercises at The Bliss Retreat. At the top of the page she had written '*I am here*'. Picking up her pen she now added the words '*at last*'.

The letter reminded her that she hadn't danced in ages. She smiled at the memory of that tango with Bruno at César Manrique's. She scrolled through her phone until she found the photo Corinne had taken of the two of them.

She reached for her pad, but then decided to write in her journal instead. The only blank page was at the front, where she had written her name and the date.

> *Change is the dance of life. Sometimes I lead, sometimes I follow, sometimes my feet ache, sometimes it's magical — but I'm still dancing.*

***

Returning to the kitchen, her phone pinged. Vincent.

"Thinking of you this week K. Hope all the prep going ok?"

She knew what it would have taken for him to type that message.

Washing out the coffee plunger, Katherine heard Johnny call her. With a tea towel in hand she walked through the restaurant, straightening a place setting as she passed. She was glad she had moved that painting from the living room to the restaurant, the one she had painted during the thunderstorm at The Retreat. It looked great in the simple frame by the door.

"So what d'ya think?" Johnny asked as Katherine stepped outside, ducking to avoid his ladder.

She spied Claire and Luke coming up the footpath and waved to them before stepping into the road to get a clear view of Johnny's work.

Her throat tightened just for a moment, before excitement took hold.

"Claire, what do you think?"

It was perfect. The green looked really fresh and the white

and pink lettering glistened in the morning sun. She had made the right choice with the colours and absolutely the right choice with the name:

Kay's Place